THE HUNDRED DAYS

THE HUNDRED DAYS

Napoleon's Last Campaign
from eye-witness accounts

Compiled, edited and translated by
ANTONY BRETT-JAMES

ST MARTIN'S PRESS
New York

To
GONI

May her blue-eyed radiance never again
be chilled by wartime anxieties or her
staunch heart set racing by fear of
encompassing enemies

PLATES

CONTENTS

MAPS

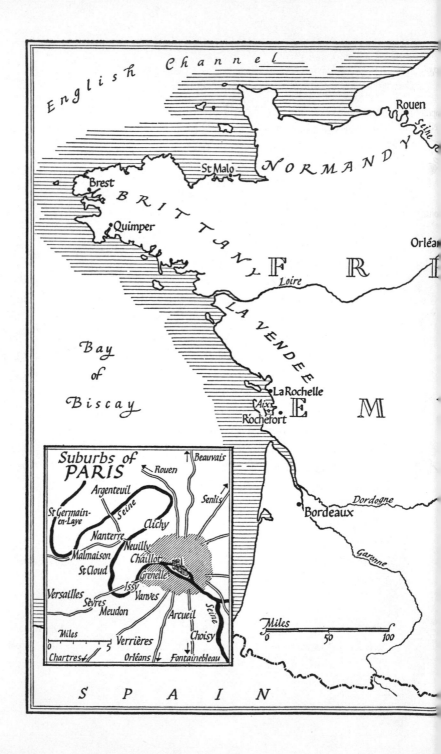

English Channel

Rouen

Seine

NORMANDY

St Malo

Brest

BRITTANY

Quimper

Orléa

F   R   I

Loire

LA VENDÉE

Bay
of
Biscay

La Rochelle

Aix

Rochefort

E   M

Dordogne

Bordeaux

Garonne

Suburbs of PARIS

↑ Beauvais

← Rouen

Argenteuil

St Germain-
en-Laye

Seine

Senlis ↗

Nanterre

Clichy

Malmaison

Neuilly

St Cloud

Chaillot

Grenelle

Versailles

Issy

Sèvres

Vanves

Meudon

Arcueil

Seine

Miles
0   5

Verrières

Choisy

Chartres ✠

Orléans ↓

Fontainebleau ↓

Miles
0   50   100

SPAIN

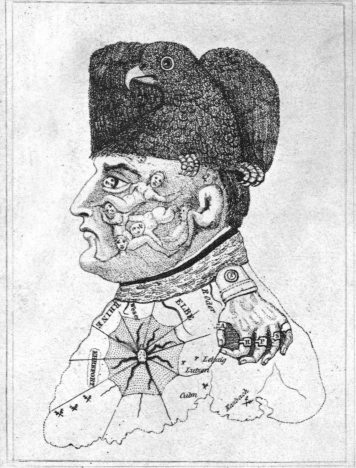

J. Kay 1814.

Description of the hieroglyphic Portrait of Buonaparte.

The French Eagle crouching forms the *chapeau en militaire*.
The Red Sea represents his *throat* illustrative of his drowning armies.
The *visage* is formed of carcases of the unhappy victims to his cruel ambition
The *hand* is judiciously placed as the epaulet drawing the Rhenish Confederacy
under the flimsy symbol of the cob-web.
The *spider* is a symbolic emblem of the vigilance of the Allies.

336

Napoleon in exile. A contemporary cartoon illustrating the popular attitude toward the still securely chained giant. 1814. (*Culver Pictures*)

INTRODUCTION

On hearing the news of Napoleon's abdication in April, 1814, the Hon. Mrs Frances Calvert wrote in her journal: 'We can scarce believe it possible that we are going to have peace and quiet, and an end to Bonaparte's horrors and dominion. He is to retire to Elba. I own I would rather there was an end of him. I dread his starting up again.' The fulfilment of her prophetic dread is the subject of this book, which seeks to give, through the eyes and emotions of more than a hundred people who experienced one of the most eventful and momentous crises in Europe's long history, a sense of what it felt like to be alive in that spring and summer of 1815.

In reading these accounts by eye-witnesses — British, French, German, Dutch and Belgian, women and boys as well as military and civilian men — who have a superiority in being there, we have the advantage of knowing what happened next, of how it all turned out in the end, of what was going on everywhere else. We know who will come through unscathed and who will perish or be disabled. We know that when the spirits of Parisians rise at the good news of a victory at Ligny, they will shortly droop terribly at the grim tidings of Waterloo.

There are, of course, discrepancies between one account and another, and minor errors of fact. Names are spelt wrongly or without consistency, and accounts of the battle reveal considerable divergence about the time of day at which events took place. The documentation on the Hundred Days is immense and dozens of narratives from which passages might have been taken have had to be discarded for lack of space, or in order to avoid undue repetition, or in the interests of maintaining as far as possible a high standard in eye-witness stories. Certain political aspects of the French scene prior to Napoleon's last campaign have been kept in the background. The role of the Belgian and Dutch troops deserves more prominence, but narratives of quality are hard to come by. Contributions by the leading actors in the drama have deliberately been limited, and some of the best known descriptions do not appear,

ix

though Creevey and Mercer must have a place. However, a preponderance of the accounts written by Belgian, French and German participants are now translated for the first time, and many of them have not been used by British writers on the period. The source of any extract can be traced by means of the key and Bibliography at the end. In the introductory sections a brief account of the relevant events is provided as a background against which the individual pieces can be set, though the book is not a full survey or detailed analysis of the Hundred Days.

Why 'the Hundred Days'? On the afternoon of July 8th, 1815, Gilbert-Joseph-Gaspard, Comte de Chabrol-Volvic, stood at the barrier of St Denis. As Prefect of the Seine for the third time he awaited the return of Louis XVIII to Paris. When the King reached the barrier, Comte de Chabrol made a speech of welcome, of which one phrase has survived by giving the title to a compelling human and historical drama: 'A hundred days have passed since the fatal moment when Your Majesty left his capital. . . .'

The Prefect's calculation was approximate, since too precise a count of the days involved would have spoilt the phrase. From March 20th, when King Louis hurried away from the Tuileries, until July 8th cannot be counted as less than 110 days, though it is true to say that the defeated Emperor left Malmaison for the west coast at Rochefort on the 101st day.

* * *

I wish to record my gratitude to Monsieur Jean Copin for his kindness in affording me the benefit of his profound knowledge of the Napoleonic era and of the Waterloo campaign and battlefield, in obtaining several books and documents for me, and in showing me round Brussels; to Monsieur Robert Macoir, who introduced me to several helpful people in Belgium and went to considerable trouble himself on my behalf; to members of the Temmermans family, who allowed me to see inside Hougoumont; to Monsieur Robert Merget, editor of the excellent *Waterloo illustré* series, for information on various points of detail; to Mr John Mollo, who lent me a copy of Captain Edmund Walcot's manuscript diary, and to Mrs Constance Macness for permission to quote from it; to Sir Brian W. Barttelot, Bart., Coldstream Guards, for allowing me to include an unpublished letter written by Lieutenant Henry Boldero; to the Office of the Household Brigade Funds for permission to reprint part of Private Matthew Clay's narrative from *The Household Brigade Magazine*; to Brigadier Peter Young, D.S.O., M.C., F.S.A., who made numerous valuable suggestions; to Monsieur Théo Fleischman and the Société Belge d'Études Napoléoniennes for permission to quote from Pierre-Jean Tellier's account; to the Marquess of Anglesey and Jonathan Cape Ltd., for permission to quote from *The Capel Letters*; to H.M. Stationery Office, for permission to quote from the *Report on the Manuscripts of the late Reginald Rawdon Hastings*, edited by Francis Bickley; to John Murray Ltd., for permission to quote from *Creevey's Life and Times*, edited by John Gore; to Librairie Plon, Paris, for permission to quote from *Souvenirs d'un Officier de la Grande Armée*, by Captain J. B. Barrès, and from *Souvenirs militaires, 1802–1815* by Colonel Octave Levasseur; and to Miss Joan Pring for her help with the index.

A. B.-J.

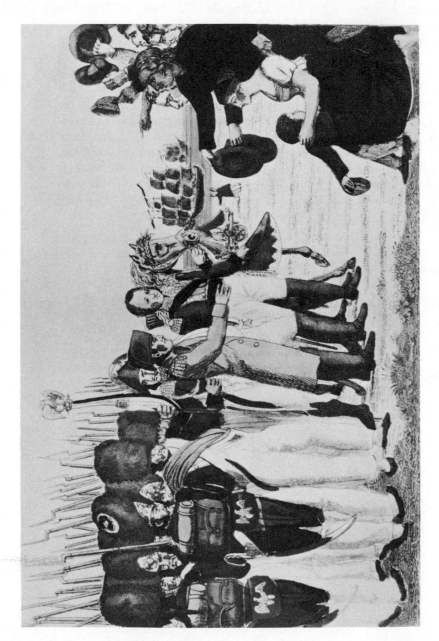

Napoleon's landing at Cannes on March 1, 1815. Popular print.

THE EMPEROR RETURNS FROM ELBA

It was no plot within France that summoned Napoleon from Elban exile. He left because he assessed correctly the national mood under the Bourbon Restoration. 'All France regrets me and wants me,' he observed on the island; 'I shall reach Paris without firing a shot,' he prophesied at sea; and he was right. Instead of bloodshed, a fervent welcome from peasantry and soldiers alike, though it must be conceded that many an officer remained loyal to the Bourbon king, and large bodies of troops were infected by popular clamour rather than inspired to disobedience by Bonapartist leanings.

After the Restoration of 1814 the French people had been exhausted by catastrophe, bewildered by political convulsions. True it is that the affairs of France had been settled with despatch and leniency: no war indemnity to be paid, no major colonial possessions to be surrendered, no Allied control of the new government. But there was no real government, only a group of ministers, many of them returned *émigrés* working with the King and too often out of touch with the nation's sensibilities. True it is that Louis XVIII came back as a constitutional monarch with a parliament of two chambers, and a charter guaranteed there would be no return to the *Ancien Régime*. Yet the new Bourbon king was to most people barely a name. Did not Chateaubriand say: 'When I described the royal family to my countrymen, it was as though I had enumerated the children of the Emperor of China'?

Then the transformation from France's position astride Europe in 1812 to the drab realities of 1814 was hard to bear, especially since the very people who should have taken pains to wound no powerful interests or sentiments were all too good at rekindling old social resentments. For instance, the *émigré* nobles and in particular their ladies despised without concealment the titles of the Empire, and did anything but soothe ruffled pride. Thanks to provocations, tactless actions and petty humiliations, disgust for the Bourbons mounted. When the Duc de Berry remarked to a distinguished general: 'The French soldier must be happy these days. His long campaigns are over, and we have peace,' he was disconcerted by the curt reply: 'Do you call "peace" a halt in the mud?'

Lack of money had caused severe reductions in the army. Soldiers, bereft of barracks and the ordered communal life, often felt lost in civil life and, being equipped for no alternative career, lived too frequently in idle misery, pawning their weapons when money ran short. Officers, twelve thousand of them on half pay or in retirement, did better; but some were so poor that a group of friends might be forced, for lack of clothes, to share a hat and greatcoat, taking turns to go out in public. And for thousands the humiliations of 1814 meant an end to swift promotion, a dashing of bright hopes of a marshal's *bâton*. They had much time for criticism and many targets on which to vent their spleen. Despite the reductions in the army, the seven foreign regiments were not disbanded and an eighth was added; *émigrés* who had fought against rather than for their country now filled the posts of men sent into retirement; the King's personal guards were largely foreigners rather than Frenchmen. As for the Legion of Honour, it was cheapened by prodigal distribution to civilians and by the re-establishment of the orders of the Saint Esprit and Saint Louis.

Many believed that Napoleon would return, and in that expectation they kept as sacred relics the eagles and tricolour cockades, several regiments preferring to burn the silk and drink the ashes rather than hand in their colours. The discontent, the grievances, the dwelling upon past glories — these were fanned by returning prisoners of war, by undefeated garrisons who marched home from Germany, from Italy and beyond, by officials who had administered the Imperial territories from Dalmatia to the Netherlands.

Napoleon's instinct was right, and the King's was not. How could so rash a venture prosper? Louis was confident in the outcome — at first. A week was devoted to the granting of concessions designed to satisfy or soothe, and Louis even wore the Legion of Honour for the first time. But the concessions came too late. Reports were arriving from all parts that the troops would not fight for the King and would transfer their allegiance to Napoleon; they would neither harm the monarch nor fire at '*le Petit Caporal.*' At court the mood was changed by news that Lyons could not be held. What to do? Where to go? Lille, Britanny, La Rochelle, La Vendée? Or another siege of Paris? And when it became known that Marshal Ney, having promised to bring Napoleon to Paris in a cage of iron, had deserted with his 6,000 men, the Court decided upon flight. With Napoleon already at Fontainebleau, Louis XVIII left Paris secretly in the early hours of March 19th and travelled first to Lille, then north to Ostend and finally to Ghent, where the Prince of Orange offered him refuge and where he established a court in exile.

Twenty-one hours afterwards the Emperor returned to his capital. He had left Elba on February 26th with a thousand and fifty men, had landed in the Golfe de Juan on March 1st, and gained success by the surprise of his arrival and the speed of his progress. There had been a momentary check at Antibes; a perilous climb in falling snow across the mountains to Digne; the failure of troops from Marseilles to reach Sisteron in time to cut off his small army. Apprehension was trans-

Louis XVIII in power, by Gros *(The Bettmann Archive)*

Napoleon acclaimed by the people on his arrival at the Tuileries, March 20, 1815

formed into warm triumph at the Laffrey defile when Napoleon called to the 5th of the Line drawn up in his path: 'If there is one soldier among you who wishes to kill his Emperor, here I am!' and no shot was fired. At Grenoble, when peasants broke down the gates, the garrison did nothing but cheer, and Napoleon was enabled to say: 'As far as Grenoble I was nothing but an adventurer. At Grenoble I was a prince.' Neither Louis XVIII's unpopular brother nor Marshal Macdonald could stem the tide of acclaim at Lyons, and the latter barely escaped capture by hostile hussars.

Napoleon in his turn issued popular decrees, by which, *inter alia*, he ended the Bourbon rule, forbade the white flag and ordered that the tricolour cockade be worn.

While on St Helena he several times affirmed his belief that he made a grave mistake in leaving Elba as soon as he did. He would, he felt sure, have done better to wait until the Congress of Vienna had broken up; then the difficulties of arranging to act in concert would have been far greater for the powers and the occasion of serious delay, whereas they were settled while the rulers and their representatives were in session.

Colonel Marie Antoine de Reiset, an officer in the King's Bodyguard at the Tuileries Palace, wrote in his journal for March 5th:

An astounding piece of news arrived yesterday. We learnt, by telegraph, that Bonaparte had landed at Cannes, near Fréjus.

Monsieur de Vitrolles[1] had come back to his office at about one o'clock, after the Sunday court, when Monsieur Chappe[2] brought him, for handing to His Majesty, a sealed dispatch which had just been transmitted by means of the apparatus he had invented. The Director of Telegraphs seemed extremely agitated. He is a large and corpulent man and had run so fast that he was all out of breath and unable to speak. When he was eventually in a state to articulate a few words, he merely begged Monsieur de Vitrolles personally to take the message, as the news was important. The King, who is very unwell, is at present suffering from an attack of gout which principally affects his hands, so much so that he had great difficulty in opening the envelope. Having read the contents he remained silent, then spent several moments with his head in his hands, deep in thought.

[1] Eugène François, Baron de Vitrolles (1774–1854) was Secrétaire des Conseils du Roi.
[2] Ignace-Urbain-Jean Chappe (1760–1828) administered the French telegraph system invented by his brother Claude.

'Do you know what this telegraph contains?' he at length asked Monsieur de Vitrolles, who was waiting for orders.

'No, Sir, I do not.'

'Well, I will tell you. It is revolution once more. Bonaparte has landed on the coast of Provence. Have this letter taken instantly to the Minister of War, so that he can come and speak to me at once and decide what steps are to be taken.'

And as Monsieur de Blacas[1] was protesting at the folly of such an attempt, and on the little danger it constituted, His Majesty interrupted him with considerable impatience. 'Blacas, my friend, you are a very pleasant fellow, but that is not enough to make you sensible. You have been wrong on many past occasions, and I am very much afraid that you are once again deluding yourself.'

Colonel Louis-Florimond Fantin des Odoards had not been home to Embrun in the Hautes-Alpes for fourteen years, having served at Austerlitz, Friedland and Corunna, and endured the retreat from Moscow. He intended to remain a month or two, but after only five days vague rumours arrived that Napoleon had landed. They were soon confirmed.

I now found myself in a perplexing predicament. On the one hand, the general commanding the department of the Hautes-Alpes wanted to place under my orders the National Guards he was going to mobilize to meet any eventuality. On the other, the Emperor's supporters told me I must place myself at the head of the movement which would certainly come out on his side in our mountains. I was going to find myself between the hammer and the anvil. I took a quick decision, made my farewells in haste, and, accompanied by a young cavalry officer who was on leave in Embrun, I mounted the first horse I could procure. Thus I found myself hurrying along the road to Gap,[2] with every intention of rejoining the regiment to which I still belonged, and there awaiting the outcome of the great events which were bound to result from the Emperor's incursion.

We reached Gap at eight o'clock the same evening, March 8th, and asked for post horses to continue our journey at full speed to Grenoble; but while the horses were being got ready, the Emperor

[1] Pierre, Comte de Blacas d'Aulps (1771–1839) was Minister of the King's Household.

[2] Twenty-five miles to the west.

suddenly dropped like a bomb in the middle of the town, escorted by those of his henchmen who had been able to keep up with his rapid progress. Shouts of *Vive l'Empereur!* were instantly to be heard on every side as excited inhabitants thronged the streets. The shadows gave way to an improvised illumination, and almost at once the inn where I was waiting for horses filled with members of the Imperial Guard in search of a bed and a meal.

I was in the throes of a painful struggle. Honour and duty dictated that I should persist in my resolve not to break the recent oaths binding me to a government which I disliked but had promised to serve loyally; yet my personal wishes and my memories tugged me towards Napoleon. Concealed in an obscure back room, I felt my heart throbbing violently, and at each pulse beat I was on the point of emerging from my hiding-place and throwing myself into the arms of old comrades of the Guard whose voices I recognised, and of saying to them: 'Take me to Napoleon.'

I can conceive of no more poignant state of indecision. How sweet it would have been to have thrown myself at the feet of the great man and offered him my sword! How he would have welcomed a former officer of his Guard! What joy I would deprive myself of by departing! I was on the point of giving way when my young travelling companion, who, being very junior in the service, could not possibly thrill to the shout of *Vive l'Empereur!*, and was most impatient to be off, informed me that the horses were ready and that we should be on our way. Had I been on my own I should have gone to Napoleon. But I had promised this young man to travel with him. I had told him to go where the call of duty led, and a sudden change of front would have given me cause to blush in his presence. I took a grip on myself, shut my ears to the shouts of joy which could still be heard, and went out by a back door so as to avoid being recognised by those with whom I had shared past glories and dangers. I mounted my horse and put it to a gallop without looking back.

After the Emperor's abdication in 1814 Captain Jean-Roch Coignet had found himself retired on half pay. Inactivity lay hard on a man who had served with gallantry at Marengo, who, on June 14th 1804, had been the first other rank to be decorated with the cross of the Legion of Honour — from the hands of the Emperor in

B

the Invalides — who had survived the retreat from Moscow, as well as campaigning in Poland, Germany and Spain. Intense, then, were Coignet's pride and pleasure when reports surged through Auxerre that Napoleon was marching north.

Everyone was filled with consternation; but the report became a certainty when, early in the morning, a fine regiment of the line, the 14th, arrived with Marshal Ney at its head. It was said that he was going to arrest the Emperor. 'It cannot be possible,' I said to myself, 'that the man whom I saw at Kowno [1] take a gun and with five men keep the enemy at bay — this marshal whom the Emperor called his lion — can lay hands on his sovereign.' The very thought of it made me tremble. I kept my ears open and did some eaves-dropping. I felt restless. Eventually the Marshal went to the office of the Prefect. A proclamation was drawn up and published throughout the town. The Commissioner of Police, accompanied by a full escort, announced that Bonaparte had returned, and that the Government had ordered his arrest. There were shouts of '*A bas Bonaparte!*' '*Vive le Roi!*' My God! how I suffered! But this fine 14th of the Line put the shakos on their bayonets and shouted '*Vive l'Empereur!*' What could the Marshal have done without soldiers? He was obliged to give in.

That evening the advance guard returned to the townhall, but not as it had left it: white cockades in the morning and tricolour ones in the evening. They took possession of the townhall, and by torchlight the same commissioner went through the town to pub-lish another proclamation and shout at the top of his voice, '*Vive l'Empereur!*' I must say that I just about ruptured my spleen.

The next day, March 17th, everybody assembled on the road to St. Bris [2] to see the Emperor arrive in his carriage with a fine escort. The snowball had grown; seven hundred of his old officers formed a battalion, and troops came in from every direction. On reaching the Place Saint-Étienne, the 14th of the Line formed a square and were reviewed by the Emperor, who afterwards called his officers into a circle and, seeing me, called me to him. 'So here you are, old grumbler?' 'Yes, sir.' 'What rank did you hold on my staff?' 'Baggage-master of General Headquarters.' 'Very well. I appoint you Quartermaster of my Palace and Baggage-master-general of Headquarters. Have you a horse?' 'Yes, sir.' 'Then follow me.'

[1] On December 12th, 1812, Ney and a few hundred men served as rearguard in Kowno, west of Vilna, and held back the Cossacks till nightfall.
[2] St Bris-le-Vineux, to the south-east.

When news of Napoleon's landing reached Gex, just north of Geneva, Colonel Girod de l'Ain, who had recently married, was busy levelling and planting his garden.

As soon as I learnt that the Emperor had entered Grenoble, I felt that I could not delay taking up my post again with General Curial,[1] to whom I still remained aide-de-camp. But as I had no news of him and did not know which side he would be on in the grave and delicate circumstances, I decided to go to Paris, thinking that I would be better placed there to rejoin him wherever he might be. So I left Gex on March 16th, but from the very outset my journey was delayed by the difficulties which the diligence met with in crossing the Col de la Faucille. That winter the snows had fallen heavily in our mountains, and my departure coincided with a tremendous thaw which put the pass almost out of action. Up at Pailly the driver, seeing that the horses were chest deep in water and certainly could not go on, invited me and my travelling companions to get out. Thus it was on foot, floundering in snow up to our waists, dripping with perspiration and quite exhausted, that we eventually reached the top of La Faucille. There we managed to collect about thirty active men who, armed with shovels and taking it in turns, cleared a way for us as far as the staging post at Les Rousses. But as a result of our slow progress we missed the Besançon diligence which should have picked us up at Dôle, and we lost twenty-four hours there.

As can well be imagined, the whole country was in a turmoil. I travelled in uniform, but I took the precaution of providing myself with *two* cockades, one *white*, the other *tricolour*, and according to which colour flag I saw flying from the belfries of any town or village we passed through, I hurriedly adorned my hat with the appropriate cockade. Such a precaution was by no means needless, because on the stretch of road as far as Dijon, and particularly at Dôle, we were subjected to questioning by the makeshift and exceedingly zealous authorities, whom we encountered at every step and who were all on the lookout for suspects of one or other colour, depending upon whether they had adopted the tricolour cockade again or had kept to the white one.

At Troyes I learnt with great satisfaction that General Curial had slept the previous night there. He was on his way to Paris,

[1] Philibert-Jean-Baptiste-François-Joseph, Comte Curial (1774–1829) was principal colonel of the Infantry Chasseurs of the Old Guard.

intending to enter the capital with the Emperor, whom he would join at Auxerre, provided that he was not outstripped by the latter's rapid progress. My first thought was to leave the diligence at Troyes and hurry after the General, but I reflected that I should probably serve him better by getting to Paris ahead of him and then going back down the road to meet him with whatever news I had been able to gather and even with orders which I would request, on his behalf, from General Drouot.[1]

Accordingly I continued my way by diligence and reached Paris on the evening of March 20th, some hours after the Emperor himself had entered the Tuileries.

By no means every officer was glad to hear of the Emperor's return, and many were faced with deep divisions of loyalty and by embarrassing dilemmas. One of those who remained loyal to King Louis XVIII was the Comte Alfred-Armand de Saint-Chamans. His officers and men were, he admits, already discontented at having been sent from Paris, early in February, to garrison Béthune, 125 miles to the north-west.

Such were the circumstances in which we heard the news that the Emperor had landed. I learnt of it on the morning of March 9th and went immediately to the barracks, paraded the squadrons, and spoke strongly to the men of the King's acts of kindness towards them. I told them to hold themselves ready to set off on campaign, because I believed that we were going to fight the ex-Emperor. Finally, I did not wait for Government orders before doing my utmost to gain support for the King's cause, and I flattered myself that I had succeeded. I learnt later that on the very same day some of the officers and non-commissioned officers of my regiment had met together to drink the Emperor's health and to swear to support him in his undertaking with every means at their disposal.

[*Saint-Chamans' regiment, the 7th Chasseurs, reached St. Quentin on March 12th without trouble.*]

At this point someone came to warn me that several officers who had assembled in the *café* had resolved to take their troops over to

[1] Antoine Drouot (1774–1847), son of a baker in Nancy, had returned from Elba with Napoleon. During the Waterloo campaign he had effective command of the Imperial Guard.

join the light infantry of the Guard so as to support the Emperor in his venture; that others were busy having tricolour flags made which they proposed to distribute to the men next morning, and thereby provoke a mutiny. I was also warned that these same officers planned to visit me at daybreak in order to declare categorically that they wanted the Emperor Napoleon as their leader and that the whole regiment was ready to follow them.

I began to see the true state of affairs and to feel the wretchedness of my own position. What could I do? There I was, with eight or ten trusted officers, alone with my views in the midst of an entire regiment composed of veterans who were longing for their original leader.

I spent a terrible night. Any hopes I had hitherto entertained of presenting to the King a fine and loyal regiment to support the throne at this fateful hour were evidently dashed to the ground.

[*Saint-Chamans led his men to Paris in good order, but he then resigned his command, ostensibly on grounds of ill-health, because he could no longer serve the King's cause with the regiment.*]

Marshal Nicolas-Charles Oudinot, Duc de Reggio, was military Governor of the vital frontier fortress of Metz, garrisoned by part of the former Imperial Guard, when Napoleon returned to France. He sent a column of grenadiers towards Toul, some forty miles away, and then he and his wife Eugénie, who relates this sequel for their children, set off by carriage for the same destination.

It was dark when we arrived at a hotel in the Place d'Armes. It was full of officers. The largest room had been reserved for us, but it was just one room, with not a corner into which I could retire.

The generals soon came in response to a summons. Without finding out precisely what he would say to the troops, my husband asked these gentlemen how the soldiers would react to a speech ending up with a 'Vive le Roi!' 'Try, Monsieur le Maréchal, just try,' said General Roguet. The others said nothing. 'Very well, issue my orders,' said the Marshal. 'Tomorrow, at dawn, I shall inspect the men and then address them.'

These generals had scarcely left the room when General Trommelin came in alone. He had just been watching and listening to emissaries of the Emperor in the cafés of Toul, and collecting unequivocal proof that officers of all ranks had been drawing up plans. 'But what about my inspection tomorrow?' said your father. 'And my shout of *Vive le Roi!* which was to conclude the proceedings? I cannot compromise on that. I shall have to settle this matter once and for all, and without delay. Go and tell those generals to send me every officer from second lieutenant to colonel immediately. I want to speak to them. The situation must be clarified.'

A few minutes later these officers crowded into our room, forming a circle three ranks deep with the Marshal in the centre. He waited until they were quiet, and then spoke in more or less the following terms: 'Gentlemen, in the circumstances in which we now find ourselves, I appeal to your loyalty. We shall march, wearing the white cockade. I intend to inspect you tomorrow before we leave. How would you and your men respond if I were to shout *"Vive le Roi!"*?'

Complete silence followed these words. I never witnessed anything more striking. Hidden behind a curtain, I was compelled to watch this unique scene. Two torches lit the room sufficiently for me to miss nothing, and their pale gleam on those sombre masculine faces had an indescribable effect. This silence, expressive as it was, could not be taken by the Marshal for an answer. I sensed that a storm was about to break. Each second seemed like a century. Eventually the Marshal managed to get out the words: 'Well, gentlemen?' At this a young and junior officer stepped forward and said '*Monsieur le Maréchal*, yes, we must give an answer. No one here will contradict me. To your *"Vive le Roi!"* the men and we ourselves will all reply *"Vive l'Empereur!"*' 'Thank you, sir,' replied the Marshal. Then he saluted them and they went off one by one without a word being uttered.

That same day the Marshal travelled as far as Jeand'heurs,[1] where he left me, and next morning continued the march of his troops, who still wore the same colours as he did, because even though insurrection undoubtedly stirred in every heart, no outward sign, not a single act of indiscipline had as yet given the Commander-in-Chief cause to believe that his soliders were in the opposing camp. But how bitterly, how anxiously the Marshal approached the crisis! It broke at Chaumont.

[*Oudinot remained loyal to the Bourbon cause and retired to his estates until after Louis XVIII's second Restoration.*]

---

[1] The property he had bought in 1808 near Bar-le-Duc.

During March Captain Edmund Walcot, Royal Horse Artillery, set off from London for Paris, acting as secretary to Mr Robert Jenkinson who was to visit the headquarters of the French Royal Army, then supposed to be in Lyons. They reached Paris on the 16th and stayed in the Hôtel 'Les Puissances Alliées' in the Rue de la Paix.

Finding the idea of joining a French Royal Army at an end, there being only one Army and that for Buonaparte, we determined to remain in Paris and wait events. This day the King went in state to the Legislative Body to explain his sentiments as to the situation of France. Buonaparte was at this time in possession of Lyons, and the accounts were gloomy.

The procession very fine, the street and bridge from the Tuileries to the Senate House lined with Soldiers, regulars on one side, and the National Guard on the other. . . .

On Sunday the 19th the reports of the successes and the rapidity of Buonaparte's march caused a very general sensation and the reports became more and more discouraging to the Royal cause. At half past four, walking on the *Carousal*,[1] I saw the King come in from a drive in his coach-and-eight, and a great number of Aides-de-Camp and Cavalry. This was a denial of the report of the Royal Family being about to leave Paris, but the next morning, again going to my usual place, the Garden of the Tuileries, I saw the White Flag no longer on top of the Palace. No longer the busy scene of a Palace inhabited by Royalty, but a gloomy appearance of its being deserted, with a straggling sentry here and there. The windows, the day before crowded with soldiers, and the courts, with carriages, gave place to silence and gloom. The fact spoke for itself: the King had left Paris.

As soon as this became known, the King's pictures, which the day before had ornamented the shops, gave place to the pictures of Buonaparte. The white ribbon disappeared, and the red, and in some places, the tricolour, usurped the place of it. About 12 o'clock the tricolour flag was hoisted on the principal buildings. At one, Buonaparte's advanced guard, consisting of about 80 or 90 Sous-Officiers, 3 pieces of Artillery, a coach containing, as was said, his cooks, and about 30 Dragoons of different Regiments, arrived, marched round the Boulevards down the Place Vendôme to the

[1] The Place du Carrousel between the Tuileries Palace and the Louvre.

Tuileries, shouting *'Vive l'Empereur'*, attended by a number of boys and the lower ranks uttering the same cry.

The City at this time had, as it had the day before, the appearance of a fair, not the slightest alteration in the occupations of the people, except that it seemed a general holiday.

Colonel Armand-Alexandre-Hippolyte de Bonneval was in command of a company of the Bodyguard at Melun, south-east of the capital; but on March 20th he happened to be crossing the Tuileries on his way to the Hôtel des Gardes on the Quai d'Orsay.

The carriage in which the King would travel was already waiting at the door. I learnt that in the general bewilderment no one had remembered to arrange for an escort, so, being on horseback, I hurried to the Quai d'Orsay where my company, in anticipation of some grave incident, was assembled and ready to mount. I immediately called out a detachment and led it back to the King's carriage. He took the road for Ghent, and we followed him for as long as the strength of our horses allowed.

. . . The princes had met together at Béthune, and we escorted them as far as we could. I remember how one day I was at the head of a troop of those brave Guards and was sent for by the Count of Artois.[1] We spoke of the melancholy events of the moment, all the while riding through the frightful mud of Béthune in which our horses sank to their girths. Deep in conversation, I failed to notice a hole full of water. My horse stepped in it and splashed the mud so high that the poor prince had his face plastered. I was in despair and profuse in my apologies, but he replied: *'Mon pauvre ami, what is this compared to what lies in store for us!'*

Hippolyte Carnot, fourteen-year-old son of the great 'Organiser of Victory', the man who had created the armies of the First Republic, was at school at the Lycée Louis-le-Grand when the news of Napoleon's landing became known in Paris.

A sense of anxious expectation seemed to predominate in people's minds. I cannot do better than compare it to the feeling experienced when one watches a hunter leaping from rock to rock on a path

[1] King Louis XVIII's brother, afterwards Charles X.

beside a precipice. Will he reach his target? Will he fall a victim to his daring? Everyone holds his breath.

The streets and boulevards were crowded with people who looked sombre and dejected, though their eyes held a glimmer of hope. They talked in pairs, looking round distrustfully. The hawkers seemed to have no voice left for hailing prospective customers, and the shopkeepers did little except watch the passers-by. Paris had the characteristic air of a great city which feels itself to be on the eve of a catastrophe.

For us schoolboys it was by now impossible to study. How could one memorise verses by Horace and leaf through a dictionary so as to translate some letter written by Caesar to Atticus, when we had before our eyes the spectacle of Livy in action? Books like *Rudiments de Latin* and *Gradus ad Parnassum*[1] lay neglected on our desks. What impositions would have been given out if the masters had not been just as preoccupied as their pupils were! Even during the break we did not play games, but gathered in groups to talk quietly.

. . . Our classroom had a window from which one could see in the distance the top of the Vendôme Column, and my desk stood immediately in front of this window. On the afternoon of March 20th we were at work, but my eyes stared out of the window more often than they looked down at my books. Suddenly I gave a yell which was taken up by the whole class. The white flag had just been lowered, and the tricolour flew in its place. We jumped over the benches, threw open the doors, cheered, embraced one another — we were wild with excitement.

On learning that the Emperor was approaching Paris, Antoine-Marie, Comte Lavallette resumed control of the postal services.

The senior officials and clerks of every rank were all delighted to see the Bourbons in flight and, like me, were convinced that we should never see them again. For already the Bourbons were forgotten to such an extent that the eleven months' reign seemed to be nothing but a bad dream which had lasted for a few hours.

After reorganising the services in the Emperor's interests, I went to the Tuileries, where I found five or six hundred half-pay officers walking in the vast courtyard, embracing and congratulating one

[1] This was a dictionary designed to help students writing Latin verses.

another on the prospect of seeing Napoleon once more. Indoors the Emperor's two sisters-in-law,[1] the Queen of Spain and the Queen of Holland, awaited him in a state of deep emotion. Soon they were joined by their ladies in waiting and those of the Empress. Everywhere the bees had given place to the fleurs-de-lis. However, one of these ladies, on looking carefully at the immense carpet which covered the floor of the throne-room, noticed that one of the fleurs-de-lis appeared to be loose. She tore it, and soon the bee was revealed. All the ladies set to work, and in less than half an hour, amid shouts of laughter from the whole company, the carpet became an imperial one again.

. . . Officers arriving from Fontainebleau in advance of the Emperor told us that it was very difficult to make headway along the road, because dense crowds of peasants were lining, or rather, had taken possession of, each side. Their enthusiasm was immense. No one could tell what time he would arrive. It was to be hoped that no one would recognize him, for an assassin's hand might reach him through all this enthusiasm and tumult. But he and the Duke of Vicenza[2] had adopted the expedient of jumping into a shabby carriage provided with a hood, and at last, at nine o'clock in the evening, this vehicle came to a standstill in front of the entrance near the railings of the Quai du Louvre. Scarcely had he set foot on the ground than there rose a shout of '*Vive l'Empereur*', a tremendous shout, a shout to split the heavens. It came from the half-pay officers who were crowded to suffocation in the entrance-hall and all the way up the staircase.

The Emperor was wearing his famous grey overcoat. I went forward to meet him, and the Duke of Vicenza called to me: 'For God's sake, stand in front of him so that he can get through the crowd.' He began to walk up the stairs. I went one step in front, walking backwards and watching him with deep emotion, my eyes bathed in tears. I was in such a state of exultation that I kept saying over and over again: '*Quoi! C'est vous! C'est vous! C'est enfin vous!*' As for Napoleon, he walked up slowly, his eyes closed and his hands outstretched, as a blind man walks, and showing his happiness by his smile alone.

[1] Joseph Bonaparte's wife, Julie Clary, and Hortense Beauharnais, who had married Louis Bonaparte, King of Holland.
[2] Armand de Caulaincourt (1773–1827) was Master of the Horse to Napoleon.

Lieutenant J. L. Henckens, a Dutch officer who served for ten years with the French army in Italy before taking part in the Russian campaign and being wounded near Leipzig in 1813, relates that his regiment became known, at the time of the Bourbon Restoration, as the Chasseurs de Berry, being in the Duc de Berry's service. On March 16th, 1815, the regiment set out from Senlis for Paris.

Here we were brigaded with the 1st Hussars and the 1st Chasseurs à cheval under the command of General [Edmond de] Talleyrand de Périgord, Duc de Dino. On the 19th the force, still sporting the white cockade, marched on Fontainebleau to oppose Napoleon. We found the King's army bivouacked beside the Rungis, near the acqueduct of Arcueil.[1] We were detailed to billets in nearby villages, with orders to be at the camp by five o'clock next morning.

At the appointed time the regiment paraded without a single absentee, but a large part of the royal army, as well as troops which had left Paris with us, had gone over to join the disembarked 'comrade', taking their arms and baggage and still under the command of their officers.

General de Périgord returned to Paris and the entire regiment followed him. We met still more troops on their way to offer their services to the Emperor. At Villejuif General Sébastiani[2] of the General Staff in Paris informed Colonel de Talhouet[3] that King Louis XVIII had left the capital and that the Emperor Napoleon had been proclaimed. In the town hawkers of tricolour cockades, selling at two sous each, held them under our noses and asked: 'Isn't this worth two sous?'

Colonel de Talhouet paraded the regiment in battle order, called the officers to the front, and said to us, his voice clearly audible to the whole assembly: 'Gentlemen, a new order has been established. I must hand in my resignation on grounds of ill-health, but I beg of you to take your places in the column which is going to rejoin the Emperor and to uphold the honour of the corps at all times.'

[1] Arcueil is on the southern outskirts of Paris, near the Porte d'Orléans. Rungis is further south, near the present Orly Airport. Villejuif lies between the two. The acqueduct dates from the early seventeenth century and was built to convey water to the Jardin du Luxembourg.
[2] François-Horace, Comte Sébastiani, had commanded a cavalry corps in Russia.
[3] Auguste-Frédéric, Baron de Talhouet, had commanded the 6th Chasseurs in Russia.

He embraced a few of the officers — I was included in this honour; then he left.

We had no time even to discuss the matter. The Emperor was at our heels in a post chaise and did not even ask us whether we wanted to follow him again. He enquired the number of the regiment, and we became the 6th Chasseurs à cheval once more. He ordered us to set out via Paris for the northern frontier and invited the officers to attend at the Tuileries next morning, March 21st, at ten o'clock.

There we found our Colonel again. 'Henckens,' he said, 'you realise perfectly well that it is nothing to do with my health that keeps me back, but I am no chameleon and I have come here to tender my resignation to the Emperor. As for the rest of you, I think you should follow the general trend.'

At an audience which the Emperor granted him before receiving the officers, the Colonel handed his sword to Napoleon, who said to him: 'Talhouet, are you going to fight against me?' 'Never, sir!' 'Well, to avoid other resignations I order you to retire until further orders to one of your family estates in Normandy.'

Napoleon, escorted by a few grenadiers of the Guard whose uniforms were no longer new and whose fur bonnets were a bit scorched, sat his horse and harangued the officers, but as the circle was a very large one, we could not hear what he said.

Captain Jean-Baptiste Barrès, who commanded the voltigeurs in the 3rd battalion of the 47th of the Line, was on half pay at home in Auvergne; his account indicates how quickly public support could alter.

On the day we heard the news that the Emperor had reached Paris, I went with my brother to the Prefecture in Le Puy to see our elder brother, Pierre-Maurice, who was Secretary-General of the Haute-Loire. We were both in uniform. Near the entrance to the building we were assailed by a crowd of wretches dressed in rags, who fell on us with shouts of '*Vive l'Empereur!* Down with the white cockade!' And without giving us time to reply, they shoved us around, snatched our shakos, tore off our cockades and hurled insults at us. My brother and I drew our swords in self defence, but as we were seized from behind too, we could not use them. The Prefecture Guard came out and rescued us from the hands of these madcaps, who would have finished up by doing us serious injury. My God, I was angry! I was in tears with rage.

Next day I collected my route and orders for rejoining my regiment in Brest. . . . At Quimper-Corentin my battalion commander, who was garrisoned there, picked a quarrel with us because we still wore Henri IV's effigy on our crosses of honour. Yet this same man had, only a few months earlier, wanted to have me arrested for not having changed Napoleon's effigy and substituted for the imperial eagle the fleurs-de-lis of the old régime.

THE ARMIES ASSEMBLE

FOR the first month after reaching Paris, Napoleon hoped that peace could be maintained, and he tried to open negotiations with Britain, Russia, Austria and Prussia. In vain. A decision at arms became inevitable when these Powers, hurriedly composing their differences at Vienna, pledged themselves to crush Napoleon and drive him once and for all from the throne of France.

The plan was for six armies to cross the French frontier simultaneously: Wellington's of 93,000 and Blücher's 117,000 Prussians, 150,000 Russians, over 200,000 Austrians, Bavarians and Hessians — all heading for Paris from Belgium and the Upper Rhine; and two Austrian-Piedmontese armies, which would cross the Alps and occupy Lyons and Provence.

To meet this formidable coalition of more than half a million troops, Napoleon bent all his energies. He found some 200,000 men under arms. Louis XVIII had recently gained some popularity by abolishing conscription, so the Emperor hesitated to re-introduce what would obviously be an unpalatable measure. Nevertheless, he did recall 100,000 men, some of them deserters or soldiers on long leave; another proclamation produced 150,000 National Guards; and 25,000 retired veterans rejoined the army on invitation.

There was a greater scarcity of materials than of men. Muskets, ammunition, horses' shoes, harness were required. Workshops were quickly set up to make uniforms and to manufacture or recondition weapons. Horses were requisitioned by the thousand. Fortified places were put in a state of defence, though they were to play very little part in the impending campaign. All this reorganisation demanded immense sums of money, energy and control, and these were forthcoming. Indeed, the tremendous galvanising work achieved by Napoleon during these weeks of preparation disposes of the theory that his activity, alertness and vigilance had been seriously diminished. After all, he was only forty-six, and had spent ten restful if frustrating months in the congenial climate of Elba.

It can be argued that certain generals had lost some of the boldness and confidence which had contributed so much to the success of earlier campaigns; or that having tasted peace for a year they were reluctant to exchange home life for the discomforts of bivouac and the dangers of battlefield. Napoleon on St Helena accused them of being faint-hearted men. There is also much to be said for the view that he did not make the best use of the senior commanders available. Some had too patently supported the King or followed him to Ghent; others were less compromised and could be placed in backwater posts; others had pleaded fatigue or illness and retired to the country.

Marshal Suchet, a popular figure, a fine administrator, and one of the best all-rounders, was kept hundreds of miles from the decisive theatre of war, and Napoleon afterwards bemoaned the fact that he had not given to Suchet the command entrusted to Grouchy. Murat, the renowned cavalry leader, was allowed no command, largely thanks to his untimely and abortive attack on the Austrians while King of Naples earlier in the year; yet Napoleon later admitted: 'The victory might have been ours had we had Murat.' Ney was not summoned till two days before the fighting began, and was given no time for preparation. The Emperor's later verdict was that he had been very wrong to employ Ney, who had lost his head. The trusted and experienced Chief of Staff, Marshal Berthier, having fallen to his death from a window on June 1st, was not available, so Marshal Soult, although he had been Minister of War under the Bourbons, was given the post instead of getting a field command; but he had no time to play himself into a part for which he was scarcely fitted by experience, and some of the muddles and delays on the battlefield stem from this fact. As for Marshal Grouchy, on whom so much was to depend, he was at first assigned to command the reserve cavalry, but was very soon placed in command of the right wing of the army and, newly promoted as he was, had no time to get used to his post and added responsibilities or to gain confidence in dealing with his resentful subordinates, Generals Gérard and Vandamme. The latter, rough, disagreeable but zealous, had commanded a division as far back as 1797, at the age of twenty-eight, whereas Gérard had been a colonel at Austerlitz, a brigadier-general at Jena, and, with Marshal Ney, a hero of the rearguard retreating from Moscow. On St Helena Napoleon said to General Gourgaud: 'More vigour and promptness were needed than Grouchy had as a general; he was good only at a splendid charge of cavalry.'

All Napoleon's corps and divisional commanders were under fifty. Of the senior Prussian commanders, Blücher the Mecklenburger was seventy-two, Bülow was sixty, and the brilliant Chief of Staff, Gneisenau, was fifty-five. George Dubislaw Ludwig von Pirch from Magdeburg was three years younger, and he had a brother, Otto Karl Lorenz, commanding a brigade in the corps led by Graf von Zieten, who was only forty-five. The other corps commander, Johann Adolf, Freiherr von Thielmann, born in Dresden fifty years before, had fought on the French side in Russia in 1812, leading a Saxon cavalry brigade under Latour-Maubourg and distinguishing himself at Borodino in particular. Apart from Prussian infantry battalions, Uhlans and Hussars,

Blücher's army included Landwehr cavalry and infantry units from Westphalia, Schleswig, the Elbe, Neumark, Kurmark and Pomerania. The age structure of the British leaders was satisfactory. Wellington, like Napoleon, was forty-six. Lord Hill was forty-two, the Earl of Uxbridge forty-seven. The average age of the divisional and brigade commanders was forty-three, with Sir Thomas Picton, who reached Brussels only the day before Quatre Bras, the oldest at fifty-seven, and Major-General Frederick Adam the youngest at thirty-four. Of Wellington's British battalion commanders, the average age was thirty-seven.

Only a third of his troops were British, and even of these a great many were untried in battle. Of the sixteen British cavalry regiments, five only had served in the Peninsula and another three in southern France. The infantry position was more favourable. Three battalions in Lambert's brigade arrived just in time for Waterloo, having landed from America and hurried to the field: they were Peninsular veterans. Of the remaining twenty-two battalions, fifteen had fought in Portugal and Spain, and another had served in Holland in 1814. However, the 3rd/14th Regiment was composed chiefly of young recruits, and fourteen officers and over three hundred men had not attained the age of twenty. Most of the Royal Artillery and Royal Horse Artillery had war service, but the Royal Engineers, apart from a few officers and men who had campaigned in Holland, notably at the storming of Bergen-op-Zoom in March, 1814, had not been in action.

The King's German Legion provided two regiments of light dragoons, three of hussars, six line battalions and two light battalions. The five Hanoverian brigades comprised field battalions from Bremen, Lüneberg, Verden and other towns, and militia from Hildesheim, Minden, Hameln, Osnabrück and elsewhere. These Hanoverians numbered 16,000, and in addition Wellington disposed of 29,000 Dutch–Belgian soldiers, 6,800 Brunswickers, and nearly 3,000 from Nassau. The loyalty of some of these contingents was uncertain, since they had been raised in territory which for the past few years had been subject to France, and some had even served in the French Army. In 1819, walking over the battlefield with Sir John Jones, a prominent Engineer, the Duke remarked: 'I had only about 35,000 men on whom I could thoroughly rely; the remainder were but too likely to run away.' When, five weeks after the battle, an old friend from Indian days observed that Wellington had had more than half his troops of other nations, he received the reply: 'That did not signify, for I had discovered the secret of mixing them up together. Had I employed them in separate corps I should have lost the battle.'

In the words of Sir Henry Hardinge: 'This army is not unlike a French pack of hounds: pointers, poodles, turnspits, all mixed up together and running in sad confusion.'

Lieutenant Frederick Mainwaring of the 51st Foot was with his regiment in Portsmouth when the news came that Napoleon had left Elba for southern France.

One morning in March I was seated with two or three others at breakfast in the mess-room; the Bugle-Major came in with the letters and as usual laid the newspaper upon the mess-table. Someone opened it, and glanced his eyes carelessly and coldly for a few moments over its contents, when suddenly his countenance brightened up, and flinging the newspaper into the air like a madman, he shouted out: 'Glorious news! Nap's landed again in France! Hurrah!' In an instant we were all wild — 'Nap's in France again' spread like wildfire through the barracks — the men turned out and cheered — nay, that night at mess, the moment the cloth was removed, the President rose and drank success to old Nap with three times three — our joy was unbounded, and few, I believe, went to bed that night sober.

Captain Cavalié Mercer, whose 'G' Troop, Royal Horse Artillery was stationed at Colchester when the news arrived of Napoleon's return from Elba, relates that reductions to put the troop on a peace establishment had already begun when orders came for immediate re-equipment for foreign service.

To do this effectually, another troop, then in the same barracks, was broken up, and we got the picked horses of both, thus making it the finest troop in the service; and such diligence was used, that although our equipment fell little short of a complete reorganisation, Major Sir A. Fraser, commanding the horse-artillery in Colchester, was enabled to report on the third day that the troop was ready to march at a moment's warning.

Meantime the town of Colchester (situated as it is on the great road from Harwich to London) presented a scene of bustle and anxiety seldom equalled — couriers passing to and fro incessantly, and numerous travellers, foreign and English, arriving day and night from the Continent, many travelling in breathless haste, as if fearful, even here, of Napoleon's emissaries.

The reports spread by these fugitives were various and contradictory, as might be expected. According to some, Louis XVIII had been arrested in Paris; according to others, he had sought

c

refuge in the Pays Bas; and again, it was asserted that His Majesty was at Ostend, awaiting permission to pass the sea and return to his old and secure quarters in England.[1]

In the midst of all this, on the 8th April, the post brought our order to march forthwith to Harwich, there to embark for Ostend — an order received with unfeigned joy by officers and men, all eager to plunge into danger and bloodshed, all hoping to obtain glory and distinction.

On the morning of the 9th, the troop paraded at half-past seven o'clock with as much regularity and as quietly as if only going to a field-day; not a man either absent or intoxicated, and every part of the guns and appointments in the most perfect order. At eight, the hour named in orders, we marched off the parade. The weather was fine, the scenery, as we skirted the beautiful banks of the Stour, charming, and the occasion exhilarating.

Near Manningtree we halted a short time to feed our horses, and then, pursuing our route, arrived at Harwich about three o'clock in the afternoon. Here we found the transports — the *Adventure*, *Philarea*, and *Salus*, in which last I embarked — awaiting us; but the tide being unfavourable, although we immediately commenced operations, we only succeeded in embarking the horses of one division and those of the officers; the remainder were therefore put up in the barracks for the night.

. . . With day-break on the morning of the 12th came a favourable wind, though light, and again we took up our anchors and proceeded to sea. . . . Our keel had scarcely touched the sand [at Ostend] ere we were abruptly boarded by a naval officer (Captain Hill[2]) with a gang of sailors, who, *sans cérémonie*, instantly commenced hoisting our horses out, and throwing them, as well as our saddlery, etc., overboard, without ever giving time for making any disposition to receive or secure the one or the other. To my remonstrance his answer was, 'I can't help it, sir; the Duke's *orders are positive that no delay is to take place in landing the troops as they arrive, and the ships sent back again; so you must be out of her before dark.*' It was then about 2 p.m.; and I thought this a most uncomfortable arrangement.

The scramble and confusion that ensued baffle all description. Bundles of harness went over the side in rapid succession, as well as horses. In vain we urged the loss and damage that must accrue

[1] The French king had lived at Hartwell House near Aylesbury.
[2] John Hill was the senior officer of the Transport Service at Ostend.

from such a proceeding. 'Can't help it — no business of mine — Duke's orders are positive,' etc. etc., was our only answer. Meantime the ebb had begun to diminish the depth of water alongside, and enabled us to send parties overboard and to the beach to collect and carry things ashore, as well as to haul and secure the horses. The same operation commenced from the other vessels as they arrived, and the bustle and noise were inconceivable. The Dragoons and our men (some nearly, others quite, naked) were dashing in and out of the water, struggling with the affrighted horses, or securing their wet accoutrements as best they could. Some of the former were saddling their dripping horses, and others mounting and marching off in small parties.

Mr George Jackson, who had been sent in April, 1813, to Berlin as Chargé d'Affaires to the King of Prussia, wrote to his mother on March 27th:

The first news of the reappearance of Bonaparte was treated by the people of Berlin generally as a false report, and they were inclined to attribute it to the Saxons. But when the confirmation arrived, which it did on the very same evening, the whole city was in a state of agitation and alarm. Europe united, it was supposed, had really vanquished 'the invincible', and Prussia was fairly freed from the yoke of her oppressor; but here he was again, and the work of the last year and a half had to be gone through once more. Who should dare to venture to predict its result. A calmer feeling now prevails; still his successful advance causes considerable uneasiness in the public mind, which the reports of the French Government, disparagingly as they speak of Bonaparte and his rash incursion into the French territory, do not greatly allay. With reference to them, on his getting possession of Lyons it was acutely remarked by some, 'What! with only *eight* thousand followers? without cannon, arms, or ammunition! If so, the country must be with him, and we may look forward to another war; to desolate homes, and the ruin of our country, even if victory should be with us'; for Prussia already suffers from such wide-spread misery and poverty that half a century will hardly suffice for the restoration of the people and the state to their former condition of ease and prosperity.

. . . However, the preparing for war is always animating, and as already the first beat of the reveille has been heard, Berlin is the livelier for it. Yet, curses on the author of this new mischief are freely growled forth by many a man who has to take up the knapsack he has just cast off, and to buckle on the sword he had hoped to turn into the much needed ploughshare and pruning hook.

. . . By letters from Vienna, we learn that when that city is no longer honoured by royal visitors, when *les grands seigneurs et les grandes dames* no longer display their *grandes toilettes* on the promenade of the Bastion, when every European order, uniform and costume, that for months past have made it so brilliant, together with the last renowned statesman and distinguished warrior, shall have taken their departure, then the Viennese ladies mean to do penance. Instead of figuring in velvets, laces, and jewels, they propose to wear, until peace shall be restored, a dress of some homely material, I suppose the nearest approach that can be obtained to a sort of ladylike sackcloth.

The ladies of Berlin and other German towns have been invited to do likewise, and this reform in dress has found favour in their eyes. No silk dresses or any jewels or ornaments are to be worn; one sad sober tint is to prevail throughout the land, until husbands, brothers, and sons, return from the wars with fresh laurels.

Franz Lieber, who was born the son of a business man in Berlin and afterwards had to seek political asylum in America, where he became Professor of History and Political Economy in South Carolina College and later Professor of Political Science at Columbia College, New York, has left an account, written in English, of how he enlisted in the Prussian army for the Waterloo campaign.

'Boys, clean your rifles,' said my old and venerable father, entering the room, where I was studying Loder's Anatomical Tables. 'He is loose again.' 'Napoleon?' 'He has returned from Elba.' My heart beat high; it was glorious news for a boy of sixteen, who had often heard with silent envy the account of the campaigns of 1813 and '14 from the lips of his two brothers, both of whom had marched in 1813, in common with most young men of good families, as volunteer riflemen, and returned as wounded officers.

The one, cured of his wounds, rejoined his regiment; another of my brothers and myself followed the call of government to enter the army as volunteers, though our age would have exempted us from all obligation. Which regiment should we choose? Of course, one which was garrisoned near the enemy's frontier, so that we were sure not to have a peaceable campaign in a distant reserve. There was a regiment among the troops near the frontiers of France which enjoyed a peculiarly high and just reputation; its name was *Colberg*, bestowed upon the brave band in honor of its valiant defence of the fortress of Colberg,[1] in the year 1806 — the only Prussian fortified place at that wretched time which did not surrender to the French. It was composed of brave and sturdy Pomeranians, a short, broad-shouldered, healthy race. In more than twenty 'ranged' engagements[2] during the campaign of '13 and '14, they had shown themselves worthy of their honorable name. My brother and I selected this regiment.

When the day appointed for the enlistment of the volunteers arrived, we went to my father and said, 'Well, then, we go; is it with your consent?' 'Go to your mother', he replied. We went to her; our hearts were big; she had suffered so much during the first campaign. With a half-choked voice I said, 'Mother, we go to be enrolled, shall we?' She fell into our arms, that noble woman, worthy of the best times of Rome, and sobbed aloud. 'Go' was all her bleeding heart allowed her to utter; and had she been the mother of twenty sons, she would have sent them all.

A table was placed in the centre of a square in the city of Berlin, at which several officers were enlisting those who offered themselves. We had to wait from ten to one o'clock before we could get a chance to have our names taken down, the throng was so great.

In the beginning of the month of May we were marched from Berlin to our regiments. . . . My father accompanied us to the place of rendez-vous. When the bugle called us to the lines, we looked for him, to take the last leave; he had stolen himself away. A great many people accompanied us out of the city; the beautiful Brandenburg Gate was soon behind us; we began to sing.

. . . On the 2nd of June we had our first parade with the regiment [near Namur], and the colonel declared that we had the bearing of old soldiers; he was satisfied with us. We longed to be tried. I saw on that day, for the first time, the woman who was sergeant in our regiment, and distinguished herself so much that she could boast of three orders on her gown, when, after the peace, she was married, in Berlin, to another sergeant.

---

[1] A town on the Baltic coast, between Stettin and Danzig.
[2] 'Pitched battles' would be a more usual phrase.

This letter, written on May 18th in the Belgian town of Hove by Lieutenant-Colonel Alexander Lord Saltoun, 1st Regiment of Foot Guards, to his wife Catherine indicates the life and mood of the assembling army.

The Duke of Wellington has been for some days back riding a good deal, and we used to say in Spain that whenever the Beau, meaning the Duke, took to riding, it was time to look out. However, I believe this time he is only looking at his troops, which have been much increased lately by several battalions of Hanoverian landwehr,[1] who are tolerably good-looking men in general, but, of course, from their having been raised by conscription since the breaking out of this business, are a good deal in want of drill and other necessary training. The spirit which the French call *morale* is very good in them, and they are pleased at acting with the British, whom they consider as countrymen. John Bull, however, does not by any means admit them to that honourable distinction, but calls them 'rid Jarmins', from their being dressed in red.

At present Enghien is quite gay. Some of our officers are good cricket players, and at present a match is going on from A to G — that is, men whose names begin with any letter from A to G inclusive — against the rest of the alphabet, including the Duke of Richmond[2]. . . . The A to G beat the others hollow yesterday and they are to try it again to-day.

On May 8th Wellington wrote in a letter to Lieutenant-General Lord Stewart, formerly his Adjutant-General in the Peninsula:

I have got an infamous army, very weak and ill equipped, and a very inexperienced Staff. In my opinion they are doing nothing in England. They have not raised a man; they have not called out the militia either in England or Ireland; are unable to send me any thing; and they have not sent a message to Parliament about the money. The war spirit is therefore evaporating as I am informed.

[1] The *Landwehr* was a citizens' militia, created in 1813.
[2] Charles, 4th Duke of Richmond and Lennox (1764–1819), was living in Brussels with his family.

He told Lieutenant-General Sir Lowry Cole on June 2nd:

I wish I could bring every thing together as I had it when I took leave of the Army at Bordeaux [June, 1814], and I would engage that we should not be last in the race.[1]

We learn from the memoirs of Colonel Scheltens that when he was a sergeant in the 7th Belgian battalion of the line, one company was detailed each day to guard King Louis XVIII in Ghent.

I thus had opportunities to admire his appetite, and we were often obliged to chase little urchins who used to heave themselves up on to the window sills on the street side of the house and would count out loud the number of dishes and glasses the King swallowed. Sometimes the greed with which he ate and drank were such as to bring him out in a sweat, and the people of Ghent made a very unkind pun on the subject, nicknaming him 'Louis di zweet!'[2]

Rees Howell Gronow left Eton in 1812 and was commissioned as an Ensign in the 1st Regiment of Foot Guards. He served for some months in Spain, but when the imminence of renewed war hung over June, 1815, Gronow saw no prospect of seeing action, since his battalion remained in London. However, he had the good fortune to be introduced to Sir Thomas Picton, who was going out to take command of the 5th Division.

He was very gracious, and, on his two aides-de-camp — Major Tyler and my friend Chambers, of the Guards[3] — lamenting that I was obliged to remain at home, Sir Thomas said, 'Is the lad really anxious to go out?' Chambers answered that it was the height of my ambition. Sir Thomas inquired if all the appointments to his staff were filled up; and then added, with a grim smile, 'If Tyler is killed, which is not at all unlikely I do not know why I should not take my young countryman: he may go

---

[1] In 1819 he said to Sir John Jones, the distinguished Engineer: 'If I had had the same army as in the south of France the battle [Waterloo] would have been won in three hours.'

[2] This is Flemish for 'Louis who sweats'. Its pronunciation is akin to 'Louis dix-huit'.

[3] Captain J. Tyler, 93rd Foot, was wounded, and Captain Newton Chambers, 1st Foot Guards, was killed at Waterloo.

over with me if he can get leave.' I was overjoyed at this, and, after thanking the general a thousand times, made my bow and retired.

I was much elated at the thoughts of being Picton's aide-de-camp, though that somewhat remote contingency depended upon my friends Tyler, or Chambers, or others, meeting with an untimely end; but at eighteen *on ne se doute de rien.* So I set about thinking how I should manage to get my outfit, in order to appear at Brussels in a manner worthy of the aide-de-camp of the great general. As my funds were at a low ebb I went to Cox and Greenwood's,[1] those staunch friends of the hard-up soldier. Sailors may talk of the 'little cherub that sits up aloft', but commend me for liberality, kindness, and generosity to my old friends in Craig's Court. I there obtained £200, which I took with me to a gambling-house in St. James's Square[2], where I managed, by some wonderful accident, to win £600; and, having thus obtained the sinews of war, I made numerous purchases, amongst others two first-rate horses at Tattersall's for a high figure, which were embarked for Ostend, along with my groom. I had not got leave; but I thought I should get back, after the great battle that appeared imminent, in time to mount guard at St. James's.

Major-General Baron Carl von Müffling was posted to British Headquarters in Brussels with the appointment of liaison officer between Wellington and Blücher, and he proved to be a great deal more successful than his predecessor in the post.

Little as this appointment accorded with my wishes, and slight as were my expectations of being able to render important services in this post, I readily obeyed, although in my early studies of the English language I had not got beyond the 'Vicar of Wakefield' and Thomson's 'Seasons'.[3]

On my departure General von Gneisenau warned me to be much on my guard with the Duke of Wellington, for that by his relations with India, this distinguished general had so accustomed himself to duplicity, that he had at last become such a master in the art as even to outwit the Nabobs themselves. . . .

---

[1] The Army agents, with offices in Craig's Court, Charing Cross.
[2] From 1807 to 1816 a certain George Raggett ran a gambling-house at No. 21, named the Union Club.
[3] Oliver Goldsmith's book appeared in 1766. James Thomson's *The Seasons* was published in 1730.

I perceived that the Duke exercised far greater power in the army he commanded than Prince Blücher in the one committed to his care. The rules of the English service permitted the Duke's suspending any officer and sending him back to England. . . . Amongst all the generals, from the leaders of corps to the commanders of brigades, not one was to be found in the active army who had been known as refractory.

It was not the custom in this army to criticise or control the Commander-in-Chief. Discipline was strictly enforced; every one knew his rights and his duties. The Duke, in matters of service, was very short and decided. He allowed questions, but dismissed all such as were unnecessary. His detractors have accused him of being inclined to encroach on the functions of others, — a charge which is at variance with my experience.

His Military Secretary and Quarter-master-General[1] were tried men; his aides-de-camp and *galopins*[2] were young men in the best families in England, who thought it an honour to devote to their country, and its greatest commander, all the energies of their will and intellect. Mounting the best horses of England's famous breed, they made a point of honour, whenever the Duke added 'Quick!' to a message, of riding three German miles in the hour, or one mile[3] in eighteen minutes.

A fortnight, or perhaps three weeks before the battle of Waterloo, Mr Thomas Creevey and his two step-daughters were walking in the Park at Brussels when the Duke of Wellington joined them. After a few remarks had been exchanged, Creevey said: 'Will you let me ask you, Duke, what you think you will make of it?'

He stopt, and said in the most natural manner: — 'By God! I think Blücher and myself can do the thing.' — 'Do you calculate,' I asked, 'upon any desertion in Buonaparte's army?' — 'Not upon a man,' he said, 'from the colonel to the private in a regiment — both inclusive. We may pick up a marshal or two, perhaps; but not worth a damn.' — 'Do you reckon,' I asked, 'upon any support from the French King's troops at Alost?' — 'Oh!' said he, 'don't mention such fellows! No: I think Blücher and I can do the

---

[1] Lieut.-Colonel Lord Fitzroy Somerset and Colonel Sir William de Lancey.
[2] Errand-boys; gallopers.
[3] The equivalent of four English miles.

business.' — Then, seeing a private soldier of one of our infantry regiments enter the park, gaping about at the statues and images: — 'There,' he said, pointing at the soldier, 'it all depends upon that article whether we do the business or not. Give me enough of it, and I am sure.'

William Gibney, Assistant Surgeon to the 15th Hussars quartered near Ghent, says that they expected every day to get orders to march into France and anticipated hard fighting before much longer.

It was wonderful with what indifference we spoke or rather joked with each other on coming events. To one, tall and big, the information was vouchsafed that his chances of being hit were good, so huge an individual forming a target not to be missed. To another, with an unusually prominent nasal organ, its liability to attract the enemy's attention to him was pointed out; and so on everlastingly. The jokes were more personal than polite, and fell hard on such as rode badly, or, rather, who were not thoroughly at home in the saddle.

Little did we think whilst thus laughing, joking and growling at the delay in advancing, that the enemy were close upon us; but it was so. Our information was bad in the extreme; at any rate, we were kept in the dark by the authorities as to what was going on elsewhere, and nothing ever came from the peasantry in the way of news. They knew nothing, and seemed to care less. However, the order to march came at last, and that very suddenly.

THE OPENING MOVES

Two plans were open to Napoleon. He could maintain a strictly defensive attitude until July, mass troops round Paris and near Lyons, and fight it out among the network of military strongholds — in many respects a repetition of the 1814 campaign, but with twice the number of men at his disposal and with Paris strongly fortified and resolutely defended. To this end he had appointed Marshal Davout as Governor of the capital as well as Minister of War. Against this plan was the fact that he would have to leave undefended a third of his territory, of which the resources would fall to his enemies and the inhabitants be subjected to a second invasion within eighteen months. Moreover, the effect upon French morale would be bad, arousing despondency and, more serious, hostility in the Chamber and probably fresh insurrections in the west and south. Not until April 16th had the last centres of royalist resistance given in, and a subsequent revolt in La Vendée had obliged Napoleon to despatch troops there.

The second and bolder plan was to attack the enemy before he could concentrate, to beat in turn the Anglo-Dutch and Prussian armies, who constituted the only immediate threat but seemed likely to remain in Belgium until their allies had reached the frontier; and then, joining up with the army he had left in the east, Napoleon would bear down on the Austrian and Russian forces and seek to defeat them or to induce their rulers to sue for peace. After balancing the factors involved, the Emperor decided to attack Wellington and Blücher in the middle of June.

The two Allied armies were holding a front of nearly a hundred miles. The Duke, with headquarters in Brussels, drew his supplies from Ostend and Antwerp, while the Prussian line of communication stretched away in the opposite direction, from Blücher's headquarters in Namur through Liége to Coblenz on the Rhine. Napoleon calculated that if either army were to retreat, it would move towards its own base, and to do so would entail marching away from its ally. His aim was to smash at the vulnerable junction of the two armies — Charleroi; drive a wedge between them, and destroy each in turn, meanwhile pinning down the other with one of his wings. It seemed likely that the Prussians, nearer to the frontier, would be the first to concentrate, and this probability was increased, in French eyes, by the nature of the two enemy commanders-in-chief. To quote General Gourgaud: 'The hussar habits of

Marshal Blücher, his activity and decided character, formed a strong contrast with the cautious dispositions, the deliberate and methodical manner of the Duke of Wellington.' Napoleon expected that the Prussians would offer battle at or near Fleurus, and that he would be able to overcome them before they could be joined by the Anglo-Dutch army. Indeed, he went so far as to tell Gourgaud on St Helena: 'I felt sure when I attacked the Prussians that the English would not come to their assistance, while Blücher, who is hot-headed, would have hastened to support Wellington, though he had only two battalions.'

By nightfall on June 14th the Emperor had concentrated his army, which had been extended between Lille and Metz, opposite to the Belgian frontier by Charleroi — five corps and Grouchy's cavalry reserve, totalling some 120,000 troops. Wellington and Blücher had foreseen this aim, and had planned to assemble at Gosselies and Fleurus respectively, but Napoleon's remarkable skill and secrecy deprived them of the three days' warning on which they counted. Rumours of French moves had not brought them from widely dispersed cantonments, and demonstrations along the frontier had achieved their object of spreading false alarms among the Allied outposts.

Early next day the French crossed the Sambre and encountered Zieten's corps, whose stubborn resistance gave time for Blücher to concentrate the rest of his army at Sombreffe, only four miles further back. French cavalry entered Charleroi at noon to a largely sympathetic welcome, but the French right wing, now under Grouchy's command, was then held up for close on five hours until Napoleon infused some vigour into the assault. Zieten's men withdrew to Fleurus, and the leading French corps bivouacked north of Châtelet and Charleroi, where the Emperor spent the night.

Meanwhile, on the left wing, 50,000 troops under Ney had crossed the Sambre at Marchienne and marched without urgency the six miles to Gosselies, pushing out the Prussians, but not obeying Napoleon's categoric order to seize the vital cross-roads to which Quatre Bras owes its name. Fortunately, Prince Bernhard of Saxe-Weimar, perceiving the danger, took it upon himself to place his Orange-Nassau brigade there, an action which was soon confirmed by General Perponcher, commanding the 2nd Dutch–Belgian Division.

Still uncertain of the direction of Napoleon's main thrust, Wellington was late in learning of the French attack, and, being very sensitive to a possible threat to his links with the coast, did not order an immediate concentration on his left flank, beside the Prussians. Instead, at five o'clock on the afternoon of June 15th, he ordered the cavalry to Vilvorde and Ninove, with the infantry divisions to Enghien, Ath, Braine-le-Comte and Grammont. The two reserve divisions in Brussels were to be in readiness 'to march at a moment's notice', and the Prince of Orange was to collect two of the Low Countries divisions at Nivelles.

Thus the Duke ordered his troops to concentrate *away* from Blücher, to cover the roads from Mons and Ath — a decision influenced in part by deliberate French sorties made from places such as Lille and Dunkirk so as to convey the impression that an attack was about to be launched against the exposed British flank. Subsequent orders issued at ten that evening brought the cavalry and two infantry divisions in to Enghien, and two others moved eastwards to Nivelles and Braine-le-Comte. If Wellington can be accused of leisurely handling on the 15th, or of underestimating or misunderstanding the enemy's build-up, it would soon be the turn of his opponents to waste precious time and to under- or overestimate.

On June 14th Blücher's Chief of Staff, Graf Neithardt von Gneisenau, wrote from Namur to a friend named Justus Gruner.

We are still standing idle here while the enemy is increasing his strength. The blame for this lies in our suspicious policy.

General Zieten,[1] who commands our corps positioned closest to the enemy, has today reported that (1) Bonaparte reached Maubeuge last night, (2) the 2nd French Corps under Reille[2] has already arrived in Maubeuge, (3) the Guards coming from Avesnes have joined Bonaparte, (4) troops have already crossed the Sambre and the frontier villages are full of them. Orders have already been issued for our corps to concentrate and to prepare for any eventuality.

Volunteer Henri Niemann, of the 6th Prussian Black Hussar Regiment in Lützow's[3] brigade of the 1st Army Corps, relates that on June 15th it became known to Blücher's men that the first three shots of heavy ordnance would signal the opening of hostilities.

I was lying on a bundle of straw when, early in the morning of 15 June, I heard those three shots. This was three o'clock in the morning, and about three hours after we marched towards the frontier again. We passed through Gasly and took position on the

[1] Hans Ernst Karl, Graf von Zieten (1770–1848).
[2] Honoré-Charles-Michel-Joseph, Comte Reille (1775–1860), commanded the 2nd Corps d'Armée. He was a veteran of Italy, Wagram and the Peninsula.
[3] Ludwig Adolf Wilhelm, Freiherr von Lützow (1782–1834) gave his name to the famous 'Free Corps' of patriotic volunteers, 'the Black Jäger' which he raised in Prussia during the War of Liberation, 1813.

other side of it. Napoleon came nearer with his army; firing began. My heart began to beat, but I soon forgot I might be shot. By command of General Ziethen we engaged the French; but it was nothing more than a feint; they retreated before us. Not having yet removed our wounded from the field, they renewed the fight with a stronger force. Fighting, we slowly retired. We were obliged to cover our retreat, and the hail of balls in covering our artillery from the enemy's attack was not very pleasant. However it was of no use to make long faces; we lost in all about three thousand men. Towards evening of that day our brigade, four regiments of cavalry, reached Fleurus; we bivouacked before the city, but an order came to break up. We marched through Fleurus and bivouacked on the other side that night. I would have paid five francs for a glass of water. On the right of the road was a windmill.[1]

Captain Fritz —— (1786–1859), whose name it has not been possible to trace, came from an ancient and titled family in Pomeranian Mecklenburg, which for many generations had always joined the Army. His father Wilhelm, having been decorated with the rare 'Pour le Mérite' Order, died in battle with the French in 1793, while serving in Blücher's Hussars. One ancestor had commanded a cavalry regiment under Gustavus Adolphus of Sweden. Another had been killed at the battle of Fehrbellin, where in 1675 the Great Elector with his Prussian troops had beaten the Swedish army. Fritz's grandfather had served in Frederick the Great's Black Hussars, who wore the skull and crossbones badge. Fritz himself had fought at Auerstadt and Eylau, and been wounded in street fighting in Lübeck.

In the Waterloo campaign he found himself commanding a squadron of Westphalian Landwehr, and records in his memoirs that he and his men bivouacked for the night of June 15th in thick corn.

We could look forward with certainty to a bloody day on the morrow, and many of our Westphalian militiamen who had a wife and children at home and had never been in action looked very solemn, and their gay songs and chatter died steadily away. Many tried to write a note to their distant loved ones, using pencil or pale ink on coarse paper, and many of them knelt for this purpose

[1] The mill of Bussy, a mile west of Ligny village. This mill was Blücher's station during much of the battle on June 16th.

before a drum or a block of wood which had to serve as writing-desk. I too wrote to my Louise, my beloved fiancée in the East Prussian pastor's house, and I laid the sheet of paper on the saddle of my stallion as I did so.

Sergeant Hippolyte de Mauduit of the Old Guard describes the scene at Charleroi that same evening.

Our battalion (the 2nd of the 1st Regiment of Grenadiers), on duty with the Emperor, bivouacked in the courtyard of a small *château* on the banks of the Sambre, not far from the bridge. Napoleon had selected it for his Headquarters. Duties were carried out with the same punctuality as at the Tuileries Palace, with this difference, that we now had six hundred men instead of the sixty which we provided in Paris.

. . . Having installed ourselves in the courtyard of this Imperial Headquarters, we busied ourselves cooking food for a morning meal as well as for the evening, because we had been either on the march or else in positions for nearly eighteen hours without being able so much as to unhook our cooking-pots, and all the signs indicated that the same thing would happen on the next day. So each man took steps to obtain rations and also to snatch a few hours' rest before marching off to attack the waiting enemy. We all wanted our revenge for the losses we had incurred during the day.

Aides-de-camp and staff officers constantly came and went in the courtyard of this makeshift palace, and in the course of dashing about they often knocked over several piles of our muskets and set our old grenadiers cursing; they had a soft spot for the weapon which so often served as a mirror on festival days and as a crutch and a sheet anchor on days of fatigue and battle.

That same day Captain Harry Ross-Lewin of the 32nd Regiment dined in Brussels with his brigade commander, Sir James Kempt, who had distinguished himself in Holland, Egypt, at Maida and in the Peninsula, and who, at Waterloo, succeeded to the command of the 5th Division when Picton was killed.

Coffee and a young aide-de-camp from the Duke of Wellington came in together. This officer was the bearer of a note from the

Duke, and while Sir James was reading it, said: 'Old Blücher has been hard at it; a Prussian officer has just come to the Beau [a nickname for Wellington], all covered with sweat and dirt, and says they have had much fighting.' Our host then rose and, addressing the regimental officers at the table, said: 'Gentlemen, you will proceed without delay to your respective regiments, and let them get under arms immediately.'

On my way I found several of our officers sitting at a coffee-house door, and told them Sir James Kempt's orders. They seemed at first to think that I was jesting, being hardly able to credit the tidings of so near and so unexpected an approach of the French; but they soon perceived that I spoke seriously, and dispersed each to his own quarters. In a few minutes, however, the most incredulous would have been thoroughly undeceived, for then drums began to beat, bugles to sound, and Highland pipes to squeal in all quarters of the city.

Wellington's Quartermaster-General, Colonel Sir William Howe De Lancey, had married at the beginning of April Miss Magdalene Hall, and his new bride accompanied him to Brussels. They arrived on Thursday, June 8th, and were billeted in the Rue Royale, facing the Park. Lady De Lancey afterwards described the following Thursday, June 15th.

That forenoon was the happiest day of my life; but I cannot recollect a day of my short married life that was not perfect. We little dreamt that Thursday was the last we were to pass together, and that the storm would burst so soon. Sir William had to dine at the Spanish Ambassador's, the first invitation he had accepted from the time I went; he was unwilling to go, and delayed and still delayed, till at last when near six, I fastened all his medals and crosses on his coat, helped him to put it on, and he went. He turned back at the door and looked at me with a smile of happiness and peace. It was the last!

I watched at the window till he was out of sight, and then I continued musing on my happy fate; I thought over all that had passed, and how grateful I felt! I had no wish but that this might continue; I saw my husband loved and respected by everyone, my life gliding on, like a gay dream, in his care.

When I had remained at the window nearly an hour, I saw an

aide-de-camp ride under the gateway of our house. He sent to enquire where Sir William was dining. I wrote down the name; and soon after I saw him gallop off in that direction. I did not like this appearance, but I tried not to be afraid. A few minutes after, I saw Sir William on the same horse gallop past to the Duke's, which was a few doors beyond ours.[1] He dismounted and ran into the house — left the horse in the middle of the street. I must confess my courage failed me now, and the succeeding two hours formed a contrast to the happy forenoon.

About nine Sir William came in; seeing my wretched face, he bade me not be foolish, for it would soon be all over now; they expected a great battle on the morrow; he would send me to Antwerp in the morning, and desired me to be ready at six. He said that though he expected it would be a decisive battle, and a conclusion of the whole business, he thought it best I should keep the plan of going to Antwerp, to avoid the alarms that he knew would seize everyone the moment the troops were gone; and he said he would probably join me there, or send for me to return the same evening. He said he would be writing all night, perhaps; he desired me to prepare some strong green tea in case he came in, as the violent exertion requisite to setting the whole army in motion quite stupefied him sometimes. He used sometimes to tell me that whenever the operations began, if he thought for five minutes on any other subject, he was neglecting his duty. I therefore scrupulously avoided asking him any questions, or indeed speaking at all. I entreated to remain in the room with him, promising not to speak. He wrote for several hours without any interruption but the entrance and departure of the various messengers who were to take the orders. Every now and then I gave him a cup of green tea, which was the only refreshment he would take, and he rewarded me by a silent look. My feelings during these hours I cannot attempt to describe, but I preserved outward tranquillity.

He went to the office, and returned near twelve, much fatigued, but he did not attempt to sleep; he went twice to the Duke's; the first time he found him standing looking over a map with a Prussian general [Müffling], who was in full-dress uniform — with orders and crosses, etc. — the Duke was in his chemise and slippers, preparing to dress for the Duchess of Richmond's ball; the two figures were quite admirable. . . . About two, Sir William went again to the Duke, and he was sleeping sound! [Cf. top of page 41.]

[1] Number 54, Rue Royale.

D

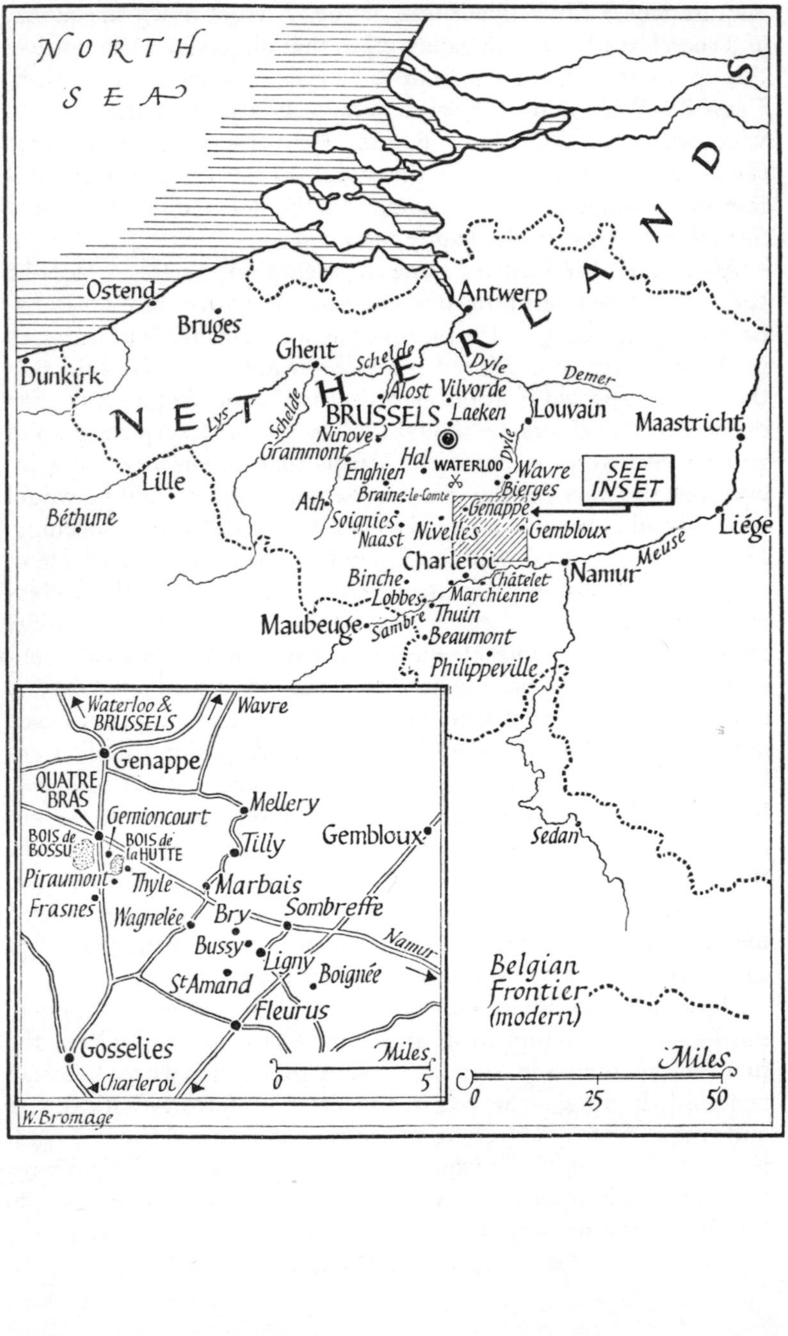
NORTH SEA
NETHERLANDS
Ostend
Bruges
Antwerp
Ghent
Dunkirk
Schelde
Dyle
Demer
Alost
Vilvorde
Laeken
Louvain
Lys
BRUSSELS
Maastricht
Ninove
Grammont
Hal
WATERLOO
Wavre
Enghien
Bierges
SEE INSET
Lille
Braine-le-Comte
Ath
Genappe
Béthune
Soignies
Nivelles
Gembloux
Liége
Naast
Charleroi
Meuse
Namur
Binche
Châtelet
Marchienne
Lobbes
Thuin
Maubeuge
Sambre
Beaumont
Philippeville
Sedan
Belgian Frontier (modern)
Miles
0
25
50
Waterloo & BRUSSELS
Wavre
Genappe
QUATRE BRAS
Mellery
Gemioncourt
BOIS de BOSSU
BOIS de la HUTTE
Tilly
Gembloux
Piraumont
Thyle
Marbais
Frasnes
Wagnelée
Bry
Sombreffe
Bussy
Namur
Ligny
Boignée
St Amand
Fleurus
Gosselies
Charleroi
Miles
0
5
W. Bromage

Arthur Wellesley, 1st Duke of Wellington, by Goya. ca. 1812
(*National Gallery of Art, Washington, D.C., Gift of Mrs. P. H. B. Frelinghuysen*)

Caroline Gordon, Duchess of Richmond, by Lawrence (*New York Public Library Print Collection*)

THE DUCHESS OF RICHMOND'S BALL

THERE was a sound of revelry by night,
And Belgium's capital had gather'd then
Her Beauty and her Chivalry, and bright
The lamps shone o'er fair women and brave men. . . .

Ah! then and there was hurrying to and fro,
And gathering tears, and tremblings of distress,
And cheeks all pale, which but an hour ago
Blush'd at the praises of their own loveliness.

Byron: *Waterloo*

Captain William Verner of the 7th Hussars was an old friend of the Duke and Duchess of Richmond and stayed with them several times in Brussels during this period. One day in June the Duchess confided to Captain Verner her intention of giving a ball, and asked whether he would be good enough to deliver invitations to various cavalry officers. This he gladly undertook to do. The Duchess then placed the invitations in his hands and observed:

'It might appear extraordinary me giving a ball at such a time, when all the papers as well as all the private communications announced that the French Army had marched to the frontier, and when it was not known the moment our Army might not be ordered out to meet them. I said to the Duke of Wellington, "Duke, I do not wish to pry into your secrets, nor do I ask what your intentions may be. I wish to give a ball, and all I ask is, may I give my ball? If you say, 'Duchess, don't give your ball', it is quite sufficient, I ask no reasons." "Duchess, you may give your ball with the greatest safety, without fear of interruption."

[*Verner returned to his regiment near Grammont and gave out the invitations as promised.*]

On the day appointed for the Ball, Captain O'Grady[1] and I proceeded to Brussels in a cabriolet; we went in our usual uniform,

[1] Standish O'Grady (1792–1848) was the son of Viscount Guillemore, Chief Baron of the Exchequer in Ireland.

39

taking with us Evening Dress for the Ball. We put up at an Hôtel de Swede[1] in the lower town, which was at no great distance from the Duke of Richmond's residence,[2] and having dined and dressed, we proceeded to the ball.

Just as we entered the State room, and before we had time to go into the ball-room, we were met by Lord George Lennox, who, knowing me intimately from having been brother Aide de Camp with his father, said, 'Verner, the Prussians have been attacked and defeated, and I am going to order the Duke's horses, who is going off immediately.' Hearing this startling news, I turned to O'Grady, saying: 'Let us go into the room, to have it to say we were in the ball-room.' It is scarcely necessary to say that the room was in the greatest confusion and had the appearance of anything but a ball-room. The officers were hurrying away as fast as possible, in order that nothing might prevent their joining their regiments. At this moment Lord Uxbridge came to the door and said, 'You gentlemen who have engaged partners had better finish your dance, and get to your quarters as soon as you can.' Turning to my companion, I observed, 'Standish, this is no time for dancing, let us try and secure a cabriolet without loss of time, and be off as soon as we can.'

Major-General Baron von Müffling recorded his recollections of that night.

Towards midnight the Duke entered my room and said: 'I have got news from Mons, from General Dörnberg,[3] who reports that Napoleon has turned towards Charleroi with all his forces, and that there is no longer any enemy in front of him; therefore orders for the concentration of my army at Nivelles and Quatre Bras are already dispatched. The numerous friends of Napoleon who are here (as towards evening the cannonade could be distinctly heard before the gates of Brussels), will raise their heads; the well-disposed must be tranquillized; let us therefore go, all the same, to the ball of the Duchess of Richmond; after which, about five o'clock, we can ride off to the troops assembled at Quatre Bras.'

[1] The Hôtel la Reine de Suède, 29 Rue de l'Évêque.
[2] In the Rue de la Blanchisserie.
[3] Wilhelm Kaspar Ferdinand von Dörnberg (born 1768) commanded the 3rd (Light) Cavalry Brigade composed of the 1st and 2nd Light Dragoons of the King's German Legion and the 23rd Light Dragoons. He was severely wounded in a charge on June 18th.

All took place accordingly; the Duke appeared very cheerful at the ball, where all the great people of Brussels were collected; he remained there till three o'clock, and about five we were on horse-back.

Lady Georgiana Lennox, afterwards Lady de Ros, who had been living in Brussels since 1814 with her parents, the Duke and Duchess of Richmond, set down many years later her memories of the ball.

My mother's now famous ball took place in a large room on the ground-floor, on the left of the entrance, connected with the rest of the house by an ante-room. It had been used by the coach-builder, from whom the house was hired, to put carriages in, but it was papered before we came there; and I recollect the paper — a trellis pattern with roses. My sisters used the room as a schoolroom, and we used to play battledore and shuttlecock there on a wet day. . . .

When the Duke arrived, rather late, at the ball, I was dancing, but at once went up to him to ask about the rumours. He said very gravely, 'Yes, they are true; we are off tomorrow.' This terrible news was circulated directly, and while some of the officers hurried away, others remained at the ball, and actually had not time to change their clothes, but fought in evening costume. I went with my eldest brother the Earl of March (A.D.C. to the Prince of Orange) to his house, which stood in our garden, to help him pack up, after which we returned to the ball-room, where we found some energetic and heartless young ladies still dancing. . . .

It was a dreadful evening, taking leave of friends and acquain-tances, many never to be seen again. The Duke of Brunswick, as he took leave of me in the ante-room adjoining the ball-room, made me a civil speech as to the Brunswickers being sure to distinguish themselves after 'the honour' done them by my having accom-panied the Duke of Wellington to their Review! I remember being quite provoked with poor Lord Hay,[1] a dashing, merry youth, full of military ardour, whom I knew very well, for his delight at the idea of going into action, and of all the honours he was to gain; and the first news we had on the 16th was that he and the Duke of

---

[1] Ensign James, Lord Hay, 1st Foot Guards, aide-de-camp to Major-General Maitland, was the Earl of Errol's eldest son and aged seventeen.

Brunswick were killed. At the ball supper I sat next to the Duke of Wellington, who gave me an original miniature of himself, painted by a Belgian artist.

Another guest, Lady Hamilton Dalrymple, wrote in her journal:

Although the Duke affected great gaiety and cheerfulness, it struck me that I had never seen him have such an expression of care and anxiety on his countenance. I sat next to him on a sopha a long time, but his mind seemed quite pre-occupied; and although he spoke to me in the kindest manner possible, yet frequently in the middle of a sentence he stopped abruptly and called to some officer, giving him directions, in particular to the Duke of Brunswick and Prince of Orange, who both left the ball before supper. Despatches were constantly coming in to the Duke.

On December 29th, 1845, Mr Julian Young dined with a friend in Brunswick Square, London, and there met Sir Henry Webster who, as a lieutenant in the 9th Light Dragoons, had served as aide-de-camp to the Prince of Orange. Young wrote down his recollections of what Sir Henry said when the question was being discussed as to whether Wellington had been taken by surprise at Waterloo.

At three o'clock, while he was eating an early dinner, the Prince of Orange galloped up to his hotel to tell him that the French were advancing by the valley of the Sambre on Brussels. He received the intelligence with his usual calmness. At five o'clock he had matured his plan of operations, and had his orders to the chief commanding officers ready-written on cards, intending them to be distributed, after supper, at the Duchess of Richmond's ball.

The Prince had himself been actively engaged that day in helping the Prince of Saxe-Weimar (whose brigade of Netherlanders had been driven in on Quatre Bras) to defend the farm-house there. He had then ridden on to Brussels to see the Duke, and to attend the ball; but before doing so, he told me to remain where I was, and bring him certain despatches which he expected, the instant they arrived. At ten o'clock ——, the minister, came to me, telling me that the advanced guard of the Prussians had been driven in at Ligny; and ordered me, without a moment's delay, to convey the despatch he put into my hand to the Prince of Orange. 'A horse ready-saddled awaits you at the door,' he said, 'and another has been sent on, half an hour ago, to a half-way house, to help you on the faster. Gallop every yard! You will find your chief at the Duchess of Richmond's ball. Stand on no ceremony; but insist on seeing the Prince at once.'

I was in my saddle without a second's delay; and, thanks to a fine moon and two capital horses, had covered the ten miles I had to go within the hour! The Palace at Brussels was all ablaze with light; and such was the crowd of carriages, that I could not well make way through them on horseback; so I abandoned my steed to the first man I could get hold of, and made my way on foot to the porter's lodge. On my telling the Suisse I had despatches of moment for the Prince, he civilly asked me if I would wait five minutes; 'for,' said he, 'the Duchess has just given orders for the band to go upstairs, and the party are now about to rise. If you were to burst in suddenly, it might alarm the ladies.' On that consideration I consented to wait.

I peeped in between the folding doors and saw the Duchess of Richmond taking the Prince of Orange's arm, and Lady Charlotte Greville[1] the Duke's, on their way to the ballroom. The moment they had reached the foot of the stairs, I hastened to the Prince's side and gave him the despatch. Without looking at it, he handed it behind him to the Duke, who quietly deposited it in his coat-pocket. The Prince made me a sign to remain in the hall. I did so. All the company passed by me, while I hid myself in a recess from observation for fear of being asked awkward questions. As soon as the last couple had mounted the *première étage*, the Duke of Wellington descended, and espying me, beckoned me to him, and said, in a low voice, 'Webster! Four horses instantly to the Prince of Orange's carriage for Waterloo!'[2]

One officer who attended the ball was Captain George Bowles, Coldstream Guards, who afterwards wrote to the Earl of Malmesbury the following account:

The Prince of Orange came back suddenly, just as the Duke of Wellington had taken his place at the supper table, and whispered

---

[1] The youngest daughter of the 2nd Earl of Warwick.
[2] Sir Hussey Vivian wrote to his wife on June 23rd: 'So little did the Duke of Wellington expect an advance of the enemy that he was to have given a ball on June 21, the anniversary of the battle of Vitoria [1813].'

some minutes to his Grace, who only said he had no fresh orders to give, and recommended the Prince to go back to his quarters and go to bed. The Duke of Wellington remained nearly twenty minutes after this, and then said to the Duke of Richmond, 'I think it is time for me to go to bed likewise'; and then, whilst wishing him good night, whispered to ask him if he had a good map in his house. The Duke of Richmond said he had, and took him into his dressing-room [his study], which opened into the supper-room. The Duke of Wellington shut the door and said, 'Napoleon has *humbugged* me, by G——! he has gained twenty-four hours' march on me.' The Duke of Richmond said, 'What do you intend doing?' The Duke of Wellington replied, 'I have ordered the army to concentrate at Quatre-Bras; but we shall not stop him there, and if so, I must fight him *here*' (at the same time passing his thumb-nail over the position of Waterloo). He then said adieu, and left the house by another way out. . . . The conversation in the Duke of Richmond's dressing-room was repeated to me, two minutes after it occurred, by the Duke of Richmond, who was to have commanded the reserve, if formed, and to whom I was to have been aide-de-camp. He marked the Duke of Wellington's thumb-nail with his pencil on the map.

THE CALL TO ARMS

AND there was mounting in hot haste: the steed,
The mustering squadron, and the clattering car,
Went pouring forward with impetuous speed,
And swiftly forming in the ranks of war;
And the deep thunder peal on peal afar;
And near, the beat of the alarming drum
Roused up the soldier ere the morning star;
While throng'd the citizens with terror dumb,
Or whispering, with white lips — 'The foe! They come! they come!'

                                    Byron: *Waterloo*

*Miss Charlotte Waldie, who with her brother and sisters had crossed
from Ramsgate to Ostend, arrived in Brussels on June 15th and
lodged in the Hôtel de Flandre.*

Scarcely had I laid my weary head on the pillow, when the
bugle's loud and commanding call sounded from the Place Royale.
'Is that the call to arms?' I exclaimed, starting up in the bed. My
sister laughed at the idea; but it was repeated, and we listened with
eager and anxious suspense. For a few moments a pause of doubt
ensued. Hark! again! it sounded through the silence of the night,
and from every quarter of the town it was now repeated, at short
and regular intervals. 'It is the call to arms!' I exclaimed. Instantly the drums beat; the Highland pibroch sounded — It was
the call to arms! Oh! never shall I forget the feelings of that moment! Immediately the utmost tumult and confusion succeeded to
the silence in which the city had previously been buried. At half-
past two we were roused by a loud knocking at our room door, and
my brother's voice calling to us to get up instantly, not to lose a
moment — that the troops were under arms — were marching out
against the French — and that Major Llewellyn[1] was waiting to
see us before he left Brussels. Inexpressibly relieved to find that
this nocturnal alarm was occasioned by the departure of Major

[1] Major Richard Llewellyn, 28th Foot.

45

Llewellyn, not by the arrival of the French, which, in the first startling confusion of my thoughts, and trepidation of my mind, had actually entered my head; and much better pleased to meet an old and kind friend, than to run away from a furious enemy, we got up with the greatest alacrity, and hastily throwing some clothes about us, flew to see Llewellyn, who was waiting on the stairs. Short and agitated indeed was our meeting under such circumstances. By the light of a candle in my brother's room, we sat down for a few minutes on some boxes, scarcely able to believe our senses, that all this was real, and almost inclined to doubt whether it was not a dream: but the din of war which resounded in our ears too painfully convinced us that it was no illusion of phantasy: — we could scarcely even 'snatch a fearful joy', for not for a single moment could we banish from our minds the impression, that in a few moments we must part, perhaps for ever, and that this hurried interview might prove our last. We could only gaze intently upon each other, as if to retain a lasting remembrance of the well-known countenance, should we indeed be destined to meet no more: we could only utter incoherent words or disjointed speeches. While he still lingered, we heard his charger, which his servant held in the court-yard below, neighing and pawing the ground, as if impatient of his master's delay, and eager to bear him to the field. Our greetings and adieus were equally hurried. We bade him farewell, and saw him go to battle.

. . . Just as he left us, the dawn appeared, and, by the faint twilight of morning, we saw the Place Royale filled with armed men, and with all the tumult and confusion of martial preparation. All was 'hurry skurry for the field'. Officers were looking in vain for their servants — servants running in pursuit of their masters — baggage waggons were loading — bât horses preparing — trains of artillery harnessing. — And amidst the clanking of horses' hoofs, the rolling of heavy carriages, the clang of arms, the sounding of bugles, and the neighing of chargers, we distinctly heard, from time to time, the loud, deep-toned word of command, while the incessant din of hammers nailing 'gave dreadful note of preparation'.

. . . As the dawn broke, the soldiers were seen assembling from all parts of the town, in marching order, with their knapsacks on their backs, loaded with three days' provision. Unconcerned in the midst of the din of war, many a soldier laid himself down on a truss of straw, and soundly slept, with his hands still grasping his firelock; others were sitting contentedly on the pavement, waiting the arrival of their comrades. Numbers were taking leave of their wives and children, perhaps for the last time, and many a veteran's rough cheek was wet with the tears of sorrow. One poor fellow, immediately under our windows, turned back again and again, to bid his wife farewell, and take his baby once more in his arms; and I saw him hastily brush away a tear with the sleeve of his coat, as he gave her back the child for the last time, wrung her hand, and ran off to join his company, which was drawn up on the other side of the Place Royale.

Captain John Kincaid of the 95th Rifles remembered the civilians during that anxious night.

Waiting for the arrival of the other regiments, we endeavoured to snatch an hour's repose on the pavement; but we were every instant disturbed by ladies as well as gentleman; some stumbling over us in the dark — some shaking us out of our sleep, to be told the news — and not a few conceiving their immediate safety depending upon our standing in place of lying. All those who applied for the benefit of my advice, I recommended to go home to bed, to keep themselves perfectly cool, and to rest assured that, if their departure from the city became necessary (which I very much doubted,) they would have at least one whole day to prepare for it, as we were leaving some beef and potatoes behind us, for which, I was sure, we would fight, rather than abandon!

The previous evening Lieutenant Basil Jackson of the Royal Staff Corps had been sent by the Quartermaster-General with an important letter to the village of Ninove, and he did not return to Brussels until about four o'clock in the morning.

Threading the Rue de la Madeleine, I reached the beautiful Place Royale, and heard sounds of movement in the park adjacent. On entering it, I found a large body of our troops in line, which their commander, the redoubtable Picton, was inspecting, accompanied by his staff. I reined in my horse, and awaited the termination of the ceremony. It was truly a splendid division [the 5th], of which Picton might feel proud. The order was given for the whole to form sub-divisions, and then 'quick march'. I posted myself at

the Hotel Bellevue[1] to see them pass. First came a battalion of the
95th Rifles, dressed in dark green, and with black accoutrements.
The 28th Regiment followed, then the 42nd Highlanders, marching so steadily that the sable plumes of their bonnets scarcely
vibrated. The 79th and 92nd, both Highlanders, were also there.
I thus saw something of 'the pomp and circumstance of glorious
war', and heard the last of the measured tread of the troops, which
alone disturbed the stillness of the morning. Forth they went by
the Porte de Namur.

*Lieutenant-Colonel Sir Augustus Frazer, who commanded the Royal
Horse Artillery, having been out to a nearby village to celebrate
the promotion of a brother officer and having then gone to bed, thus
missing the ball, wrote, at six o'clock on the morning of June 16th,
to his brother-in-law living at Great Bealings in Suffolk.*

I have been sleeping very sound. We have a beautiful morning.
I have sent to Sir George Wood's[2] to hear if we are to move, which
I conclude we are of course to do. . . .

I have just learned that the Duke moves in half an hour. Wood
thinks to Waterloo, which we cannot find on the map: this is the
old story over again. I have sent Bell to Delancey's office, where
we shall learn the real name, &c. The whole place is in a bustle.
Such jostling of baggage, of guns, and of waggons. It is very useful
to acquire a quietness and composure about all these matters; one
does not mend things by being in a hurry.

Adieu! I almost wonder I can write so quietly. But nothing can
be done to-day. My horse is ready when the signal for mounting
shall be given.

[*Later that day he finished another letter addressed to Great Bealings.*]

Bonaparte has moved; and in consequence we are moving too.
It may be hardly worth while to describe what I hardly yet understand, but to-day will unravel the mystery; to-morrow we may try
the fate of arms. Our troops are concentrating. I suspect the scene
of the struggle will be in the vicinity of Braine l'Aleud near Hal.
Whilst I write I receive your letters: shall I continue to describe

[1] Number 9 in the Place Royale.
[2] Colonel Wood (1767–1831) commanded the Royal Artillery in the
Waterloo campaign.

movements and battles, or shall I read the delicious pages of affection? can I hesitate?

I accept your challenge at Dutch billiards, and care not how soon I play with balls amusing and harmless: can one avoid making the contrast with those here? . . .

Ought a man who should think of nothing but Braine l'Aleud and Bonaparte to bestow one thought on Bealings and billiards? methinks he ought, and without doubt he will. Fancy will turn; the heart, you know, untravelled will turn. A flower girl has just brought me a parting bouquet of roses: was it possible to receive it and not think of the dear boys [two sons], and the flowers which *may*, nay which *must* wither? and to what, and to how many reflections does not the idea lead?

I have written you a shabby return for your letter; but when I wrote this late last night, I little thought of having so much time as I now expect to have to-day. I have never less to do than previous to an action; there are then no difficulties, no littlenesses to be plagued with; in truth, at present every preparation in my power has already been made, and I never felt lighter or easier.

Now for Bonaparte, the disturber of all the great, as well as of all the little folks of this lower world.

What, meantime, of the British troops quartered at a distance from Brussels? Ensign George Thomas Keppel, later sixth Earl of Albemarle, had joined the third battalion of the 14th Regiment, in which fourteen of the officers and three hundred of the men were under twenty years of age. The battalion was training hard in a village two miles from Grammont.

June 15th. I was this afternoon, about sunset, one of a group of officers who assembled near the principal inn at Acren, when a Belgian, dressed in a blouse, told us that the French had crossed the frontier. I well remember the utter incredulity with which his statement was received by us all, but it proved to be perfectly correct. At daylight that morning Napoleon opened the campaign by attacking the first corps of the Prussian army, commanded by Count Zieten, in the neighbourhood of Charleroi.

June 16th. The following morning as I was proceeding to fall in with my company as usual, I found the regiment in heavy marching order, and all ready for a start. They had received the 'route' to Enghien. . . .

Hurrying back to my billet, I swallowed hastily a few mouthfuls of food, and with the assistance of my weeping hostesses packed up my baggage. I then placed it on my bât horse and consigned it to the care of the baggage guard. I had taken my final leave of both horse and baggage. Thus, when I entered upon the Waterloo campaign, all my worldly goods consisted of the clothes on my back.

As we passed through the village, our drums and fifes playing 'The Girl we left behind us',[1] or some such lively air, we were greeted with the cheers of the men and the wailing of the women. Their leave-taking was as if we were their own countrymen, sallying forth in defence of a common 'Vaderland'.

Captain Mercer, commanding 'G' Troop, Royal Horse Artillery, in the village of Strytem, noted in his diary on June 16th that the Quartermaster-General of the cavalry appeared to enjoy disturbing people at very unreasonable hours.

I was sound asleep when my servant, bustling into the room, awoke me *en sursaut*.[2] He brought a note which an orderly hussar had left, and ridden off immediately. The note had nothing official in its appearance, and might have been an invitation to dinner; but the unceremonious manner in which the hussar had gone off without his receipt looked curious. My despatch was totally deficient in date, so that time and place were left to conjecture; its contents pithy — they were as follows, viz.: —

'Captain Mercer's troop will proceed with the utmost diligence to Enghien where he will meet Major M'Donald,[3] who will point out the ground on which it is to bivouac to-night.

Signed,   *   *   *
D.A.Q.M.-Gen.'

---

[1] 'The Girl I left behind me' dates from about 1759. The second verse runs:

> The hour I remember well
> And constancy shall prove me;
> For what I felt there's none can tell,
> When first she own'd she loved me.
> But now I'm bound to Brighton Camp,
> Kind Heaven then pray mind me;
> And send me home, safe back again,
> To the girl I left behind me.

[2] 'With a start.'
[3] Lieut.-Colonel A. Macdonald commanded the six troops of Royal Horse Artillery attached to the Cavalry.

That we were to move forward, then, was certain. It was rather sudden, to be sure, and all the whys and wherefores were left to conjecture; but the suddenness of it, and the importance of arriving quickly at the appointed place, rather alarmed me, for upon reflection I remembered that I had been guilty of two or three imprudences. First, all my officers were absent; secondly, all my country waggons were absent; thirdly, a whole division (one-third of my troop) was absent at Yseringen. 'Send the sergeant-major here,' was the first order, as I drew on my stockings. 'Send for Mr Coates' (my commissariat officer), the second, as I got one leg into my overalls. 'William, make haste and get breakfast,' the third, as I buttoned them up. The sergeant-major soon came, and received his orders to turn out instanter, with the three days' provisions and forage[1] in the haversacks and on the horses; also to send an express for the first division. He withdrew, and immediately the fine martial clang of 'boot and saddle' resounded through the village and courts of the château, making the woods ring again, and even the frogs stop to listen.

The commissary soon made his appearance. 'What! are we off, sir?' 'Yes, without delay; and you must collect your waggons as quickly as possible.' 'I fear, Captain Mercer, that will take some time, for St Cyr's[2] are gone to Ninove.' My folly here stared me full in the face. Mr Coates said he would do his utmost to collect them; and as he was a most active, intelligent, and indefatigable fellow, I communicated to him my orders and determination not to wait, desiring him to follow us as soon as he possibly could. My first-enumerated care was speedily removed, for I learned that the officers had just arrived and were preparing for the march, having known of it at Brussels ere we did. The two divisions in Strytem were ready to turn out in a few minutes after the 'boot and saddle' had resounded, but, as I feared, the first kept us waiting until near seven o'clock before it made its appearance. This delay allowed us time to make a hearty breakfast; and, in the uncertainty of when we should get another meal, we each stowed away a double portion of Walsdragen's[3] fine eggs. At length the first division arrived, and the animating and soul-stirring notes of the 'turn-out' again awoke the echoes of the hills and woods. Up jumped my old dog Bal, and away to parade and increase the

[1] We had been ordered nearly a fortnight ago to keep this quantity ready, and the hay rolled, etc., etc. [Mercer]
[2] A local farmer.
[3] Mynheer Walsdragen had the nearby château farm.

bustle by jumping at the horses' noses and barking, as parade formed. Away went the officers to inspect their divisions, and Milward[1] is leading my impatient charger Cossack up and down the court.

Ensign Edward Nevil Macready, brother of the celebrated actor, William Charles Macready, relates how his battalion the 30th Foot had been billeted in the neat little town of Soignies, head-quarters of Sir Charles Alten's 3rd Division, since May 20th.

Here we were drilled out of all patience, and, like the soldiers of ancient Rome, I longed for war as a respite from fatigue.

About June 12th all intercourse between France and Belgium was suspended, we consequently expected soon to march, and were all in a charming state of anxiety. As a group of us were standing in the square of Soignies discussing the probable events of the approaching campaign about four o'clock on the evening of June 15th, a rumour got afloat that the French had crossed the frontier. We were looking at each other with a half-credulous and half-apprehensive smile, when General [Sir Colin] Halkett galloped up, and called out, 'Are any light infantry officers among you?' 'Yes, sir,' said I. 'Parade your company in ten minutes' time on this spot,' was his reply, and I went away to arouse the men. I ordered my servant to put the baggage, and a box of light infantry appoint-ments that had just arrived, on my pony, and by the time specified, Rumley, Pratt,[2] and I, were on the ground with the company. Lieutenant-Colonel [Charles A.] Vigoureux was ordered to plant us on picket at a village called Naast, about a league from Soignies. As we marched to our post, we met several regiments of our divi-sion hurrying to the town; it was evident that the game was a-foot.

. . . The night passed quietly. About eight o'clock next morning, it was agreed that I should ride over to the regiment to order out a few necessaries; and accordingly away I went. I cantered on unconsciously and pulling up in the market-place, was thunder-struck. Not a soul was stirring. The silence of the tomb reigned where I expected to have met 10,000 men. The breath left my body as if extracted by an air pump. I ran into a house and asked, 'Where are the troops?' 'They marched at two this morning,' was the

[1] Mercer's groom.
[2] These lieutenants, both named John, were wounded.

chilling reply. 'By what road?' 'Towards Braine le Compte,' was
all I heard, when, jumping on my pony's back, I endeavoured by
sympathetic heel to convey the rapidity of my ideas into his carcase.
But vain were my efforts; Soignies was his home, and his obstinacy
invincible. So getting off, I made the best of my way on foot, lugging
him by the bridle. On reaching Naast, I found Rumley and Pratt
in deep consultation with the burgomaster, who had informed them
that the French had passed the Sambre, and occupied Charleroi;
that the Prussians were falling back and our troops hastening up
to support them. Our patrols had examined the country on every
side, and not a soldier was to be seen.

We were most unpleasantly situated; ignorant whether we were
left here by mistake or design, and dreading equally the consequences of quitting our post without orders, or the division being
engaged during our absence. Our commissions were safe by remaining where we were; but we were determined to risk them, and
all the hopes of young ambition, rather than be absent from the
field of glory. Away we marched towards Braine le Compte. There
we learned that the troops had struck off to Nivelles and we followed
their route. We soon got among the baggage of the army, passed it,
and quickened our pace on hearing a noise like distant peals of
thunder. 'The Dutch artillery are practising,' said a young soldier
in a tremulously inquisitive tone. 'They've redder targets than
your cheeks, my boy, that fire those guns,' replied a swarthy
veteran, who had learned this music in Spain.

THE BATTLE OF QUATRE BRAS

CONFRONTING Ney at Quatre Bras that Friday morning of June 16th was only Count Perponcher-Sedlnitzky's division of 8,000 men, sixteen guns and a mere fifty hussars from Silesia — a weak obstacle against the 19,000 infantry, sixty guns and 3,000 horsemen at Ney's disposal. Admittedly the farm buildings, long slopes and dense woods, especially the Bois de Bossu, were readily defensible; but the two-mile line could not be anything but thinly held and was dangerously weak on the left flank — the flank which covered the vital road communicating with Blücher at Ligny.

The Prince of Orange knew that reinforcements were hastening to his support, but he could not be aware that the French marshal still had his two corps outstretched all the way from Frasnes back to the Sambre — nine miles and more; and that even the head of Reille's corps was still an hour's march from Quatre Bras. The Prince had to hold out against whatever came, and he gave thanks to Ney for every idle hour. Usually bold to a fault, the Frenchman now seemed apathetic, made no attempt to reconnoitre the front, and allowed himself to be persuaded by the cautious, unenterprising Reille that Quatre Bras might well turn out to be 'one of those Spanish battles in which the English never show themselves till the right moment comes' — in other words, a typical Wellingtonian position with most of the troops concealed on a reverse slope. This indicates that one of Wellington's assets was a well-established moral ascendancy over his old antagonists. Unpalatable memories of Peninsular setbacks gave Ney cause for hesitation and misgiving, but he should at least have concentrated his troops in readiness to act upon fresh orders from Napoleon.

Not until eleven o'clock, when such orders were brought in, did Ney bestir himself, and even then two hours elapsed before his leading infantry moved clear of Frasnes. The Prince of Orange still had 8,000 men to hold 3,000 yards. At two o'clock the French guns opened fire. Reille's divisions attacked the weak left flank and took the hamlets of Piraumont and Gemioncourt east of the Brussels road. The outnumbered allied line began to give, except by the Bois de Bossu; yet even here, when Ney sent up a third division, the stubborn defenders were forced back among the trees. The crisis was extreme, for Perponcher could not long have held the crossroads. But Wellington returned from seeing Blücher, a Dutch–Belgian cavalry brigade rode up

54

from Nivelles, and by half past three Picton's division, with twelve guns and nearly 8,000 men, British and Hanoverian, came on the scene from Brussels and quickly deployed along the Namur road to the east.

When French infantry advanced, the Prince of Orange set his cavalry to charge them. In vain. The horsemen were routed, six guns fell into French hands, and the situation looked grave again. But now the Duke of Brunswick's 4,000 reached the field of battle, and both sides had an almost equal strength in sheer numbers, though not in cavalry or guns. Soon the Brunswickers were engaged and driven back, their Duke having been killed while leading the first charge. Of the Bois de Bossu one corner only remained to the allied defenders, but east of the road the French infantry achieved much less. Quite suddenly they were fired on by Picton's men hidden in the tall standing rye, and a counterattack sent them to Piraumont in disorder. When French cavalry intervened, Kempt's brigade successfully formed square. Pack's brigade had also to withstand cavalry assaults, and here the 42nd, caught while forming square, were mauled, and the 44th suffered grievous loss. Yet the lancers were repulsed.

It was now five o'clock. More reinforcements arrived, 8,000 of them, Halkett's British brigade and Kielmansegge's scarlet Hanoverians and green-clad Nassauers, with two field batteries. As for Marshal Ney, learning from Napoleon that the fate of France was in his hands, he tried to force a decision with Kellermann's cuirassiers. Only one of the four brigades had arrived forward — that was Ney's fault; and thus to storm some 30,000 Allied troops in defended positions resembled folly. Kellermann, stung by Ney's jibes, led the premature charge with reckless courage and crashed against Halkett's brigade. Two battalions, the 30th and 33rd, just had time to form a protective square, but the 69th, unwisely stopped from so doing by the Prince of Orange, were caught in disarray and lost a colour. Kellermann tore a breach in the Allied line, but the charge got out of control and swept on to Quatre Bras, only to be caught by a troop of horse artillery which hurriedly un-limbered and poured in close-range salvos. The horsemen fell or turned away. Kellermann's mount was killed. His men rushed back, straight into a French infantry division on its way up with belated support. Such confusion reigned that another French division was obliged to halt; while Kempt's battalions repulsed further charges by *chasseurs* and lancers.

At half past six Ney rallied his disordered infantry and led an attack against Pack's brigade. It failed. Wellington's force was now swollen by the arrival from Enghien of two brigades of Foot Guards under Maitland and Byng and of the Brunswick artillery. While the Guards attacked the Bois de Bossu on the right, Kempt and the Hanoverians tackled Piraumont on the left, and Halkett and Pack headed down the main road for Gemioncourt. The French resisted this general advance with ferocity, and fighting was ebb and flow for an hour, but at last the weight of numbers told, and by nine o'clock the battle was over.

French casualties totalled 4,000, those of the Allies about 600 more. Ney, though he had missed his chance of a morning victory and a telling break-through, had at least prevented Wellington from going to the aid of Blücher.

Ensign Robert Batty of the 1st Foot Guards wrote a letter on June 21st in which he told of his experiences during the battle. His battalion had marched early on the 16th from Enghien, and halted at Nivelles, where the men began to make fires and cook.

During the whole of this time, and as we approached the town, we heard distinctly a constant roar of cannon; and we had scarcely rested ourselves, and commenced dressing the rations which had been served out at Enghien, when an aide-de-camp from the Duke of Wellington arrived, and ordered us instantly under arms, and to advance with all speed to *Les Quatre Bras*, where the action was going on with the greatest fury, and where the French were making rapid strides towards the object they had in view, which was to gain a wood called 'Bois de Bossu'; a circumstance calculated to possess them of the road to Nivelles, and to enable them to turn the flank of the British and Brunswickers, and to cut off the communication between them and the other forces which were coming up. The order was, of course, instantly obeyed; the meat which was cooking was thrown away, the kettles, &c. packed up, and we proceeded, as fast as our tired legs would carry us, towards a scene of slaughter, which was a prelude well calculated to usher in the bloody tragedy of the 18th.

We marched up towards the enemy, at each step hearing more clearly the fire of musquetry; and as we approached the field of action we met constantly waggons full of men, of all the various nations under the Duke's command, wounded in the most dreadful manner. The sides of the road had a heap of dying and dead, very many of whom were British: such a scene did, indeed, demand every better feeling of the mind to cope with its horrors; and too much cannot be said in praise of the division of Guards, the very largest part of whom were young soldiers, and volunteers from the militia, who had never been exposed to the fire of an enemy, or witnessed its effects. During the period of our advance from

Nivelles, I suppose nothing could exceed the anxiety of the moment with those on the field. The French, who had a large cavalry and artillery (in both of which arms we were quite destitute, excepting some Belgian and German guns), had made dreadful havock in our lines, and had succeeded in pushing an immensely strong column of tirailleurs into the wood I have before mentioned, of which they had possessed themselves, and had just begun to cross the road, having marched through the wood, and placed affairs in a critical situation, when the Guards luckily came in sight. The moment we caught a glimpse of them we halted, formed, and having loaded and fixed bayonets, advanced, the French immediately retiring; and the very last man who attempted to re-enter the wood was killed by our Grenadiers.

At this instant our men gave three glorious cheers, and though we had marched fifteen hours without anything to eat and drink, save the water we procured on the march, we rushed to attack the enemy. This was done by the 1st brigade, consisting of the 2d and 3d battalions of the first regiment; and the 2d brigade, consisting of the 2d battalion of the Coldstream and third regiment, were formed as a reserve along the chaussée.

As we entered the wood, a few noble fellows, who sunk down overpowered with fatigue, lent their voice to cheer their comrades. The trees were so thick, that it was beyond anything difficult to effect a passage. As we approached, we saw the enemy behind them, taking aim at us: they contested every bush, and at a small rivulet running through the wood they attempted a stand, but could not resist us, and we at last succeeded in forcing them out of their possessions. The moment we endeavoured to go out of this wood (which had naturally broken us), the French cavalry charged us; but we at last found the third battalion, who had rather *skirted* the wood, and formed in front of it, where they afterwards were in hollow square, and repulsed all the attempts of the French cavalry to break them. Our loss was most tremendous, and nothing could exceed the desperate work of the evening; the French infantry and cavalry fought most desperately; and after a conflict of nearly three hours (the obstinacy of which could find no parallel, save in the slaughter it occasioned), we had the happiness to find ourselves complete masters of the road and wood, and that we had at length defeated all the efforts of the French to outflank us and turn our right, than which nothing could be of greater moment to both parties.

Another account of the fighting comes from the pen of Sergeant James Anton, 42nd Highlanders in Sir Denis Pack's brigade.

We now descended to the plain by an echelon movement towards our right, halted on the road (from which we had lately diverged to the left), formed in line, fronting a bank on the right side, whilst the other regiments took up their position to right and left, as directed by our general. A luxuriant crop of grain hid from our view the contending skirmishers beyond, and presented a considerable obstacle to our advance. We were in the act of lying down by the side of the road, in our usual careless manner, as we were wont when enjoying a rest on the line of march, some throwing back their heads on their knapsacks, intending to take a sleep, when General Pack came galloping up, and chid the colonel for not having the bayonets fixed. This roused our attention, and the bayonets were instantly on the pieces. . . .

Our pieces were loaded, and perhaps never did a regiment in the field seem so short taken. We were all ready and in line — 'Forward!' was the word of command, and forward we hastened, though we saw no enemy in front. The stalks of the rye, like the reeds that grow on the margin of some swamp, opposed our advance; the tops were up to our bonnets, and we strode and groped our way through as fast as we could. By the time we reached a field of clover on the other side we were very much straggled; however, we united in line as fast as time and our speedy advance would permit. The Belgic skirmishers retired through our ranks, and in an instant we were on their victorious pursuers.

Our sudden appearance seemed to paralyse their advance. The singular appearance of our dress, combined, no doubt, with our sudden début, tended to stagger their resolution: we were on them, our pieces were loaded, and our bayonets glittered, impatient to drink their blood. Those who had so proudly driven the Belgians before them, turned now to fly, whilst our loud cheers made the fields echo to our wild hurrahs.

We drove on so fast that we almost appeared like a mob following the rout of some defeated faction. Marshal Ney, who commanded the enemy, observed our wild unguarded zeal, and ordered a regiment of lancers to bear down upon us. We saw their approach at a distance, as they issued from a wood, and took them for Brunswickers coming to cut up the flying infantry; and as cavalry on all occasions have the advantage of retreating foot, on a fair field, we were halted in order to let them take their way; they were approaching our right flank, from which our skirmishers were extended, and we were far from being in a formation fit to repel an attack, if intended, or to afford regular support to our friends if requiring our aid. I think we stood with too much confidence, gazing towards them as if they had been our friends, anticipating the gallant charge they would make on the flying foe, and we were making no preparative movement to receive them as enemies, further than the reloading of the muskets, until a German orderly dragoon galloped up, exclaiming, 'Franchee! Franchee!' and, wheeling about, galloped off.

We instantly formed a rallying square; no time for particularity; every man's piece was loaded, and our enemies approached at full charge; the feet of their horses seemed to tear up the ground. Our skirmishers having been impressed with the same opinion that these were Brunswick cavalry, fell beneath their lances, and few escaped death or wounds; our brave colonel[1] fell at this time, pierced through the chin until the point of the lance reached the brain. Captain [Archibald] Menzies fell, covered with wounds, and a momentary conflict took place over him; he was a powerful man, and, hand to hand, more than a match for six ordinary men. The Grenadiers, whom he commanded, pressed round to save or avenge him, but fell beneath the enemies' lances.

Of all descriptions of cavalry, certainly the lancers seem the most formidable to infantry, as the lance can be projected with considerable precision, and with deadly effect, without bringing the horse to the point of the bayonet; and it was only by the rapid and well-directed fire of musketry that these formidable assailants were repulsed.

Colonel [Robert Henry] Dick assumed the command on the fall of Sir Robert Macara, and was severely wounded. Brevet-Major [George] Davidson succeeded, and was mortally wounded; to him succeeded Brevet-Major [John] Campbell. Thus, in a few minutes, we had been placed under four different commanding officers.

An attempt was now made to form us in line; for we stood mixed in one irregular mass — grenadier, light, and battalion companies — a noisy group; such is the inevitable consequence of a rapid succession of commanders. Our covering sergeants were called out

[1] Sir Robert Macara was being carried off the field by four of his men when they were surrounded by the French, who, seeing from his decorations that Macara was of high rank, cut him down.

on purpose that each company might form on the right of its sergeant; an excellent plan had it been adopted, but a cry arose that another charge of cavalry was approaching, and this plan was abandoned. We now formed a line on the left of the Grenadiers, while the cavalry that had been announced were cutting through the ranks of the 69th Regiment. Meantime the other regiments to our right and left, suffered no less than we; the superiority of the enemy in cavalry afforded him a decided advantage on the open plain, for our British cavalry and artillery had not yet reached the field.

We were at this time about two furlongs past the farm of Quatre Bras, as I suppose, and a line of French infantry was about the same distance from us in front, and we had commenced firing at that line, when we were ordered to form square to oppose cavalry. General Pack was at our head, and Major Campbell commanded the regiment. We formed square in an instant; in the centre were several wounded French soldiers witnessing our formation round them; they doubtless considered themselves devoted to certain death among us seeming barbarians, but they had no occasion to speak ill of us afterwards; for as they were already incapable of injuring us, we moved about them regardful of their wounds and suffering.

Our last file had got into square, and into its proper place, so far as unequalised companies could form a square, when the cuirassiers dashed full on two of its faces; their heavy horses and steel armour seemed sufficient to bury us under them, had they been pushed forward on our bayonets.

A moment's pause ensued; it was the pause of death. General Pack was on the right angle of the front face of the square, and he lifted his hat towards the French officer, as he was wont to do when returning a salute. I suppose our assailants construed our forbearance as an indication of surrendering; a false idea; not a blow had been struck nor a musket levelled, but when the general raised his hat, it served as a signal, though not a preconcerted one, but entirely accidental; for we were doubtful whether our officer commanding was protracting the order, waiting for the general's command, as he was present. Be this as it may, a most destructive fire was opened; riders cased in heavy armour, fell tumbling from their horses; the horses reared, plunged, and fell on the dismounted riders; steel helmets and cuirasses rang against unsheathed sabres as they fell to the ground . . .

Major-General Sir Colin Halkett's brigade, comprising the 30th, 33rd, 69th and 73rd Regiments, entered the field of battle at Quatre Bras at about three o'clock, having marched some twenty-seven miles under a burning sun. Sergeant Thomas Morris of the 73rd describes his battalion's part in the fight, and the ordeal of an officer's wife.

The ground, for a considerable distance, being covered with rye, and of an extraordinary height, some of it measuring seven feet, prevented us from seeing much of the enemy; but, though we could not see them, they were observing us. We continuing to advance, the glittering of the tops of our bayonets guided towards us a large body of the enemy's cuirassiers, who, coming so unexpectedly upon us, threw us in the utmost confusion. Having no time to form a square, we were compelled to retire, or rather to run, to the wood through which we had advanced; and when we rallied, the 69th unfortunately lost their king's colours.

We were again led to the charge, in conjunction with the 'Black Brunswickers', commanded by the Duke of Brunswick, and this time we were successful, and drove the enemy, against whom we were pitted, a considerable distance across the plain. In this charge we lost several officers and about thirty men.

. . . Ensign [Thomas] Deacon, of our regiment, was on my right, close to me, when we were charging the enemy, and a private on my left being killed by a musket-ball, through the temple, the officer said, 'Who is that, Morris?' I replied, 'Sam Shortly,' and, pointing to the officer's arm, where a musket ball had passed through, taking with it a portion of the shirt-sleeve, I said, 'You are wounded, Sir.' 'God bless me! so I am,' said he, and dropping his sword, made the best of his way to the rear. After getting his wound dressed, he went in search of his wife, who, with her three children, he had left with the baggage guard. During the whole night he sought her in vain; and the exertion he used was more than he could bear, and he was conveyed by the baggage-train to Brussels.

The poor wife, in the meantime, who had heard from some of the men that her husband was wounded, passed the whole night in searching for him among the wounded, as they passed. At length, she was informed that he had been conveyed to Brussels, and her chief anxiety then was how to get there. Conveyances, there were none to be got; and she was in the last state of pregnancy;

but, encouraged by the hope of finding her husband, she made the best of her way on foot, with her children, exposed to the violence of the terrific storm of thunder, lightning, and rain, which continued unabated for about ten hours. Faint, exhausted, and wet to the skin, having no other clothes than a black silk dress and light shawl, yet she happily surmounted all these difficulties; reached Brussels on the morning of the 18th, and found her husband in very comfortable quarters, where she also was accommodated; and the next day gave birth to a fine girl, which was afterwards christened 'Waterloo Deacon'.

Ensign Edward Macready, one of Halkett's officers, gives a vivid account of a company of the 30th Foot on the march and in battle.

After passing Nivelle, we started double quick, for the firing increased, and we soon came up with the division of Guards. They jeered us about 'our hurry', and our fellows taunted them in return. 'Shall I carry your honour on my pack?' said one of ours to a Guardsman as he was falling out. 'Haven't you some gruel for that young gentleman?' shouted another. 'It's a cruel shame to send gentlemen's sons on sich business,' continued a third.

We cut across the road through the interval between two of their battalions, and as an officer rowed us well for doing so, [Lieutenant John] Rumley made us strike into the fields to the right. Many of our poor fellows tumbled over, quite done up, and at length, after some whispering communications among themselves, as if by word of command, off went every knapsack in the company from right to left but those of two or three who felt still strong enough to carry them. After scrambling through a thick plantation, we found ourselves close to a body of men with whose uniform we were unacquainted. A wood stretched in front of and half a mile beyond them, and over it was a heavy cloud of smoke, with birds in all directions flying and squealing about it. We loosened our ammunition, loaded, and went up to these men. They belonged to the Nassau Contingent, and had been driven from the wood (of Bossu). We made for it, and came up with a staff officer with long light hair, who had just escaped from the lancers. He told us our regiment had entered the field about a quarter of an hour before, and that they were on the other side of the wood which we must pass on the left, as the enemy occupied nearly the whole of it.

This we were soon convinced of by several round shot coming from it, one of which splashed mud and dirt over the whole company. This was what they called 'our baptism'.

We soon reached Quatre Bras, and on turning the end of the wood found ourselves bodily in the battle. The roaring of great guns and musketry, the bursting of shells, and shouts of the combatants raised an infernal din, while the squares and lines, the galloping of horses mounted and riderless, the mingled crowds of wounded and fugitives (foreigners), the volumes of smoke and flashing of fire, struck out a scene which accorded admirably with the music. As we passed a spot where the 44th, old chums of ours in Spain, had suffered considerably, the poor wounded fellows raised themselves up and welcomed us with faint shouts, 'Push on old three tens — pay 'em off for the 44th — you're much wanted, boys — success to you, my darlings.' Here we met our old Colonel riding out of the field, shot through the leg;[1] he pointed to it and cried, 'They've tickled me again, my boys — now one leg can't laugh at the other.' . . .

Hamilton showed us where our regiment was, and we reached it just as a body of lancers and cuirassiers had enveloped two faces of its square. We formed up to the left and fired away. The tremendous volley our square, which in the hurry of formation was much overmanned on the sides attacked, gave them, sent off these fellows with the loss of a number of men, and their Commanding-Officer. He was a gallant soldier, and fell while crying to his men, '*Avancez, mes enfants — courage — encore une fois, Français.*' I don't know what might have been my sensations on entering this field coolly, but I was so fagged and choked with running and was crammed so suddenly into the very thick of the business, that I can't recollect thinking at all, except that the poor Highlanders (over whom I stumbled or had to jump almost every step) were most provokingly distributed.

On our repulse of the cavalry, a General outside the square (said to be Sir Thomas Picton) thanked us warmly, and some seconds after, in still louder terms, damned us all for making such a noise, and asked if we had no Officers amongst us. We were half a minute in the square laughing and shaking hands with all about us, when we were ordered to pursue, and dashing out, were soon brought

---

[1] Lieut.-Colonel Alexander Hamilton. It was thought necessary to amputate his leg, and three times a tourniquet encircled the limb in readiness for the operation, but each time the surgeon was called away. The doctors then decided to let the leg take its chance. The Colonel lived until 1838.

up by a line of tirailleurs, with whom we kept up a briskish fire. . . .
The cannonade and skirmishing were lively on both sides, while
the heavy fire from the wood in our rear showed that the Guards
and the enemy were hotly disputing it.

*On the French side Captain Bourdon de Vatry, aide-de-camp to
Jérôme Bonaparte, ex-King of Westphalia, relates that a fierce
bayonet battle was fought in the Bois de Bossu.*

Prince Jérôme was struck on the hip, but fortunately the ball
hit the massive gold scabbard of his sword first and did not penetrate, so he came off with nothing worse than a severe bruise which
made him turn pale. Mastering his pain, the Prince remained on
horseback at the head of his division, thereby giving us all an
example of courage and self-sacrifice. His coolness had an excellent
effect. The 8th Cuirassiers, commanded by Colonel Garavaque,[1]
were about to launch a strong attack on a Scottish square; the
regiment gave the Prince an ovation, and the brave horsemen,
having broken the square and captured the enemy's colours, presented this trophy to the ex-King.

The position at Quatre Bras had just been taken by Kellermann's cavalry. Marshal Ney was impatiently awaiting the arrival
of d'Erlon's corps, when he learnt that the Emperor had altered
the direction of this corps and summoned it to join him at Saint-
Amand. At the same moment an unaccountable panic seized
Kellermann's cavalry, which fled back hell for leather after knocking over their commander. Kellermann had the presence of mind
to cling to the bits of two of his cuirassiers' horses and so avoid
being trampled underfoot.

As the infantry of the 1st Corps did not come, since it had been
sent for to the battlefield of Ligny, the enemy reoccupied the
Quatre Bras position and we were only too happy to prevent the
English from going to the aid of the Prussians. This was all we
could do in the face of the considerable forces then holding Quatre
Bras.

People set to work to bandage the wounded, and we bivouacked
for the night. Unfortunately there were no rations, so the soldiers
began to wander about the countryside, marauding in order to live.
The Marshal invited Jérôme to supper. The table was laid on a

[1] Garavaque was unhorsed during Kellermann's great cavalry charge.

plank supported on empty barrels and lit by candles stuck into bottlenecks.

Night had fallen.

We were just beginning our frugal meal when Comte de Forbin-Janson was brought in to Ney with an order from the Emperor to march on Bry. Here is the text of this order by the Chief of Staff:

> Before Fleurus, 16th June, at a quarter past three
> *Monsieur le Maréchal*, I wrote to you an hour ago to say that the Emperor was attacking the enemy at half past two in the position he has taken up between Saint-Amand and Bry. At this moment the fighting is very heavy. His Majesty commands me to say that you must immediately manoeuvre in such a way as to envelop the enemy's right wing and pitch into him from the rear. His army is doomed if you act with vigour. The fate of France is in your hands. Therefore do not waste a moment in carrying out the move which the Emperor has ordered, and make for the heights of Bry and Saint-Amand so as to share in what may be a decisive victory. The enemy has been caught *en flagrant délit*, just when he was trying to join the English.

When Monsieur Forbin-Janson arrived, it was already dark; we were eating by candlelight. It was too late to carry out the movement indicated. Moreover, the 1st Corps had not yet rallied, and if we had taken even one pace to the rear in order to support the right of Napoleon's army, the English troops who were posted at Quatre Bras in considerable strength and whom Ney, the Prince de la Moscowa, had contained and prevented from aiding the Prussians only by prodigies of valour, would have been on the heels of the weak corps commanded by Reille and Kellermann. Thus the order arrived six hours too late, and nothing could be done without the support of d'Erlon.

Major M. Lemonnier-Delafosse, who was aide-de-camp to General Foy commanding the 8th Division, gives an account of the evening after Quatre Bras and expresses regret that he cannot describe a gastronomic feast.

At our excellent General's headquarters we had not only no pans but no cook either, and Prince Jérôme Bonaparte's table was his own. Therefore our staff lived off what it could find. Now this particular evening, having taken shelter in the hovel of a local cobbler, and swept up all the parings of leather so as to lay down straw on which to rest, I discovered under a flight of steps leading to a wood and wine cellar three bowls of milk which we hurriedly fetched up. We also asked the soldiers for some ration bread. But this milk, which we proposed to drink, was curdled. However, it was on this account even more refreshing to us whose blood ran hot after a long day's fighting. We could not dip our bread in it. We had knives, but no forks or spoons. I recall that in sweeping up the bits of leather, I brought to light a wooden spoon. We picked it out of the dust, wiped it carefully, and then it passed from hand to hand as we scooped up the curds. That was all the comfort our poor stomachs received. War makes one the reverse of fussy. One is happy enough when the little and the tolerable are not lacking.

Michel Ney, Duke of Elchingen and Marshal of France, by Maurin
(*The Bettmann Archive*)

Blücher's near escape from death at Ligny. From Christopher Kelly's *A Full and Circum-*

THE BATTLE OF LIGNY

AFTER Zieten's men had drawn back under French attack on June 15th, Blücher ordered his other three corps to march westwards to join it on a prearranged line between Saint-Amand, Ligny and Sombreffe. This defence line ran for seven miles along the winding Ligny stream and among the orchards, gardens and hedgerows of ten villages and hamlets, where many a house or farm courtyard was turned into a small fortress with loopholed walls. The 84,000 troops at Blücher's disposal were barely enough to hold such a line, but he expected Bülow's corps of 30,000, which had furthest to march and would therefore be late; and he had Wellington's promise to come to support him provided that he himself was not attacked. On forward slopes above the villages Blücher exposed the main Prussian masses — a disposition which could not fail to incur the disapprobation of Wellington, accustomed as he was to hide his men on a sheltered reverse slope.

On the French side, Napoleon had 78,000 soldiers and 242 guns — sixteen more than the Prussians had. However, Lobau's small reserve corps was still on its way to the front. The Emperor, awaiting the sound of a cannonade which would announce that Wellington was being seriously engaged at Quatre Bras, was obliged to delay attacking Blücher until after half past two. His plan was to contain the Prussian left with Grouchy's corps and smash into the centre, forcing Blücher to commit his every reserve until the moment when Ney would arrive from Quatre Bras to assail and surround the Prussians' right wing and fall on their rear. But how could Napoleon be sure of the opposition Ney would encounter at Quatre Bras, or calculate at what time he would overcome this opposition? He could hope much, but he could guarantee nothing.

The French infantry, moving forward through waist-high corn, ousted their enemies from a large part of Saint-Amand. Another French division assaulted Ligny, but here its columns were at first repulsed. The Prussians, many of them very young and inexperienced, defended with praiseworthy stubbornness. Small groups fought hand-to-hand amid the burning houses and thatch and a pall of smoke. No less savage, no less inspired by hatred or wild exasperation, was the fighting for cemetery and church or the struggle for the bridges. Soldiers fired down from upper windows. Others broke in farmhouse gates with axe or musket butt. Opponents shot each other from very close to. In a desperate artillery duel across the stream grapeshot volleys were being fired at a range of fifty yards. Villages changed hands more than once. Ligny's streets and gardens became choked with dead.

Blücher realised by now that Wellington could not help him with even a single squadron that bloodstained afternoon — a message to this effect came from General Müffling;[1] yet he resolved to act alone and drive in the French left wing. He took grave risks by leading the attack in person, but his reserve of six battalions, swelled though they were by stragglers, was simply not enough, and having recaptured one hamlet the Prussians were thrown back in disorder. All Blücher could hope for now was to hold out until nightfall and so make possible a joint effort with Wellington on the morrow.

Napoleon, for his part, was eager to deal the Prussians a death blow before dusk, and so leave himself free to deal with Wellington's army on the 17th without danger of Prussian intervention. Already time for this blow was short. For one thing, an hour had been wasted by the failure to identify d'Erlon's will o' the wisp corps: the Emperor had been obliged to halt the attack by his Guard until staff officers had ascertained just who these troops were who had been spotted to the south-west and who so unaccountably moved away again towards Quatre Bras. For another, the daylight available for a final assault against the weakened Prussian centre was reduced by a thunderstorm which broke overhead when the French artillery opened fire.

Now the weary Prussians gave way before veteran troops. With Grouchy in possession of Boignée and threatening Sombreffe, Blücher could not draw off troops from his hard-pressed left to stiffen the crumbling centre, and the only reserve now at his disposal were some squadrons at Bry. In gathering darkness the indefatigable Marshal *Vorwärts*, acting more like a Hussar colonel than a commander-in-chief, led these horsemen into a charge, but they could make little impression on the French squares, and were soon counter-attacked by cavalry. Blücher's grey charger, a present from the Prince Regent, was shot and rolled on its rider; and he, badly bruised and half conscious, was led from the battlefield to a village six miles in the rear.

Despite its bad outcome, this last effort by the Prussian cavalry did afford time for the infantry to draw off in squares and for most of the guns to be dragged away. Moreover, on the two wings the French advance was held. Spasmodic firing lasted until after midnight. Two rearguards clung to Bry and Sombreffe for several hours, while the rest of the army retreated on Wavre under Gneisenau's command.

Napoleon did not think it wise to pursue. Of Ney he had heard no news. Bülow's fresh corps must be near at hand. The two Prussian

---

[1] The suspicious and far less co-operative Gneisenau could still write on June 22nd: 'The Duke of Wellington had promised to attack the enemy in the rear, but he did not come, because his army, Heaven knows why, could not concentrate.'

wings might still offer stiff resistance. So, having ordered Grouchy to have the enemy pursued at daybreak, he rode back to Fleurus for the night, and his troops bivouacked among 20,000 dead and wounded on the field of battle. No attempt was made to keep contact with the Prussians or to watch the line of their retreat.

Whereas French casualties totalled some 12,000, the Prussian losses were close on 16,000, and twenty-one guns; and during the night another 8,000 deserted their colours — men who, coming as they did from provinces formerly in the French Empire, were sympathetic towards Napoleon or at least of doubtful loyalty. Yet when Wellington's liaison officer at Prussian headquarters sent a report on the fighting, he was able to say that Blücher's men, though beaten, were ready to fight again.

Sergeant Hippolyte de Mauduit, of the 2nd battalion of the 1st Regiment of Grenadiers, relates how at about four o'clock on the morning of June 16th he received orders to take up arms and follow the Emperor who was on the point of moving forward.

At nine o'clock we set off for Fleurus, drums and band in the lead. We wore battle order — greatcoat, trousers, unadorned bearskins; and yet for the Guard it should have been an occasion for wearing full dress, since the Guard would soon have a worthy part to play and would have to pin to our colours a hard fought victory.

. . . On reaching the village of Gilly, where the first houses border the Fleurus road, we broke off in order to take a sad look at the battlefield of the previous evening. The dead still awaited burial; the 'Jews' — those crows which follow in the wake of an army — had not had time to swoop down on their prey, and our brothers-in-arms, whose hearts had pulsed so valiantly a bare twelve hours before, still lay there, some three hundred of them, just as they had been struck down.

A dense cloud of dust enveloped us and made breathing difficult. The heat was stifling, there was no breeze to cool one's face, and the sun was right overhead. At noon we escaped from this furnace on reaching a wide and fertile plain, and there piled arms so as to allow time for each corps to get into its battle position.

Here we remained for about an hour. Each man tried to ward off the sun's rays which flashed down upon our dark mass. Several of our men were veteran grenadiers who had fought at the battle

F

of Fleurus under the Republic.[1] They explained the plan and the manoeuvres of that battle just as staff officers would have done, and they told us several unusual incidents in the picturesque style peculiar to old soldiers of the Guard.

. . . One grenadier even unfolded an old map of Flanders which he had in his pack — since when nobody knew; and there, outstretched on the rye which we had unmercifully crushed under foot, we set to discussing the day's manoeuvres.

By means of a dozen handkerchiefs tied together and suspended over a ring of piled arms, we erected a sort of tent, which provided a little shade during this lesson in strategy.

Lieutenant-Colonel Ludwig von Reiche, Chief of Staff to Zieten's 1st Corps, was present when Wellington rode over to see Blücher that afternoon at Ligny.

At one o'clock Blücher appeared on the hill by the mill of Bussy, and not long afterwards the Duke of Wellington rode up. He wore a simple blue overcoat without decorations, an ordinary three-cornered hat with three cockades side by side — one black and two red, the Spanish and Portuguese, with a red and white plume, fastened, as was then the English custom, between the two brims of the hat. Otherwise he was very quietly dressed. For this reason none of our troops recognised him for who or what he was; but as I knew him already from the review at Grammont, I was able to tell them, and every man standing near turned to look at the famous war hero.

After some discussion he was convinced that the enemy's main force was directed against us and not against Quatre Bras; moreover there could no longer be any uncertainty about the direction of the enemy's attack.

From the hill Wellington could overlook our positions in every direction, and he enquired what measures had been taken or were in hand. At this moment we noticed in the distance a party of the enemy, and Napoleon was clearly distinguishable in the group. Perhaps the eyes of the three greatest military commanders of the age were directed on one another.

Having promised powerful support and co-operation, Wellington left soon after half past one to return to his own army. The horse

[1] The Austrians had been defeated there in 1794.

which he rode on this occasion attracted a good deal of attention. A small valise had been strapped to the back of the saddle, and according to one of his staff officers this contained a change of clothes; in addition, a portfolio and pen and ink had been fastened in place of the pistol holster — indications of the way in which English industry knows how to be compendious and practical.

It must have been soon after two o'clock in the afternoon when we saw two enemy columns march out of the wood behind Fleurus.

Wellington afterwards told Lord de Ros how he had ridden over to see Blücher's position and had there met Lieutenant-Colonel Sir Henry Hardinge, British Commissioner at the Prussian head-quarters.

I found them drawn up on the slope of the ground with their advanced columns close down to the rivulet of Ligny, the banks of which were so marshy that the French could only cross it at the bridges of three or four villages that lie along its course. I told the Prussian officers, in presence of Hardinge, that, according to my judgment, the exposure of the advanced columns and, indeed, of the whole army to cannonade, standing as they did displayed to the aim of the enemy's fire, was not prudent. The marshy banks of the stream made it out of their power to cross and attack the French, while the latter, on the other hand, though they could not attack them, had it in their power to cannonade them, and shatter them to pieces, after which they might fall upon them by the bridges at the villages. I said that if I were in Blücher's place with English troops, I should withdraw all the columns I saw scattered about in front, and get more of the troops under shelter of the rising ground. However, they seemed to think they knew best, so I came away very shortly. It all fell out exactly as I had feared. . . .

Colonel Fantin des Odoards, commanding the 22nd of the Line in Vandamme's 3rd Corps, played a distinguished part in the battle.

I had reason to be satisfied with the conduct of my new regiment on this brilliant day. Having dislodged the Prussians from Saint-Amand after repeated attacks, the brigade composed of the 70th and ourselves was ordered to deploy beyond the village to act as a screen. At the approach of enemy cavalry we prepared to receive them in squares, regiment by regiment, and chequerwise. The 70th, on my left, were attacked by the Prussians with great determination, but in my view the enemy would not have driven home their charge had not the wretched 70th, without even waiting for the Prussians, suddenly taken fright and retreated, only to be caught almost immediately and sabred. Had their panic infected my 22nd, then our brigade would have been lost, but my soldiers stood firm, repulsed the enemy's charge, covered the ground with men and horses they had brought down with their accurate firing, and so the situation was restored. The fugitives from the 70th were able to rally behind my square, and they soon took up their positions again on my left in the same order as before.

Tempted by the weakness of the 70th rather than deterred by my regiment's firmness and good musketry, other bodies of Prussian cavalry tried to charge us; but this time the 70th, inspired by the voice of their excellent commanding officer, Colonel Maury, did their duty, and the attackers were repeatedly beaten off and severely mauled in the process. Seeing that their efforts were useless, the Prussians took advantage of a fold in the ground to bring up two guns. These fired grapeshot at us until a sudden grand effort, in which the reserve took part — that is to say, the Imperial Guard — swept the battlefield and brought us victory.

[*This engagement had an interesting sequel next morning when the Emperor inspected the corps.*]

When he reached the left of the line, His Majesty dismounted and walked slowly from one regiment to the next, stopping to speak to each commanding officer and to ask the usual questions. I had not seen the Emperor since the day he had promoted me to colonel, nearly two years before,[1] and how much had happened in the meantime! When I saw him my heart began to beat even faster than it usually does in his presence.

I had moved to the far end of my column, on the side where the 70th were standing, and I overheard the following conversation: 'How many men on parade?' 'So many, sire.' 'Your regiment did not stand against the Prussian cavalry yesterday.' 'Sire, I have many young soldiers who had never seen the enemy before and were frightened. But the disorder was soon set to rights.' 'Yes, but without the 22nd who were on your right and did their duty

[1] Near Dresden in September 1813.

very well, how far would you have retreated? Goodbye Colonel Maury. This error must be remedied.' And the poor Colonel, blushing with embarrassment, could think of nothing to say.

The Emperor wore a stern expression when he left the 70th, but he relaxed as he walked towards me with short steps, his hands behind his back; and when I had saluted him with my sword I saw that his face had a kindly look. He fixed me with his eagle eye and said: 'I know you. You used to be in my Guard, didn't you?' 'Yes, sire, I had that honour, and I owe you all my steps in promotion.' 'Good. How many on parade?' '1830, sire.' 'How many did you lose yesterday?' '220,' 'I watched your conduct from the mill [Naveau]. You repelled the enemy's charges very gallantly. Excellent. We shall meet again The Prussians abandoned a great many muskets on the battlefield. What is being done with them?' 'Sire, we are making *jambons* [hams] of them, as is the custom (a military expression which means that one destroys the weapon by removing the butt).' 'You are wrong, quite wrong. I gave orders for these muskets to be collected with great care so that our National Guards in the interior of France could be armed with them. And the artillery has instructions to allow the soldiers three francs for each weapon collected in this way.' 'Sire, this order has not reached me yet.'

The Emperor turned to the gilded group behind him and said: 'Do you hear that? An order of this importance not yet known. Have this set right as soon as possible. Goodbye, Colonel. I am pleased with you and your regiment.'

Captain Charles François tells how the 30th Regiment of the Line which, together with the 90th, formed General Rôme's 1st Brigade, was ordered to attack Ligny village soon after three o'clock.

When within two hundred yards of the hedges which concealed thousands of Prussian sharpshooters, the regiment took up battle order while still on the march. The charge was sounded and the soldiers went through the hedges. The 1st Brigade's left half-battalion, to which I belonged, went down a hollow track blocked by felled trees, vehicles, harrows and ploughs, and we got past these only after considerable difficulty and under fire from the Prussians hidden behind the hedges, which were extremely thick. Eventually we overcame these obstacles and, firing as we went, entered the village. When we reached the church our advance was halted by a stream, and the enemy, in houses, behind walls and on rooftops, inflicted considerable casualties, as much by musketry as by grapeshot and cannon-balls, which took us from front and flank.

In a moment Major Hervieux, commanding the regiment, and two battalion commanders, Richard and Lafolie, had been killed; another battalion commander, Blain by name, was slightly wounded and had his horse killed under him; five captains were killed and three wounded, two adjutants and nine lieutenants and sub-lieutenants were killed, seven wounded, and close on seven hundred rank and file killed or wounded.

As for me, I escaped with nothing worse than bruises on my thighs and right leg. Not for a long time had I fought with such dash and devotion. The confusion into which the enemy threw us made me curse my existence. I was so angry at seeing a fight conducted so badly that I wanted to get myself killed. No one was in command. No generals, no staff officers, no aides-de-camp were in sight. The regiment lost two thirds of its strength without receiving either reinforcements or orders, and were obliged to retreat in disorder, leaving our wounded on the ground. We rallied near our batteries which were firing like hell at the enemy's guns.

Captain Christophe and I rallied what remained of the regiment, and I can say to my own glory that the troops were pleased to see me still among them, and they asked me to lead them back into action. Despite the setback, the battalion had taken some five hundred prisoners.

Just as we were busy collecting the regiment, General Rôme arrived and ordered us back into Ligny village. The men, not at all disheartened by their failure, nor disturbed by the loss of nearly two thirds of their comrades, shouted '*Vive l'Empereur!*' and advanced. Captain Christophe had the charge sounded, the battalion re-entered the village, but was repulsed. It rallied and forced its way in three times more, only to suffer the same reverse each time.

[*General Rôme led another attack and this time the Prussians had to retreat.*]

Franz Lieber of the Colberg Regiment, writing in English, says that for the first part of the battle he was in reserve, though frequently under shellfire. Eventually an aide-de-camp galloped up from the

*brigade commander with orders for the regiment to throw the
French out of the left wing of Ligny village.*

Presently the colonel rode up to us and said, 'Riflemen, you are
young, I am afraid too ardent; calmness makes the soldier; hold
yourselves in order'; then he turned round: 'March!' — and the
dull, half-suffocated drum, from within the deep column, was
heard beating such delicious music. Now, at last, was all to be
realized for which we had left our homes, had suffered so many
fatigues, had so ardently longed. The bugle gave the signal of halt;
we were in front of the village of Ligny. The signal was given for
the riflemen to march out to the right and left of the column, and to
attack.

Our ardor now led us entirely beyond the proper limits; the
section to which I belonged ran madly, without firing, towards the
enemy, who retreated. My hindman[1] fell; I rushed on, hearing
well but not heeding the urgent calls of our old sergeant. The village was intersected with thick hedges, from behind which the
grenadiers fired upon us, but we drove them from one to the other.
I, forgetting altogether to fire and what I ought to have done, tore
the red plume from one of the grenadiers' bear [skin]-caps, and
swung it over my head, calling triumphantly to my comrades. At
length we arrived at a road crossing the village lengthwise, and the
sergeant-major had now succeeded in his attempt to bring us somewhat back to our reason [senses]. There was a house around the
corner of which he suspected that a number of French lay. 'Be
cautious', he said to me, 'until the others are up', but I stepped
round and a grenadier stood about fifteen paces from me; he aimed
at me, I levelled my rifle at him. 'Aim well, my boy', said the sergeant-major, who saw me. My antagonist's ball grazed my hair on
the right side; I shot and he fell; I found I had shot through his
face; he was dying. This was my first shot ever fired in battle.

Several times I approached old soldiers in the battle, to ask them
whether this was really a good sound battle, and when they told
me, as heavy a one as Dennewitz,[2] one of the most sanguinary en-

---

[1] Riflemen, who attack as *tirailleurs* and never shoot without aiming, are
placed two by two together. These couples assist each other, one charges whilst
the other aims, and *vice versa*. One of them is called the foreman, the other
hindman. [Lieber's note.] A more usual term would be 'covering file', or 'rear
rank man'.

[2] In this battle fought south-west of Berlin on September 6th, 1813, the
Prussians defeated Ney, who lost 53 guns and 22,000 men, double the casualties
suffered by his victors.

gagements in which our regiment or, in fact, any regiment had ever fought, I was delighted. All I had feared was, that I should not have the honor of assisting in a thorough battle.

Captain von Reuter, who commanded a battery of Prussian artillery supporting Zieten's corps, had been quartered in the castle at Soirlen near Charleroi until June 15th, when the battery moved to Fleurus. During the battle his guns were positioned near Bussy windmill.

I suppose it was between two and three o'clock in the afternoon when I received an order to take four guns of my battery and accompany the 14th Regiment in its advance towards St. Amand, while the howitzers and two remaining guns took up a position opposite Ligny, so as to be able to shell the open ground beyond the village, and the village itself, too, in the event of our not being able to hold it. I halted my guns about six hundred paces from St. Amand, and opened fire on the enemy's artillery in position on the high ground opposite, which at once began to reply with a well-sustained fire of shells, and inflicted heavy losses on us. Meanwhile the 14th Regiment, without ever thinking of leaving an escort behind for us, pressed gallantly forward to St. Amand, and succeeded in gaining possession of a part of that village. I myself was under the impression that they had been able to occupy the whole of it. The battery had thus been engaged for some hours in its combat with the hostile guns, and were awaiting the order to follow up the movement of the 14th Regiment, when suddenly I became aware of two strong lines of skirmishers which were apparently falling back on us from the village of St. Amand. Imagining that the skirmishers in front of us were our own countrymen, I hastened up to the battery and warned my layers not to direct their aim upon them, but to continue to engage the guns opposite. In the meanwhile the skirmishers in question had got within three hundred paces of the battery.

I had just returned to the right flank of my command, when our surgeon, Zinkernagel, called my attention to the red tufts on the shakos of the sharpshooters. I at once bellowed out the order 'With grape on the skirmishers!' At the same moment both their lines turned upon us, gave us a volley, and then flung themselves on the ground. By this volley, and the bursting of a shell or two, every horse, except one wheeler, belonging to the gun on my left flank, was either killed or wounded. I ordered the horses to be taken out of one of my ammunition waggons, which had been emptied, and thus intended to make my gun fit to move again, while I meanwhile kept up a slow fire of grape, that had the effect of keeping the marksmen in my front glued to the ground. But in another moment, all of a sudden, I saw my left flank taken in rear, from the direction of the Ligny brook, by a French staff officer and about fifty horsemen. As these rushed upon us the officer shouted to me in German, 'Surrender, gunners, for you are all prisoners!' With these words he charged down with his men on the flank gun on my left, and dealt a vicious cut at my wheel driver, Borchardt, . . . who dodged it, however, by flinging himself over on his dead horse. The blow was delivered with such good will that the sabre cut deep into the saddle, and stuck there fast. Gunner Sieberg, however, availing himself of the chance the momentary delay afforded, snatched up the handspike of one of the 12-pounders, and with the words, 'I'll soon show him how to take prisoners!' dealt the officer such a blow on his bearskin that he rolled with a broken skull from the back of his grey charger, which galloped away into the line of skirmishers in our front.

The fifty horsemen, unable to control their horses which bounded after their companion, followed his lead in a moment, rode over the prostrate marksmen, and carried the utmost confusion into the enemy's ranks. I seized the opportunity to limber up all my guns except the unfortunate one on my left, and to retire on two of our cavalry regiments, which I saw drawn up about 600 paces to my rear. It was only when I had thus fallen back that the enemy's skirmishers ventured to approach my remaining gun. I could see from a distance how bravely its detachment defended themselves and it with handspikes and their side-arms, and some of them in the end succeeded in regaining the battery. The moment I got near our cavalry I rode up to them and entreated them to endeavour to recapture my gun again from the enemy, but they refused to comply with my request. I, therefore, returned sorrowfully to my battery, which had retired meanwhile behind the hill with the windmill on it near Ligny.

We there replenished our ammunition waggons and limber boxes, and set to rights our guns, and the battery again advanced to come into action on the height. We had, however, hardly reached the crest of the hill when the enemy issued from the village of

Ligny in overpowering numbers, and compelled all our troops which were there with us to fall back. The movement was carried out with complete steadiness and regularity. It was now about eight o'clock p.m., and the growing darkness was increased by the heavy storm clouds which began to settle down all round us. My battery, in order to avoid capture, had, of course, to conform to this general movement. I now noticed that there was an excellent artillery position about 1,500 paces behind the village of Brye, close to where the Roman road intersects the road to Quatre Bras. . . . I made for this point with all haste, so that I might there place my guns and cover with their fire the retreat of my comrades of the other arms.

A hollow road leading to Sombreffe delayed my progress some minutes. At length I got over this obstacle and attained my goal; but just as I was going to give the word, 'Action rear,' Von Pirch's (II)[1] infantry brigade began to debouch from Brye. The general saw in an instant what he took for a selfish and cowardly movement of retreat on my part, dashed his spurs into his horse, and galloped up to me nearly beside himself with passion, and shouting out, 'My God! Everything is going to the devil!' 'Truly, sir,' said I, 'matters are not looking very rosy, but the 12-pounder battery, No. 6, has simply come here to get into a position from whence it thinks it may be able to check the enemy's advance.' 'That, then, is very brave conduct on your part,' answered the general, at once mollified; 'cling to the position at all hazards, it is of the greatest importance. I will collect a few troops to form an escort to your guns.' While this short, but animated, discussion had been going on his brigade had come up close to where we were. He formed it up to cover us, and sent every one who was mounted to collect all retreating troops in the neighbourhood for the same purpose, while, as they came up, he called out to them, 'Soldiers, there stand your guns; are you not Prussians!'

During the time that a sort of rear-guard was thus formed, the battery had opened fire on the enemy's cavalry, which was coming up rather cautiously, and had forced them to fall back again. Later on, a 6-pounder field battery and half a horse artillery battery came up and joined us. The fight then became stationary, and as the darkness came on, fighting gradually ceased on both sides.

[1] Prussian general officers bearing the same family name were usually distinguished by the addition of Roman numerals. General von Pirch I commanded the 2nd Prussian Corps. His younger brother, Otto Karl Lorenz, was the brigade commander.

*A young Prussian staff officer, von Wussow by name, relates how
Blücher sent a certain Major von Winterfeldt from Ligny to
Quatre Bras to inform Wellington that the Prussian army might
have to pull back. As it turned out, Gneisenau did well to duplicate
this by ordering von Wussow to ride at full speed to Wellington
and to report on the present state of the battle.*

It was fortunate that I had followed the course of the battle
closely. I felt honoured by the great trust Gneisenau placed in me,
so I did not waste a moment in setting my horse to a gallop towards Thyle and Quatre Bras by way of Brye and Marbais. I
changed my horse for horses belonging to the cavalry detachment
which kept open the line of communication with the Duke between
Wagnelée and Quatre Bras. By the village of Thyle the Bois de la
Hutte comes close to the chaussée. The commander of the cavalry
post here informed me that the road on the far side of the wood
had already been occupied by French troops who had advanced as
far as Piraumont, and that Major von Winterfeldt had been severely
wounded there by enemy sharpshooters.

Having convinced myself of the justice of this warning, I
turned right and left the main road between Thyle and Ahyle,
intending to get back on to the Quatre Bras road as soon as possible.
I had to ride through enemy musketry, but I managed to reach the
English troops at Quatre Bras unscathed. Here I found the Duke
of Wellington on foot, holding a telescope and watching the attack
and the movements of the enemy. General von Müffling stood beside him. I reported to him first the nature of the mission I had
been entrusted with. The Duke turned to me and I said to him:

'At the time I left the battlefield we were still holding all the
villages we occupied behind the Ligny stream, from Sombreffe
through Ligny, Saint-Amand la Haye and Wagnelée, in spite of
constant French attacks and of alternately losing ground and then
regaining it. However, it appears that our losses have mounted
heavily, and as the prospect of Bülow's corps coming to our support has entirely vanished, the most we can do is to hold the battlefield until nightfall. Any greater success is not to be looked for.
Perhaps a strong offensive by the English troops could prevent
Napoleon from turning his full force against the Prussian army.'

The Duke listened to me with his characteristic serenity and
sangfroid, even though enemy cannon balls were flying about us in
all directions. He thanked me in a friendly manner for my report,

and then, as fresh troops had arrived along the Brussels road, he gave orders for a renewed advance.

The Duke instructed me to tell Marshal Blücher that so far it had been extremely difficult for him to resist the heavy attacks made by superior French forces, but that with the reinforcements that had just arrived — he believed he now had about 20,000 men on the ground — he would try to launch a powerful attack which would benefit the Prussian army.

I followed the success of the English offensive until Piraumont had been recaptured, then I rode back as fast as I had come. At the windmill of Bussy I reported to General von Gneisenau and gave him the Duke's reply. This occurred at a time when Ligny had not yet been lost.

We turn again to the recollections of Captain Fritz —— of the Westphalian Landwehr squadron, supporting the infantry.

The light of the long June day was beginning to fail when our very depleted infantry brigade was sent back into reserve. . . . The men looked terribly worn out after the fighting. In the great heat, gunpowder smoke, sweat and mud had mixed into a thick crust of dirt, so that their faces looked almost like those of mulattos, and one could hardly distinguish the green collars and facings on their tunics. Everybody had discarded his stock; grubby shirts or hairy brown chests stuck out from their open tunics; and many who had been unwilling to leave the ranks on account of a slight wound wore a bandage they had put on themselves. In a number of cases blood was soaking through.

As a result of fighting in the villages for hours on end, and of frequently crawling through hedges, the men's tunics and trousers had got torn, so that they hung in rags and their bare skin showed through. In short, anyone accustomed to judging the efficiency of a unit merely from the men's appearance on a parade ground would have been appalled to watch the 4th Westphalian Infantry Regiment of Landwehr coming out of the battle of Ligny.

*Colonel von Reiche relates how he encountered Gneisenau on the
Roman road and learnt from him that the Prussian army had
orders to retreat on Tilly.*

Although it was almost dark I could still see my map[1] clearly
enough to realise that Tilly was not marked on it. Thinking it
likely that a number of other officers would have the same map,
and that uncertainty and confusion could easily result, I proposed
that instead of Tilly another town lying further back but on the
same line of march should be named as the assembly point —
somewhere which we could assume would be shown on every other
map. I remarked that even if two withdrawal points were detailed,
they were both in the same direction, so there would be no fear of
confusion. Gneisenau agreed. On his map I found that Wavre was
just such a place.

How far my suggestion contributed to the fact that the retreat
extended as far as Wavre I must leave open.

Next I stationed the staff officers I had with me, Lieutenant von
Reisewitz, at the point on the Roman road where the track now to
be taken branched off, and instructed him to direct any troops who
arrived to follow it. The detachments which had already taken the
Roman road or the Namur road could not, of course, be recalled.
In itself this was a bad thing, yet it had the advantage that the
enemy would be deceived as to the line of our withdrawal.

. . . As the troops directed on to the road were all split up,
General Gneisenau ordered me to collect them and form them up.
Anyone who has ever been given such a task, and in similar circumstances, will know the endless difficulties one has to contend with
in order to carry it out. I tried to deal with the problem by first
halting the head of the throng and letting the rest of the men fall
in on this. When, after a great deal of trouble, I had managed to
get one group halted and was trying to stop the men who were going past in the meantime, the group broke up again; and this went
on for a while until I succeeded in attracting a few officers and
non-commissioned officers to assist me. Particularly helpful in this
business was my hat with its white plume, because in the dark
people mistook me for a general, an error I was glad to put up with.

When I had disentangled the skein to the point where the men
stood grouped under regiments and formed up in ranks and files,

[1] *Nouvelle carte des Pays-bas etc., réduite d'après celle de Ferrari* (Brussels)
[Reiche].

they marched off in good order. Feeling worn out, I lay down under a tree, holding on to the bridle of my poor horse, which had had nothing to eat or drink all day and all night. I could scarcely have credited such an animal with so much endurance, but it seems to have been one of those occasions, with him as with human beings, when one is so keyed up that one can stand unbelievable strains.

A senior Prussian officer, whose name is unrecorded, gives in his diary a glimpse of Gneisenau that night after the battle.

I found him in a farmhouse. The village had been abandoned by its inhabitants, and every building was filled with wounded. No lights, no drinking water, no rations. We were in a small room, in which an oil lamp burned dimly. On the floor wounded men lay groaning. The General himself was seated on a barrel of pickled cabbage, with only four or five people round him. Scattered troops passed through the village all night long: no one knew whence they came or whither they were going. The dispersion was as great as after the battle of Jena,[1] and the night was just as dark — but morale had not sunk. Each man was looking for his comrades so as to restore order.

In October 1837 Lord Mahon was present when Wellington and Hardinge were reminiscing about the battle of Ligny; and Mahon recorded the conversation.

'Yes,' said Hardinge, 'Blücher himself had gone back as far as Wavre [this should be Mellery]. I passed that night with my amputated arm lying with some straw in his anteroom, Gneisenau and other generals constantly passing to and fro. Next morning Blücher sent for me, calling me Lieber Freund, &c., and embracing me. I perceived he smelt most strongly of gin and of rhubarb. He said to me, *Ich stinke etwas*, that he had been obliged to take medicine, having been twice ridden over by the cavalry, but that he should be quite satisfied if in conjunction with the Duke of Wellington he was able now to defeat his old enemy. I was told that there

[1] On October 14th, 1806, the Prussian line was broken by a whirlwind charge from Murat's cavalry; resistance collapsed, and the routed troops fled and scattered in disorder towards Weimar.

had been a great discussion that night in his rooms, and that Blücher and Grolmann[1] carried the day for remaining in communication with the English army, but that Gneisenau had great doubts as to whether they ought not to fall back to Liége and secure their own communication with Luxembourg.[2] They thought that if the English should be defeated, they themselves would be utterly destroyed.'

[1] Karl Wilhelm Georg, General von Grolmann (1777–1843), was Quartermaster-General.
[2] This is an error, as the Prussian supply routes lay further north.

JUNE 17TH: THE FRENCH PURSUIT

EARLY in the morning Napoleon received his first news of the fighting at Quatre Bras and also learnt that Count Claude-Pierre Pajol's two cavalry divisions were in pursuit of the Prussians towards Namur and Liége. Though Pajol believed himself to be trailing Thielmann's corps, in fact he had before him a band of stragglers and a battery which had lost its way; so apart from taking some guns and waggons, he achieved little. The more fortunate but scarcely less supine Exelmans and his cavalry corps came upon 20,000 Prussians at Gembloux soon after nine o'clock, but failed to pass this vital piece of information to Pajol, though his colleague was only four miles away: Exelmans on his own was heavily outnumbered, but he and Pajol together could have done much to harass the retreating foe. They had not been severely exposed on June 16th. Still more serious was Exelmans' failure to send word to either Grouchy or the Emperor. As for opening fire on the Prussians or even keeping them under vigilant observation, he did neither.

When the anxious Grouchy asked for orders, Napoleon tartly snubbed him, and with a casualness he could ill afford spent some precious hours in riding about the Ligny battlefield, now talking to wounded Prussians, now congratulating his own commanders and their troops. Later he dawdled in political discussion with Grouchy and others of high rank. Only after eleven o'clock, by which time he had received reports that Wellington was still holding Quatre Bras in strength and — tardily — that French cavalry were in contact with the Prussians near Gembloux and along the Namur road, did he take constructive steps to benefit from his gains of the previous day. Grouchy was sent off to reconnoitre Blücher's march and report on his movements; but even now the Emperor was convinced that the Prussians were heading east for the Meuse, when in fact they were retreating northwards on the Dyle. He himself would march against the English at Quatre Bras whither he had already despatched Lobau's corps, the entire Imperial Guard, and three cavalry divisions.

Needless, stupid delays occurred on the march of Grouchy's corps. The early negligence which had allowed the enemy to slip away unseen by the French vedettes could still have been redeemed if only dynamic vigour had replaced fumbling and inertia. The diffident marshal should have given priority to locating Blücher's main force and then to placing his thirty-three thousand troops between it and Napoleon's right wing.

If the Prussians were bound for Brussels, a possibility which he had no right to discount, then by moving north he would surely find them. If, however, they were retreating on Liége, they were steadily drawing away from Wellington and therefore becoming less and less of a danger. If and when they did turn back to rejoin their allies, Grouchy would be well placed to intercept their march.

With speed, Grouchy's men could have reached Wavre and the Dyle by dusk, but neither of his infantry corps covered even ten miles that day. Moreover, because the rain was torrential and the roads were wretched, he halted them two hours before nightfall. Yet the Prussians, tired, soaked, and muddy as they were, pressed ahead in like conditions. Zieten and Pirch were the first to reach Wavre. Thielmann's corps came in at eight o'clock that evening and established itself north of the town, while Bülow's force, arriving later still, bivouacked several miles to the east. Blücher adjusted his lines of communication to run further north through Louvain to Maastricht. Exelmans' scouts did report a concentration of Prussians at Wavre, but their messages failed to reach Grouchy till around midnight; and in drafting his orders for renewing the pursuit next morning the Marshal appears to have believed still that the bulk of the enemy was retreating on Liége.

Meanwhile the Duke of Wellington at Quatre Bras had not learnt of the Prussian defeat and withdrawal until half past seven that morning, and he then decided to pull back to Mont St Jean, so as to keep level with the Prussians moving on Wavre. At ten the allied infantry skilfully broke contact behind a screen of cavalry and horse artillery and headed north, unmolested by the torpid Ney. Not until the Emperor arrived to inject some vigour did Ney's men bestir themselves; and the Emperor himself, riding his grey mare 'Désirée', led the belated pursuit with blazing energy. Had it not been for a torrential storm and several rearguard actions, in particular at Genappe, he might still have caught the retreating Anglo-Dutch army, but this reached safely the ridge where the morrow's battle would be fought. This position for defence had been spotted by Wellington the previous year and already reconnoitred. Here, armed with Blücher's promise to come to his support, he stood confidently at bay. Here Napoleon, no less confidently, expected to defeat Wellington before the Prussians could rally and march to his aid. He would have done well to bear in mind what he had said about Blücher to Colonel Sir Neil Campbell on Elba: 'That old devil always attacked me with the same vigour. If he was beaten, he would, a moment later, show himself ready to fight again.'

G

Captain Fritz——, commanding the Westphalian Landwehr squadron attached to Jagow's infantry brigade, relates what happened to him on June 17th.

In very bad weather we set off again in the morning to cross the Dyle. The mood of the troops was certainly grave, but not in the least disheartened, and even if one could have detected that we were on a retreat rather than a victory march, the bearing of all but a few isolated units was still very good. 'We have lost once, but the game is not up, and tomorrow is another day,' remarked a Pomeranian soldier to his neighbour who was grumbling, and he was quite right. The firm bearing of the army owed not a little to the cheerful spirit and freshness of our seventy-four-year-old Field-Marshal [Blücher]. He had had his bruised limbs bathed in brandy, and had helped himself to a large schnaps; and now, although riding must have been very painful, he rode alongside the troops, exchanging jokes and banter with many of them, and his humour spread like wildfire down the columns. I only glimpsed the old hero riding quickly past, although I should dearly have liked to have expressed to him my pleasure at his fortunate escape.

Even my Westphalian Landwehr riders did not lose their good bearing. But in the rain many new saddles swelled, and the troops, as young riders often do, sat unsteadily and lolled about during the march, with the unfortunate result that I soon had a number of horses with saddle sores. I carried out a thorough inspection and anyone who had a horse in this condition was ordered to dismount, carry his portmanteau on his back, and then go splashing through thick and thin on foot beside us. This was very unpleasant indeed for the rather easy-going Westphalians.

Lieutenant James Hope of the 92nd Regiment of Foot saw Wellington arrive at Quatre Bras early on June 17th from Genappe, where he had spent the night.

The morning being cold, and rather inclined to rain, his Grace, on alighting, came up to some of our men and said — 'Ninety-second, I will be obliged to you for a little fire.' The request had no sooner been made, than every man flew to the village, to procure the necessary materials. In a very short time, they returned, lighted the fire opposite to the door of a small hut, constructed of the boughs of trees, which they repaired in the best manner they could. For their attention, particularly the latter part of it, his Grace expressed himself truly grateful. In this splendid mansion the Field-Marshal received the Prince of Orange, Lord Hill, and a great many other officers of rank; — in that hut, he received the melancholy tidings from Prince Blücher, communicating the disaster that had befallen his army at Ligny. . . .

For some time after he had received the unwelcome news, his Grace remained closely shut up in the hut. Having issued the necessary orders for the retreat of the army, he came out of his airy residence, and for an hour walked alone in front of it. Now and then his meditations were interrupted by a courier with a note, who, the moment he had delivered it, retired to some distance to wait his Grace's will. The Field-Marshal had a small switch in his right hand, the one end of which he frequently put to his mouth, apparently unconscious that he was doing so. His left hand was thrown carelessly behind his back, and he walked at the rate of three and a half to four miles in the hour. He was dressed in white pantaloons, with half-boots, a military vest, white neckcloth, blue surtout, and cocked hat. He was dressed in a similar manner on the 16th. On the latter day, the telescope was never out of his hand, and very seldom from his eye.

Captain George Bowles had his company of Coldstream Guards nearly in front of the farmhouse at Quatre Bras.

Soon after daybreak the Duke of Wellington came to me, and, being personally known to him, he remained in conversation for an hour or more, during which time he repeatedly said he was surprised to have heard nothing of Blücher. At length a staff-officer[1] arrived, his horse covered with foam, and whispered to the Duke, who without the least change of countenance gave him some orders and dismissed him. He then turned round to me and said, 'Old Blücher has had a d——d good licking and gone back to Wavre, eighteen miles. As he has gone back, we must go too. I suppose in England they will say we have been licked. I can't help it; as they are gone back, we must go too.'

He made all the arrangements for retiring without moving from the spot on which he was standing, and it certainly did not occupy him five minutes.

[1] Colonel Gordon. See next extract.

Lieutenant Basil Jackson of the Royal Staff Corps, having spent the
night at Genappe, was back with the army before daybreak, and
as everything seemed to be quiet, he took the opportunity to go and
examine the ground which had been so fiercely contested the pre-
vious day.

On returning to the place where I had left the Duke, when I
went on my ramble round the outposts, I found him still seated on
the ground, where he remained till Gordon[1] and his escort returned with jaded horses, soon after ten o'clock. On hearing his
report, the Duke said a few words to Delancey, who, observing me
at hand, directed me to find Sir Thomas Picton[2] and tell him to
make immediate preparation for withdrawing to Waterloo. I
found Picton at a farm-house a short distance along the Charleroi
chaussée, who gave me a surly acknowledgment of the order; he
evidently disliked to retire from a position he had so gallantly held
the day before, and no wonder!

The first intimation that the army was about to retire was the
getting in of the wounded; troopers were sent to the front, who
placed such disabled men as could manage to sit, on their horses,
they themselves rendering support on foot. At times a poor fellow
might be seen toppling from side to side, requiring two men to
keep him on his seat; the horses moving gently, as if conscious that
their motions were torturing their suffering riders. Some again required to be carried in a blanket, so that every man found with life
in him was in one way or another brought in and sent to the rear.
It was about mid-day ere this important duty was completed, and
the troops then began to move off by brigades, in such a manner as
should prevent the enemy from observing what we were about.

One of the best accounts of the British rearguard's retreat comes from
Captain Mercer of the Royal Horse Artillery.

It was now about one o'clock. . . . Still the French army made
no demonstration of an advance. This inactivity was inaccountable.

[1] Lieut.-Colonel Sir Alexander Gordon, aide-de-camp to Wellington, had
been sent off some hours earlier, escorted by a squadron of the 10th Hussars, to
discover what had happened to the Prussians after Ligny.

[2] General Picton had been struck by a musket ball at Quatre Bras and had
two ribs broken, but although in pain he had his servant bind up the wound
secretly and hid the fact. His wound was not discovered until after his death on
the field of Waterloo. To add to his ill humour, he was compelled to ride a
trooper's horse, his groom having taken fright and gone off to the rear with
his horses.

Lord Uxbridge and an aide-de-camp came to the front of my battery, and, dismounting, seated himself on the ground; so did I and the aide-de-camp. His lordship with his glass was watching the French position; and we were all three wondering at their want of observation and inactivity, which had not only permitted our infantry to retire unmolested, but also still retained them in their bivouac. 'It will not be long now before they are on us,' said the aide-de-camp, 'for they always dine before they move; and those smokes seem to indicate that they are cooking now.'

He was right; for not long afterwards another aide-de-camp, scouring along the valley, came to report that a heavy column of cavalry was advancing through the opening between the woods to the left from the direction of Gembloux. At the same moment we saw them distinctly; and Lord Uxbridge, having reconnoitered them a moment through his glass, started up, exclaiming, in a joyful tone, 'By the Lord, they are Prussians!' jumped on his horse, and, followed by the two aides, dashed off like a whirlwind to meet them. For a moment I stood looking after them as they swept down the slope, and could not help wondering how the Prussians came there. I was, however, not left long in my perplexity, for, turning my eyes towards the French position, I saw their whole army descending from it in three or four dark masses, whilst their advanced cavalry picket was already skirmishing with and driving back our hussars. The truth instantly flashed on my mind, and I became exceedingly uneasy for the safety of Lord Uxbridge and his companions, now far advanced on their way down the valley, and likely to be irretrievably cut off.

My situation now appeared somewhat awkward: left without orders and entirely alone on the brow of our position — the hussar pickets galloping in and hurrying past as fast as they could — the whole French army advancing, and already at no great distance. In this dilemma, I determined to retire across the little dip that separated me from Sir O. Vandeleur, and take up a position in front of his squadrons, whence, after giving a round to the French advance as soon as they stood on our present ground, I thought I could retire in sufficient time through his intervals to leave the ground clear for him to charge. This movement was immediately executed; but the guns were scarcely unlimbered ere Sir Ormsby came furiously up, exclaiming, 'What are you doing here, sir? You encumber my front, and we shall not be able to charge. Take your guns away, sir; instantly, I say — take them away!' It was in vain that I endeavoured to explain my intentions, and that our fire would allow his charge to be made with more effect. 'No, no; take them out of my way, sir!' was all the answer I could get; and, accordingly, I was preparing to obey, when up came Lord Uxbridge, and the scene changed in a twinkling.

'Captain Mercer, are you loaded?' 'Yes, my lord.' 'Then give them a round as they rise the hill, and retire as quickly as possible.' 'Light dragoons, threes right; at a trot, march!' and then some orders to Sir Ormsby, of whom I saw no more that day. 'They are just coming up the hill,' said Lord Uxbridge. 'Let them get well up before you fire. Do you think you can retire quick enough afterwards?' 'I am sure of it, my lord.' 'Very well, then, keep a good look-out, and point your guns well.' I had often longed to see Napoleon, that mighty man of war — that astonishing genius who had filled the world with his renown. Now I saw him, and there was a degree of sublimity in the interview rarely equalled. The sky had become overcast since the morning, and at this moment presented a most extraordinary appearance. Large isolated masses of thundercloud, of the deepest, almost inky black, their lower edges hard and strongly defined, lagging down, as if momentarily about to burst, hung suspended over us, involving our position and everything on it in deep and gloomy obscurity; whilst the distant hill lately occupied by the French army still lay bathed in brilliant sunshine. Lord Uxbridge was yet speaking, when a single horseman, immediately followed by several others, mounted the plateau I had left at a gallop, their dark figures thrown forward in strong relief from the illuminated distance, making them appear much nearer to us than they really were. For an instant they pulled up and regarded us, when several squadrons, coming rapidly on the plateau, Lord Uxbridge cried out, 'Fire! — fire!' and, giving them a general discharge, we quickly limbered up to retire, as they dashed forward supported by some horse-artillery guns, which opened upon us ere we could complete the manoeuvre, but without much effect, for the only one touched was the servant of Major Whinyates,[1] who was wounded in the leg by the splinter of a howitzer shell.

It was now for the first time that I discovered the Major and his rocket troop, who, annoyed at my having the rear, had disobeyed the order to retreat, and remained somewhere in the neighbour-

---

[1] Edward C. Whinyates, later a general, had served with distinction in the Peninsula. At Waterloo he had three horses shot under him, and was twice wounded.

hood until this moment, hoping to share whatever might be going on. The first gun that was fired seemed to burst the clouds overhead, for its report was instantly followed by an awful clap of thunder, and lightning that almost blinded us, whilst the rain came down as if a waterspout had broken over us. The sublimity of the scene was inconceivable. Flash succeeded flash, and the peals of thunder were long and tremendous; whilst, as if in mockery of the elements, the French guns still sent forth their feebler glare and now scarcely audible reports — their cavalry dashing on at a headlong pace, adding their shouts to the uproar. We galloped for our lives through the storm, striving to gain the enclosures about the houses of the hamlets, Lord Uxbridge urging us on, crying, 'Make haste! — make haste! for God's sake, gallop, or you will be taken!' We did make haste, and succeeded in getting amongst the houses and gardens, but with the French advance close on our heels. Here, however, observing the chaussée full of hussars, they pulled up. Had they continued their charge we were gone, for these hussars were scattered about the road in the utmost confusion, some in little squads, others singly, and, moreover, so crowded together that we had no room whatever to act with any effect — either they or us.

Meantime the enemy's detachments began to envelop the gardens, which Lord Uxbridge observing, called to me. 'Here follow me with two of your guns,' and immediately himself led the way into one of the narrow lanes between the gardens. What he intended doing, God knows, but I obeyed. The lane was very little broader than our carriages — there was not room for a horse to have passed them! The distance from the chaussée to the end of the lane, where it debouched on the open fields, could scarcely have been above one or two hundred yards at most. His lordship and I were in front, the guns and mounted detachments following. What he meant to do I was at a loss to conceive; we could hardly come to action in the lane; to enter on the open was certain destruction. Thus we had arrived at about fifty yards from its termination when a body of chasseurs or hussars appeared there as if waiting for us. These we might have seen from the first, for nothing but a few elder bushes intercepted the view from the chaussée. The whole transaction appears to me so wild and confused that at times I can hardly believe it to have been more than a confused dream — yet true it was; — the general-in-chief of the cavalry exposing himself amongst the skirmishers of his rear-guard, and literally doing the duty of a cornet! 'By God! we are all prisoners' (or some such words), exclaimed Lord Uxbridge, dashing his horse at one of the garden-banks, which he cleared, and away he went, leaving us to get out of the scrape as best we could.

There was no time for hesitation — one manoeuvre alone could extricate us if allowed time, and it I ordered. 'Reverse by un-limbering' was the order. To do this the gun was to be unlimbered, then turned round, and one wheel run up the bank, which just left space for the limber to pass it. The gun is then limbered up again and ready to move to the rear. The execution, however, was not easy, for the very reversing of the limber itself in so narrow a lane, with a team of eight horses, was sufficiently difficult, and re-quired first-rate driving. Nothing could exceed the coolness and activity of our men; the thing was done quickly and well, and we returned to the chaussée without let or hindrance. How we were permitted to do so, I am at a loss to imagine; for although I gave the order to reverse, I certainly never expected to have seen it executed. Meantime my own situation was anything but a pleasant one, as I sat with my back to the gentlemen at the end of the lane, whose interference I momentarily expected, casting an eye from time to time over my shoulder to ascertain whether they still kept their position. There they sat motionless, and although thankful for their inactivity, I could not but wonder at their stupidity. It seemed, however, all of a piece that day — all blunder and con-fusion; and this last I found pretty considerable on regaining the chaussée. His lordship we found collecting the scattered hussars to-gether into a squadron for our rescue, for which purpose it was he had so unceremoniously left us.

General Jean-Baptiste Drouet d'Erlon records in his memoirs what took place when Napoleon arrived that morning at Quatre Bras.

The Emperor, finding me there, spoke in a grieved tone of voice the following words which are engraved on my memory for all time: 'France has been ruined. Go, my dear General, place your-self at the head of the cavalry and press the English rearguard vigorously.'

The Emperor stayed at the head of the advance-guard, and even took part in a cavalry charge as we came out of Genappe. The pur-suit went as far as the approaches to Plancenoit. When we reached a hillock on the left of the road, from which we had a view of the positions the enemy were taking up, the Emperor stood and watched their movements. In the belief that the enemy were still retreating, he said to me: 'Continue the pursuit.'

It was nearly dark. At this moment Milhaud's division of heavy cavalry came on the scene, but when it tried to get into battle order on the right of the road, and a little forward of the hillock, it was heavily shelled. The Emperor said to me: 'Have all the troops take up positions and we will see what happens tomorrow.'

The night was terrible. Rain poured down, and soaked the ground so badly that the deployment of the artillery was seriously impeded. Our soldiers spent the night without shelter, and no musket would fire. An officer whom the Emperor sent to the outposts early next morning reported that the enemy were continuing their retreat, so I was ordered to move off and follow them hard. But as I had placed quite a different interpretation on the enemy's moves, I sent my chief of staff to the Emperor to say that I thought the enemy were preparing to stand and fight.

The Emperor came at once to our forward lines and I accompanied him. We dismounted so as to be able to get close to the enemy's look-out posts, and study what was going on there. He saw that I was right, and having come to the conclusion that the allied army was taking up battle positions, he said: 'Have the troops make soup and get their arms in good order. We will see what midday brings.'

The French suffered as badly in pursuit as did their opponents in retreat. Sergeant Hippolyte de Mauduit relates how, at eight o'clock that evening, the infantry of the Guard left the main road near Genappe and branched off to the right, so as to leave the paved route clear and not impede the artillery and its parks.

The tracks were so deep in mud after the rain that we found it impossible to maintain any sort of order in our columns. In looking for easier paths a large number of men went astray, and not until daybreak did they all manage to rejoin the columns.

The Emperor had selected the farm of Le Caillou, right on the main road itself, as Headquarters. One by one the regiments of his Guard came up, but each arrived there in a state of exhaustion. During all the marches and countermarches of that frightful night there was a real helter-skelter. Regiments, battalions, even companies became muddled; and in complete darkness and drenching rain people were hunting vainly for their generals or their officers. We had constantly to push our way through quick hedges or deep ravines. Furthermore, grumbles and curses were levelled on all sides against the generals on whom was laid the blame, quite unjustly, for all this hardship. In fact, discontent rose to such a pitch that repeated shouts of '*A la trahison!*' were heard.

Driven to the limit of their patience even more than of their strength, a crowd of grenadiers and light infantry dashed into any buildings they came across, some seeking shelter from the dreadful ordeal, others a bivouac where they could dry themselves and rest for a few hours.

At about midnight the bulk of our regiment arrived, despite everything, in an orchard in which stood a farm only just converted into the headquarters of the Guard. This was definitely our bivouac. And about time too! What a day and a night!

Our greatcoats and our trousers were caked with several pounds of mud. A great many of the soldiers had lost their shoes and reached the bivouac barefoot.

THE NIGHT BEFORE THE BATTLE

Chorus of the Years

THE young sleep sound; but the weather awakes
In the veterans, pains from the past that numb;
Old stabs of Ind, old Peninsular aches,
Old Friedland chills, haunt their moist mud bed,
Cramps from Austerlitz; till their slumber breaks.

Thomas Hardy, *The Dynasts*

Mr John Gordon Smith, Assistant Surgeon of the 12th Light Dragoons, set down his recollections of that night.

We bivouacked in open clover fields, close to, and somewhat in rear of, the farm of *Mont St Jean*.

When we reached our halting place, it was probably about seven in the evening, and still daylight. The position of the general army was a short distance in front of us, and the red colouring of the scene, owing to the uniforms of our troops, exhibited an imposing sight.

. . . We were to pass the night on the spot we already occupied, but the officers were in want of food, drink, and fire. Of the first, our men had received a supply; the horses had also been, at least partially, cared for, — but water! There was a draw-well close to the village, or hamlet of *St Jean*, and that was the only resource to which thousands of thirsty ones had access. The first attack upon it was the last; for snap went the rope, and down fell the bucket, to a depth from which it could not be recovered. Disappointed in the article of water, our attention was drawn to that of fire, in procuring which we were eminently successful. The adjoining village furnished fuel in abundance. Doors, and window-shutters — furniture of every description — carts, ploughs, harrows, wheelbarrows, clock-cases, casks, tables, &c &c, were carried or trundled out to the bivouac, and being broken up, made powerful fires, in spite of the rain. Chairs were otherwise disposed of. Officers were

95

paying two francs each for them, and the men seemed, at first, to be very well able to keep up the supply. This, at last, failed, and, for one, I was fain to buy a bundle of straw.

In front of the field which the horses occupied, ran a miry cart-road (upon which the officers' fires were kindled) and by the side of this road was a drain, or shallow ditch. Here a party of us deposited our straw, and resolved to establish ourselves for the night, under cover of our cloaks; but such was the clayey nature of its bottom, that the rain did not sink into the earth, but rose like a leak in a ship, among the straw, and we were, in consequence, more drenched from below than from above.

On June 17th the Assistant Commissary-General to the 2nd Division of Infantry, Tupper Carey by name, went into Waterloo to obtain supplies, or at least to ascertain what was to be done to get them. A native of Guernsey, this efficient, gentlemanlike young man had already served in the retreat to Corunna and later as commissary to General Le Marchant's cavalry brigade.

I found nothing but bustle and confusion in the village, which was encumbered with troops, &c. I therefore determined to ride on at once to Brussels, as there only I hoped to effect my object, and at the same time to get a fresh horse, expecting to find my groom, who was on it and had orders to look out for me. It was late in the afternoon and the road was thronged with waggons loaded with supplies of bread and forage, corn, baggage, animals, and other conveyances belonging to the army. I had hardly proceeded a mile when suddenly a panic seemed to have seized every one at the cry of the enemy being at hand. It seemed ridiculous to me, who had just arrived from the front, where all was quiet, except the occasional booming of guns at long distance; but when a cry of the sort occurs among a set of men without anyone to control them, the disorder which ensues is hardly to be conceived. It gathers strength and to stem it is impossible.

Never did I witness a scene of such confusion and folly. To add to its bad effects, it was raining hard, and we were in the Forest of Soignies. The servants got rid of their baggage, let it drop on the ground, then, jumping on their animals, galloped off to the rear. Others dispersed in various directions in the wood. The peasantry, carrying provisions in the country waggons, cut the traces of the harness and ran away with the horses, abandoning the waggons. As the tumult progressed down the road with approaching darkness, the apprehension of danger became so general, with the followers of the army as well as with officers and detachments of troops on their way to join their regiments, that the whole went towards Brussels like a sudden rush of water increasing as it went.

With other mounted officers I endeavoured to get ahead of the current (seeing the impossibility of checking it) by galloping in the forest away from the road, but we were brought up so often by enclosures and other hindrances that we were obliged to return to it, and follow the stream. Thus we were obliged to creep on by degrees as the tide flowed, until two o'clock in the morning, when we at last got into Brussels. The rain was coming down in torrents the whole night, but, fortunately for myself, I had a cloak strapped on the pummel of my saddle, which helped to keep me, when on, free from a good portion of wet. Many there were, however, round about me who had not that advantage, being in their uniforms. One poor man in particular (a brother officer), who was next to me, was in full dress, with his gold epaulettes and white duck pantaloons, which from their brightness appeared to have been put on for the first time. Help him I could not.

. . . I went immediately to an inn, but it was so full that room to lie down could hardly be found. I therefore got into a quiet corner of the saloon, and after resting two or three hours, and having seen my horse well fed, went to the office of the Commissary-General [Mr Thomas Dunmore] and was there informed that all the supplies were on the road, but where they had got to was not known. Finding that I could do nothing, and that I might be considered too long absent from duty if I stayed, I started again for Waterloo, after having in vain inquired for my groom and second horse.

At three o'clock in the morning [1] *Wellington, having occasion to send a messenger to Brussels, wrote a letter to Lady Frances Wedderburn Webster, who was staying in the city with her parents, the Earl and Countess of Mountnorris.*

We fought a desperate battle on Friday, in which I was successful, though I had but very few troops. The Prussians were very

[1] At the same time he wrote to Sir Charles Stuart, who was Ambassador to the Sovereign Prince of the Netherlands and also in attendance upon Louis XVIII at Ghent: 'Pray keep the English quiet if you can. Let them all prepare to move, but neither be in a hurry or a fright, as all will yet turn out well.'

roughly handled, and retired in the night, which obliged me to do
the same to this place yesterday. The course of the operations may
oblige me to uncover Bruxelles for a moment, and may expose
that town to the enemy; for which reason I recommend that you
and your family should be prepared to move to Antwerp at a
moment's notice.

I will give you the earliest intimation of any danger that may
come to my knowledge; at present I know of none.

*The Emperor Napoleon, angry that he had been unable to attack the
Anglo-Dutch army that afternoon and thinking it probable that
Wellington and Blücher were using the night to cross the Forest of
Soignes and link up in front of Brussels, went out on foot at one
o'clock in the morning, accompanied only by his Grand Marshal,
Comte Bertrand.*

It was my intention to follow the English army in its retreat
and to endeavour to engage it, despite the darkness, as soon as it
was on the march. I walked along the line of main defences. The
Forest of Soignes looked as if it were on fire; the horizon between
this forest, Braine-la-Leud and the farms of La Belle Alliance and
La Haye was aglow with bivouac fires; complete silence prevailed.
The Anglo-Dutch army lay wrapped in profound slumber, following upon the exhausting days it had just gone through. On arriving
near to the woods of the Château de Hougoumont I heard the
sounds of a column on the march. It was half-past two. Now, at
this hour, the rearguard would be leaving its position if the enemy
were in fact retreating; but this illusion was short-lived.

The noises stopped. The rain fell in torrents. Several officers
who had been sent out on reconnaissance, and some secret agents
returning at half past three, confirmed that the Anglo-Dutch
troops were not making a move. Then at four o'clock despatch-
riders brought me a peasant who had acted as guide to an English
cavalry brigade which had gone to positions on the far left by the
village of Ohain. Two Belgian deserters, who had just left their
regiment, told me that their army was preparing for battle and
that no retreat had taken place; that Belgium was offering up
prayers for my success; and that the English and the Prussians
were both equally hated there.

The enemy commander could do nothing more contrary to the

interests of his cause and his country, to the whole mood of this campaign, and even to the most elementary rules of war, than to stay in the position he occupied. He had behind him the defiles of the Forest of Soignes, and if he were beaten any retreat would be out of the question.

The French troops were bivouacked in the mud. The officers considered it impossible for us to give battle during the day. The artillery and cavalry could not manoeuvre on the ground, so soaked was it; and they calculated that twelve hours of fine weather would be needed to dry it out.

The day began to dawn. I returned to my headquarters well satisfied with the great error which the enemy commander was making and very anxious lest the bad weather should prevent my taking advantage of it. But already the sky was clearing. At five o'clock I noticed a few faint rays of that sun which, before setting, should light up the defeat of the English army. The British oligarchy would be overthrown by it! France, that day, was going to ride more glorious, more powerful and greater than ever!

General Maximilien-Sébastien Foy, who had fought in Spain and now commanded the 9th Infantry Division in Reille's Corps, wrote as follows:

During the night of June 17–18 we were eating with Prince Jérôme at the Roi d'Espagne [in Genappe]. A waiter who was serving us said that Lord Wellington had dined in the inn the previous evening, and that one of his aides-de-camp had announced at table that the English army would await the French at the entrance to the Forest of Soignes and that it would be joined by the Prussian army which had taken the road to Wavre. This news was illuminating for Guilleminot[1] and myself. On the morning of the 18th Jérôme was with his brother at Le Caillou farm and told him what the waiter at Genappe had said. The Emperor replied: 'The Prussians and English cannot possibly link up for another two days, after such a battle as Fleurus [Ligny] and given the fact that they are being pursued by a considerable body of troops.' His Majesty added: 'We shall be only too happy if the English

---

[1] Armand-Charles, Comte Guilleminot (1774–1840) was second in command of Jérôme's division at Waterloo. On July 2–3, as commander of the 9th Cavalry Division, he negotiated and signed with Blücher the capitulation of Paris.

decide to stay. The battle that is coming will save France and will
be celebrated in the annals of the world. I shall have my artillery
fire and my cavalry charge, so as to force the enemy to disclose his
positions, and, when I am quite certain which positions the
English troops have taken up, I shall march straight at them with
my Old Guard.'

*William Gibney, Assistant Surgeon to the 15th Hussars, is another
who has described that miserable night.*

There was no choice; we had to settle down in the mud and
filth as best we could, and those having any provisions about them
were fortunate. As I had obtained a bit of tongue (but whether
cooked, or only smoked and salted, I know not) in the morning,
and had a thimble-full of brandy in my flask, I was better off than
many, and finishing the somewhat queer-tasting food, with others
I looked about for a drier place to lie down and rest the weary
limbs. It was all mud, but we got some straw and boughs of trees,
and with these tried to lessen the mud and to make a rough
shelter against the torrents of rain which fell all night; wrapping
around us our cloaks, and huddling close together, we lay in the
mud and wooed the drowsy god, and that with tolerable success.
For, notwithstanding rain, mud, and water, cold, and the
proximity of the enemy, most of us managed to sleep. As for myself, I slept like a top, but I had become seasoned to the work, and
was young and strong.

Very early on the morning of the 18th June we were ordered to
bridle up and prepare for action. This we did in darkness, wet, and
discomfort, but a night spent in pouring rain, sitting up to the
hips in muddy water, with bits of straw hanging about him, does
make a man feel and look queer on first rising. Indeed, it was
almost ludicrous to observe the various countenances of us officers,
as, smoking cigars and occasionally shivering, we stood round a
watch-fire giving out more smoke than heat. It was tedious work
waiting for orders. We were anxious to be put into motion, if it
were only to circulate our blood, for both horses and men were
shaking with cold.

*When Sir Walter Scott was gathering material for his life of Napoleon,
he talked to Jean Baptiste Decoster, who owned a little inn on the
road between Rossomme and La Belle Alliance. By diligent questioning he obtained the following particulars of Decoster's experiences during the morning of the great battle.*

About five in the morning he was taken prisoner to serve as
guide, and conducted with his hands tied behind him (that he
might not escape as a former man had done) to another house
belonging to him, opposite to which Buonaparte had slept. Observing the French soldiers plundering and destroying this house,
he cried. Buonaparte asked what he cried for. 'Because your
soldiers are destroying all my property, and my family have no-
where to put their heads.' Buonaparte said, 'Do you not know that
I am Emperor, and can recompense you an hundred times as
much?' He was placed on a horse immediately between Buonaparte
and his first Aide-de-Camp, his saddle being tied to the saddle of
a trooper behind him, that he might not escape. They proceeded
a little beyond Belle Alliance, and Buonaparte took the ground on
a small eminence on the opposite side, a sort of bodyguard of
twelve pieces of artillery, very light, surrounding them. From
this spot he could command both lines.

He first observed: 'How steadily those troops take the ground!
how beautifully those cavalry form! *regardez ces chevaux gris! Qui
sont ces beaux cavaliers? Ce sont des braves troupes, mais dans une
demi-heure je les couperai en pièces.*' Observing how the chasms in
the British squadrons were filled up the instant they were made
by his artillery, he exclaimed '*Quelles braves troupes! comme ils se
travaillent, ils travaillent très-bien, très-bien!*'

He asked Decoster the particulars of every house, tree, wood,
rising ground, &c., with which he seemed well informed, holding
a map in his left hand, and intent upon the action all the day, incessantly taking snuff from his waistcoat pocket, in large pinches,
of which he violently snuffed up about half, throwing the other
from him, with a violent exertion of the arm, and thumb and
finger, as if from vexation; this was all the refreshment he took for
fourteen hours: he frequently placed his left hand upon the back
of Decoster's horse, to speak to the Aide-de-Camp on the other
side of him. Seeing Decoster flinch at the shower of shot, he replied,
'Do not stir, my friend. A shot will kill you equally in the back as
the front, or wound you more disgracefully.'

H

*Colonel Auguste-Louis Pétiet, a hussar officer who had fought at
Austerlitz and Eylau and, as aide-de-camp to Soult, had been
severely wounded at Badajoz, was again on Soult's staff and had
opportunities for watching the Emperor at close quarters, especially
on June 18th.*

During his stay on Elba, Napoleon's stoutness had increased
rapidly. His head had become enlarged and more deeply set between his shoulders. His pot-belly was unusually pronounced for a
man of forty-five. Furthermore, it was noticeable during this campaign that he remained on horseback much less than in the past.
When he dismounted, either to study his maps or else to send messages and receive reports, members of his staff would set before him
a small deal table[1] and a rough chair made of the same wood, and
on this he would remain seated for long periods at a time. . . .

[That morning] the Emperor rode round the lines and was received as usual with cheers by his army. He dismounted and took
up his position on a fairly high mound[2] just near La Belle Alliance,
from which one could see the battlefield and the two armies ready
to come to grips. Napoleon had spread a map on his little table and
while looking at it he seemed to be deeply preoccupied with strategical plans. From the foot of the mound where I stood, I found it
hard to keep my eyes off the extraordinary man upon whom Victory had for so long showered her gifts. His stoutness, his dull white
complexion, his heavy walk made him appear very different from
the General Bonaparte I had seen at the start of my career during
the campaign of 1800 in Italy, when he was so alarmingly thin that
no soldier in his army could understand how, with so frail a body
and looking as ill as he did, he could stand such fatigue.

*Private Matthew Clay states that the Light Company of the 2nd
Battalion, 3rd Guards spent the night extended along the upper*

---

[1] This is confirmed by General Foy, who wrote: 'I saw him through my
glass, walking up and down, wearing his grey greatcoat, and frequently leaning
over the little table on which his map was spread.'

[2] William Warden, surgeon on board H.M.S. *Northumberland*, was told by
General Gourgaud at St Helena that Napoleon had ordered some trusses of
straw to be placed under his feet on this soggy mound to keep them dry and
prevent him from sliding.

Decoster told Sir John Sinclair in January 1816 that he watched Napoleon
constantly walk to and fro, sometimes with his arms crossed, but chiefly behind
his back, with his thumbs in the pockets of a slate-coloured greatcoat. He had
his eyes fixed on the battle, and pulled out his watch and snuff-box alternately.

side of the Hougoumont orchard, in a shallow ditch sheltered by a
high bush hedgerow which separated the men from the French, who
were close at hand.

When daylight appeared, all being quiet on Sunday morning, we procured some fuel from the farm of Hougoumont and then lighted fires and warmed ourselves. Our limbs were very much cramped sitting on the side of the wet ditch the entire night. The Sergeant of each section gave a small piece of bread, which was about an ounce, to each man, and inquiry was made along the ranks for a butcher. One having gone forward, he was immediately ordered to kill a pig, as there were cattle at the farmhouse. Having slaughtered it, it was divided amongst the Company and a portion of the head in its rough state was my share. I put it upon the fire, the heat of which served to dry our clothing and accoutrements, and to cook our separate portion of meat. When it became warmed through and blackened with smoke, I ate a bit but found it too raw and unsavoury. I had neither bread nor salt and I put the remainder in my haversack. I took my musket to put it in order for action; I had loaded it the previous day and the enemy had not disturbed us during the night. I fired it at an object which the ball embedded in the bank where I had purposely placed it as a target. Whilst so employed we kept a sharp look out on the enemy (who were no doubt similarly employed), and at the same time attended to those things usual for a soldier to do in the presence of the enemy when not actively engaged. For example, I examined the amount and state of ammunition remaining after previous engagements, put my musket in fighting trim and made sure that it was well flinted and oiled, etc. By the by, the flint musket then in use was a sad bore on that occasion: from the effects of the wet, the springs of the locks became wood bound and would not act correctly, and when in action the clumsy flints became useless. The quickest way of amending these failures which were very disheartening was to make an exchange from those that were lying about amongst the slain.

. . . I was now ready for the day's encounter and went to the farmyard of Hougoumont for straw to sit upon as the ground was very wet. I entered the gates facing the wood into the farmyard, and on my left was a building in which was a quantity of dry straw. It was very early in the morning and some of our troops were still resting on the top of a mow. The whole of the left side of the farmyard appeared to be composed of buildings suitable for farming purposes, such as a well of water, sheds for wagons, etc. and the whole presented a solid wall on the exterior and was mostly loop-holed.

Captain John Kincaid relates that the 95th Rifles, led by Sir Andrew F. Barnard, spent the night on the Namur road behind La Haye Sainte. The Colonel occupied a small mud-cottage as a quarter.

The weather cleared up as the morning advanced; and, though every thing remained quiet at the moment, we were confident that the day would not pass off without an engagement, and, therefore, proceeded to put our arms in order, as, also, to get ourselves dried and made as comfortable as circumstances would permit.

We made a fire against the wall of Sir Andrew Barnard's cottage, and boiled a huge camp-kettle full of tea, mixed up with a suitable quantity of milk and sugar, for breakfast; and, as it stood on the edge of the high road, where all the big-wigs of the army had occasion to pass, in the early part of the morning, I believe almost every one of them, from the Duke downwards, claimed a cupful.

About nine o'clock we received an order to retain a quantity of spare ammunition, in some secure place, and to send every thing in the shape of baggage and baggage-animals to the rear. It therefore became evident that the Duke meant to give battle in his present position.

George Keppel, a sixteen-year-old ensign in the 14th Foot, has left an account of that morning.

During the first hour after sunrise our regiment, like the rest of the troops, were occupied in cleaning and drying their arms, a very necessary business after such a night as we had passed through. That done we had a rigid inspection of every musket and ammunition-pouch. We then piled arms and fell out till the bugle recalled us to the ranks.

If I were asked what were my sensations in the dreary interval between daylight and the firing of the first cannon-shot I should say that all I can now remember on the subject is, that my mind was constantly recurring to the account my father had given me of his interview with Henry Pearce,[1] otherwise the Game Chicken, just before his great battle with Mendoza[2] for the championship of England. 'Well, Pearce,' asked my father 'how do you feel?' 'Why, my lord,' was the answer, 'I wish it was *fit* (fought).' Without presuming to imply any resemblance to the Game Chicken, I had thus much in common with that great man — I wished the fight was *fit*.

[1] Henry Pearce, born in Bristol in 1777, was bareknuckle heavyweight champion of England in 1805–6. He died of pulmonary consumption in 1809. I have been unable to trace any encounter between Pearce and Mendoza. Pearce beat Spray, Carte, Gully and Belchar in 1805.

[2] Daniel Mendoza (1763–1836), the Jewish pugilist from Whitechapel who became champion of England in 1792.

A celebrated pugilist was killed at Waterloo: John Shaw, a young Nottinghamshire farmer who, in 1807, had enlisted as a private in the Life Guards.

PHASE ONE — THE ASSAULT ON HOUGOUMONT

THE first French move in the battle was an attack to occupy the approaches to Hougoumont, with the object of diverting attention from the vital centre where the main assault would be launched, and also, it was hoped, of drawing off Wellington's reserves from that centre. Reille, the corps commander, entrusted this demonstration with very limited objectives to Prince Jérôme. Just after half past eleven the gunners fired their first shots and then four regiments marched into the outskirts of Hougoumont Wood. In the face of tenacious opposition by troops from Nassau and Hanover, the French took an hour to clear it, fighting from one thicket to the next. Though outnumbered, the defenders clung to the loopholed garden wall and fortified buildings, firing close-range volleys at the persistent French. From further back, British guns inflicted many casualties.

Despite orders from Reille to stop and consolidate, Jérôme Bonaparte persevered expensively, calling up more and more battalions and pressing the attacks with apparently reckless disregard for the losses incurred. Instead of trying to crumble or breach the walls by howitzer fire, he sent his men forward over and over again to storm the place. In vain, but heroically, they tried to implement futile tactics. Those who sought to scale the six foot garden wall were either shot or bayonetted through the loopholes. Then came a moment of precarious success: a giant, Lieutenant Legros, nicknamed '*l'enfonceur*', having smashed in a panel of the great door on the north façade, a small bold group rushed into the courtyard. Not a man escaped. A fierce struggle ensued, and the door was forced shut again. Colonel Woodford's four Coldstream companies arrived in reinforcement and drove the French back to the wood before joining the garrison. Other Frenchmen who had scrambled into the orchard were ousted by Lord Saltoun's Guardsmen.

The struggle for Hougoumont went on for most of the day, but even when the Château itself was ablaze, the defenders maintained their supremacy to such good effect that Wellington was not obliged to weaken his centre at all seriously in order to bolster his right. As for Prince Jérôme's transformation of a limited demonstration into an all-out assault, it did not materially assist the French cause.

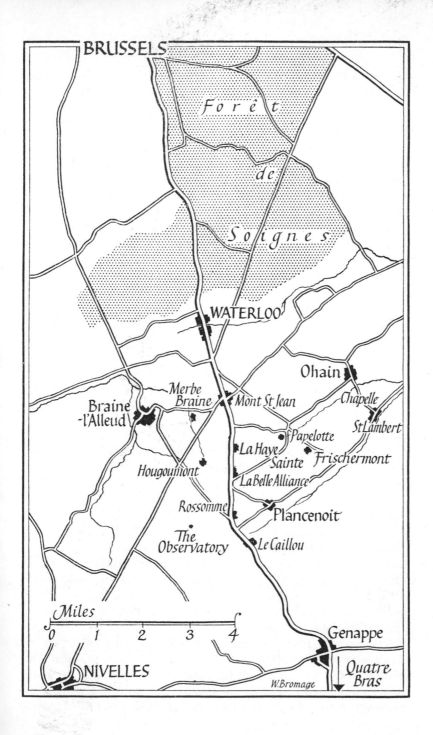

BRUSSELS

Forêt

de

Soignes

WATERLOO

Ohain

Merbe
Braine

Mont St Jean

Chapelle

Braine
-l'Alleud

StLambert

Papelotte

La Haye
Sainte

Frischermont

Hougoumont

La Belle Alliance

Rossomme

Plancenoit

The
Observatory

Le Caillou

Miles

0   1   2   3   4

Genappe

NIVELLES

Quatre
Bras

W. Bromage

Colonel Alexander Woodford of the Coldstream Guards described the farm and garden of Hougoumont.

The farm is well calculated for defence. The dwelling-house in the Centre was a strong square building, with small doors and windows. The barns and granaries formed nearly a square, with one door of communication with the small yard to the South; and from that yard was a door into the garden, a double gate into the wood, under or near the small house; and another door opening into the lane on the West.

There was also another carriage gate at the North-West angle of the great yard, leading into the barn, which conducted to the road to Braine-la-Leud.

The little garden to the South, fronting the wood, was occupied by the Guards; there were platforms in it, and I do not recollect that the Enemy ever got into it. Some few of the Enemy penetrated into the yard from the lane on the West, but were speedily driven out, or despatched. The Enemy were, of course, in possession of the wood all night.

At the time I was sent down to Hougoumont (about twelve o'clock or a little after), the Enemy had nearly got into the farm-yard. We found them very near the wall, and charged them, upon which they went off, and I took the opportunity of entering the farm by a side door in the lane.

A rising ground commanded the south-west angle of the farm. The corn was high and concealed the tirailleurs, who kept a regular fire upon the doors of communication I have mentioned, and killed several men and wounded some Officers. There was but little cannonade directed against Hougoumont; in the afternoon, however, a shell or carcass was thrown into the great barn, and the smoke and flames burst out in a most terrific manner, and communicated with rapidity and fury to the other outbuildings. Some Officers attempting to penetrate into the stables to rescue some wounded men were obliged to desist, from the suffocation of the smoke, and several men perished. The flames, as is well known, stopped at the little Chapel.

The French, never, as far as I recollect, got into the garden. They were in the orchard, but did not scale the garden walls. The platforms did not extend all the way, as in some cases the bank was high enough to enable the men to fire over the walls. The platforms were, of course, rudely constructed, Colonel Macdon-

...Waterloo! Waterloo! morne plaine!...

Lt.-Gen. Sir Thomas Picton, an English hero. From Kelly's *Waterloo*

Cruikshank's view of the Imperial defeat (*New York Public Library Print Collection*

Napoleon's retreat. From Kelly's *Waterloo*

nell[1] having to work all night to collect materials and loophole the walls.

Private Matthew Clay of the 3rd Foot Guards relates that when the French skirmishers advanced towards Hougoumont through a cornfield, he and the rest of the Light Company fired from the cover of a close hedge beside the kitchen garden.

Our Commanding Officer on his charger remained on the road between the fence of the garden and the exterior wall of the farm to our rear, and as this ground was higher he could more perfectly watch the movements of the enemy. The expected signal was given for us to retire from the garden and the front of the Company was led by Lieutenant-Colonel [Charles] Dashwood, Captains [George] Evelyn and [John] Elrington into the wood. I was in the rear subdivision on leaving the garden and on reaching the road above, Lieutenant Standon,[2] with a very determined appearance, holding his cap in one hand and his sword in the other, called our attention to join him and charge the enemy. We then went up the road towards the wood, the enemy skirmishers being under cover about the hedge on the right of the wood. Our party took advantage of cover, and I and a man of the name of R. Gann took up our positions under cover of a circular-built haystack from which we fired on the enemy. We were earnestly engaged and the intervening objects prevented us from perceiving the movements and retreat of our comrades. We were now left to ourselves and could see no one near us. The enemy's skirmishers remained under cover and continued firing at us, and we fired back and retired down the road up which we had advanced.

We now halted and I unwisely ascended the higher part of a sloping ground on which the outside wall of the farm was built. I thought that I would be able to single out the enemy's skirmishers more correctly, but I very quickly found that I had become a target for them because my red coat was more distinctly visible than theirs. Remaining in this position I continued to exchange shots

[1] James Macdonell of Glengarry, Coldstream Guards, afterwards a knight and a general. Müffling relates how towards the close of the battle he met Wellington near La Haye Sainte, holding a telescope raised in his right hand. 'He called out to me from a distance: "Well! you see Macdonell has held Hougoumont!" This was an expression of pleasure that his brave comrade had answered his expectations.'

[2] Ensign George Douglas Standen. See next piece.

with the enemy across the kitchen garden, but they, having the advantage of the fence as a covering, their shots freely struck the wall in my rear. Our Company from which we were separated had opened a fire from within the farm. My musket, now proving defective, was very discouraging but looking on the ground I saw a musket which I immediately took possession of in exchange for my own one. The new musket was warm from recent use and proved an excellent one; it had belonged to the Light Infantry of the First Foot Guards. My comrade during this time had more wisely contended with the enemy on the low ground by the garden fence. He was my senior by some years and a very steady and undaunted old soldier, and although I was but a youth I felt as though I had partaken of his courageous spirit.

I was still annoyed by the shots of the enemy who were under good cover, and we took advantage of a clover stack some distance off and beyond the extremity of the farm from which we exchanged shots. During the time we were engaged with the enemy across the garden, a party of their force had made an attack on the gates round the corner of the château, but were repulsed and our comrades still retained possession. My comrade now from his position by the stack apprised me of the enemy's advance to renew the attack and supposing that we were shut out from the farm we were for a moment or two quite at a loss as to how to act. On turning my eyes, however, towards the lower gates I saw that they were open and at the same time telling my comrade of this we hurried towards them. . . .

On entering the courtyard I saw the doors, or rather the gates, were riddled with shot holes, and it was also very wet and dirty. In its entrance lay many dead bodies of the enemy. One which I particularly noticed appeared to be a French Officer, but they were scarcely distinguishable, being to all appearance as though they had been very much trodden upon and covered with mud. On getting inside the farm I saw Lieutenant-Colonel Macdonnell carrying a large piece of wood or the trunk of a tree in his arms. One of his cheeks was marked with blood and his charger lay bleeding a short distance away. With this timber he was hurrying to bar the gates against the renewed attack of the enemy which was most vigorously repulsed.

I was now told off with others under Lieutenant Gough of the Coldstream Guards[1] and was posted in an upper room of the

[1] Dalton's *Waterloo Roll Call* lists no such officer.

château. This room was situated higher than the surrounding buildings and we annoyed the enemy's skirmishers from the window. The enemy noticed this and threw their shells amongst us and set the building which we were defending on fire. Our officer placed himself at the entrance of the room and would not allow anyone to leave his post until our positions became hopeless and too perilous to remain. We fully expected the floor to sink with us every moment and in our escape several of us were more or less injured. The enemy's artillery forced the upper gates, a part of them rushed in, but they were quickly driven back. No one was left inside except a Drummer Boy without his drum whom I lodged in the stable or outhouse. Many of the wounded of both armies were arranged side by side, and we had no means of carrying them to a place of greater safety.

Ensign George Standen belonged to the Light Company of the 3rd Foot Guards which, with the Light Company of the Coldstream, had the defence of the wood and Château of Hougoumont.

A haystack [some fifty yards south of the stables] was set fire to in one of the attacks in which our Companies were repulsed, behind which we repeatedly formed and charged; I cannot speak as to time, but think between one and two the French drove the remaining few into the house. After a severe struggle the French forced the rear gate open and came in with us. We flew to the parlour, opened the windows and drove them out, leaving an Officer and some men dead within the wall.

During this time the whole of the barn and cart house were in flames. During the confusion three or four Officers' horses rushed out into the yard from the barn, and in a minute or two rushed back into the flames and were burnt. I mention this as I had always heard horses would never leave fire; perhaps some beam or large piece of wood fell and astonished them.

The ditch at the corner of the wood leading into the orchard was full of dead bodies (we had blocked up the gate), as the French strove repeatedly and gallantly to get through in defiance of the fire from the loopholes so close to them. The anecdote of the fire burning only to the foot of the Cross [in the Chapel] is perfectly true, which in so superstitious a country made a great sensation.

I never saw such a 'bullfincher' as the hedge in front of the orchard. I cannot tell how the barn was first fired, but there was an opening sufficient for a man to get through in the wall, by which the French might with the burning hay have fired it.

*There survives a note pencilled by Wellington on ass's skin to Lieu-
    tenant-Colonel James Macdonell:*

I see that the fire has communicated from the hay stack to the Roof of the Chateau.

You must however still keep your Men in those parts to which the fire does not reach.

Take care that no Men are lost by the falling in of the Roof or floors. After they will have fallen in occupy the Ruined Walls in-side of the Garden, particularly if it should be possible for the Enemy to pass through the Embers in the Inside of the House.

*Captain Horace Seymour of the 60th Rifles, who was aide-de-camp
    to the Earl of Uxbridge, afterwards related one small incident
    which had significance in the struggle for the farm.*

Late in the day of the 18th, I was called to by some officers of the 3rd Guards defending Hougoumont, to use my best endeavours to send them musket ammunition. Soon afterwards I fell in with a private of the Waggon Train in charge of a tumbril on the crest of the position. I merely pointed out to him where he was wanted, when he gallantly started his horses, and drove straight down the hill to the Farm, to the gate of which I saw him arrive. He must have lost his horses, as there was a severe fire kept on him. I feel convinced that to that man's service the Guards owe their ammuni-tion.

PHASE TWO: D'ERLON'S CORPS
ATTACKS THE ALLIED CENTRE

At half past one eighty French guns began a half-hour bombardment, during which almost the only sufferers were the members of Bylandt's Belgian brigade, who were exposed on the forward slope within horse-pistol range of the hostile artillery. Then d'Erlon's four divisions, 18,000 men in all, marched forward, three of them in compact phalanxes, 160 to 200 files in each rank and twenty-four ranks deep — a dangerous formation against British troops and over uneven ground, and one which served to double the casualties and to hinder the ascent to the plateau. Once the soldiers had reached the valley or were beginning to climb the opposite slope, the French guns fired again in their support. So did the British guns, tearing holes in the close-ranked columns.

While part of d'Erlon's left-hand division by-passed La Haye Sainte, the rest scaled the garden wall and drove the King's German Legion from the kitchen-garden, only to be repulsed from behind solid farm walls. Far away to the right, another division secured Papelotte, and the central divisions swept back Bylandt's brigade. While the unwieldy French masses were trying to deploy along the crest thirty paces from the Ohain road, Picton saw his chance and ordered Kempt's brigade to stand up, fire a volley, and charge. Picton was killed, but his division, despite the losses incurred at Quatre Bras, drove the enemy back. Another French mass in the centre was halted by Pack's brigade, who charged with the bayonet until obliged to form square as protection against French cuirassiers who came up to support d'Erlon.

Now it was the turn of the Allied cavalry. While Vandeleur's three regiments of dragoons, aided by Dutch dragoons and Belgian hussars, forced the French from Papelotte, Somerset's brigade of Life Guards, Royal Horse Guards and 1st Dragoon Guards, under Lord Uxbridge's personal command, shattered and drove back the opposing cuirassiers. Then Sir William Ponsonby's three regiments attacked d'Erlon's columns: the Royals drove off one French brigade struggling with the 95th near the sand-pit; the Inniskillings charged another column; while the Scots Greys followed Pack's battalions which opened ranks to let the horsemen through, whereupon the French were sent back down the muddy slope in disorder. Two French eagles and 3,000 prisoners were taken. But the British cavalry threw restraint to the winds and charged headlong at the enemy's guns, silencing thirty before being overwhelmed by French counterattacks and forced to retreat. Of the 2,500 horsemen who charged, 1,000 were left behind dead or wounded.

However, by three o'clock no living soldier of France remained on the slopes of Mont St Jean, and the fighting died away except at Hougoumont and La Haye Sainte. If Wellington had gained time for the Prussians to draw nearer, his opponents had secured no foothold for their next assault.

The attack by d'Erlon's corps was watched by a young Belgian named Scheltens, who belonged to the 7th infantry battalion of the line in Bylandt's brigade.

Our battalion opened fire as soon as our skirmishers had come in. The French column was unwise enough to halt and begin to deploy. We were so close that Captain Henry l'Olivier, commanding our grenadier company, was struck on the arm by a ball, of which the wad, or cartridge paper, remained smoking in the cloth of his tunic.

. . . One French battalion commander had received a sabre cut on his nose, which was hanging down over his mouth. 'Look,' he said to me, 'how they do for us!' The good fellow might have fared much worse.

I afforded protection to two French officers in this débâcle. They gave me the masonic sign, so I had them taken to the rear, where they were not, as always happened, searched and robbed by the fighting troops and afterwards again by marauders. These two officers reached Brussels safe and sound. It was a great advantage to belong to a masonic lodge, as this enabled one to enjoy very pleasant relations with the leading inhabitants of any town in which one happened to be garrisoned and it ensured useful protection in time of war.

Captain Duthilt, an officer of the 45th Regiment of the Line, describes the great attack of d'Erlon's corps from the viewpoint of the divisional column commanded by General Pierre-Louis Binet de Marcognet.

When it was thought that the English had been sufficiently shaken by our cannonade, d'Erlon's four divisions formed up in separate columns. The third, to which my regiment belonged, had to advance like the others in deployed battalions, with only four paces between one and the next — a strange formation and one which was to cost us dear, since we were unable to form square as a defence against cavalry attacks, while the enemy's artillery could plough our formations to a depth of twenty ranks. To whom the 1st Corps owed this unfortunate formation, which proved to be one cause, maybe even *the* cause of our failure, nobody knows.

Our turn came eventually. The order to attack was greeted with a frenzied shout of *Vive l'Empereur!* The four columns moved off down the slope, with ported arms and in serried ranks. We were to mount the opposite slope where the English held the ridge and from where their batteries were blasting us. No doubt the distance involved was not great, and an average person on foot would have taken no more than five or six minutes to cover the ground; but the soft and rain-sodden earth and the tall rye slowed up our progress appreciably. As a result the English gunners had plenty of time in which to work destruction upon us.

However, we did not weaken, and when we were eventually ready to assault the position, the charge was beaten, our pace quickened, and to repeated shouts of *Vive l'Empereur!* we rushed at the batteries. Suddenly our path was blocked: English battalions, concealed in a hollow road, stood up and fired at us at close range. We drove them back at the point of the bayonet and climbed higher up the slope and over the stretches of quick hedge which protected their guns. Then we reach the plateau and give a shout of 'Victory'!

In the bloody confusion our officers did their duty by trying to establish some sort of order and to reform the platoons, since a disordered group can achieve nothing. Just as I was pushing one of our men back into the ranks I saw him fall at my feet from a sabre slash. I turned round instantly — to see English cavalry forcing their way into our midst and hacking us to pieces.

Just as it is difficult, if not impossible, for the best cavalry to break into infantry who are formed up in squares and who defend themselves with coolness and daring, so it is true that once the ranks have been broken and penetrated, then resistance is useless and nothing remains for the cavalry to do but to slaughter at almost no risk to themselves. This is what happened. In vain our poor fellows stood up and stretched out their arms: they could not reach far enough to bayonet those cavalrymen mounted on powerful horses, and the few shots fired in this chaotic mêlée were just as fatal to our own men as to the English. And so we found ourselves defenceless against a relentless enemy who, in the intoxication of battle, sabred even our drummers and fifers without mercy. That is where our eagle was captured;[1] and that is where I saw death close at hand, for my best friends fell round me and I was expecting the same fate, all the while wielding my sword mechanically.

When we could offer no further resistance, the mass of the cavalry made ready to cross the valley to seize our guns, while one group of them escorted away what remained of our division.

One member of the Scots Greys who rode in the famous charge of the Union Brigade was Corporal John Dickson, whose story was taken down by relatives in Scotland some years after the battle. He died in 1880 at the age of ninety.

Immediately after this, the General of the Union Brigade, Sir William Ponsonby, came riding up to us on a small bay hack. I remember that his groom with his chestnut charger could not be found. Beside him was his aide-de-camp, De Lacy Evans.[2] He ordered us forward to within fifty yards of the beech-hedge by the roadside. I can see him now in his long cloak and great cocked hat as he rode up to watch the fighting below. From our new position we could descry the three regiments of Highlanders, only a thousand in all, bravely firing down on the advancing masses of Frenchmen. These numbered thousands, and those on our side of the Brussels road were divided into three solid columns. I have read since that there were fifteen thousand of them under Count d'Erlon spread over the clover, barley, and rye fields in front of our centre, and making straight for us. Then I saw the Brigadier, Sir Denis Pack, turn to the Gordons and shout out with great energy, 'Ninety-second, you must advance! All in front of you have given way.' The Highlanders, who had begun the day by solemnly chanting 'Scots wha hae' as they prepared their morning meal, instantly, with fixed bayonets, began to press forward through the beech and holly hedge to a line of bushes that grew along the face of the slope in front. They uttered loud shouts as they ran forward and fired a volley at twenty yards into the French.

At this moment our General and his aide-de-camp rode off

[1] See Sergeant Ewart's account, page 119.
[2] Major Evans had served in America, capturing the Congress House in Washington, and fighting at Bladensberg, Baltimore and New Orleans. He commanded the British Legion in Spain, 1835–37, and led a division in the Crimean War. He lived until 1870.

to the right by the side of the hedge; then suddenly I saw De Lacy Evans wave his hat, and immediately our colonel, Inglis Hamilton, shouted out, 'Now then, Scots Greys, charge!' and, waving his sword in the air, he rode straight at the hedges in front, which he took in grand style. At once a great cheer rose from our ranks, and we too waved our swords and followed him. I dug my spur into my brave old Rattler, and we were off like the wind. Just then I saw Major [Thomas Pate] Hankin fall wounded. I felt a strange thrill run through me, and I am sure my noble beast felt the same, for, after rearing for a moment, she sprang forward, uttering loud neighings and snortings, and leapt over the holly-hedge at a terrific speed. It was a grand sight to see the long line of giant grey horses dashing along with flowing manes and heads down, tearing up the turf about them as they went. The men in their red coats and tall bear-skins were cheering loudly, and the trumpeters were sounding the 'Charge.' Beyond the first hedge the road was sunk between high, sloping banks, and it was a very difficult feat to descend without falling; but there were very few accidents, to our surprise.

All of us were greatly excited, and began crying, 'Hurrah, Ninety-Second! Scotland for ever!' as we crossed the road. For we heard the Highland pipers playing among the smoke and firing below, and I plainly saw my old friend Pipe-Major Cameron standing apart on a hillock coolly playing 'Johnny Cope, are ye waukin' yet?' in all the din.

Our colonel went on before us, past our guns and down the slope, and we followed; we saw the Royals and Enniskillens clearing the road and hedges at full gallop away to the right.

Before me rode young Armour, our rough-rider from Mauchline (a near relative of Jean Armour, Robbie Burns's wife), and Sergeant [Charles] Ewart on the right, at the end of the line beside our cornet, [F.C.] Kinchant. I rode in the second rank. As we tightened our grip to descend the hillside among the corn, we could make out the feather bonnets of the Highlanders, and heard the officers crying out to them to wheel back by sections. A moment more and we were among them. Poor fellows! some of them had not time to get clear of us, and were knocked down. I remember one lad crying out, 'Eh! but I didna think ye wad ha'e hurt me sae.'

They were all Gordons, and as we passed through them they shouted, 'Go at them, the Greys! Scotland for ever!' My blood

I

thrilled at this, and I clutched my sabre tighter. Many of the Highlanders grasped our stirrups, and in the fiercest excitement dashed
with us into the fight. The French were uttering loud, discordant
yells. Just then I saw the first Frenchman. A young officer of
Fusiliers made a slash at me with his sword, but I parried it and
broke his arm; the next second we were in the thick of them. We
could not see five yards ahead for the smoke. I stuck close by
Armour; Ewart was now in front.

The French were fighting like tigers. Some of the wounded were
firing at us as we passed; and poor Kinchant, who had spared one
of these rascals, was himself shot by the officer he had spared. As
we were sweeping down a steep slope on the top of them, they had
to give way. Then those in front began to cry out for 'quarter,'
throwing down their muskets and taking off their belts. The Gordons at this rushed in and drove the French to the rear. I was now
in the front rank, for many of ours had fallen. . . . We now came
to an open space covered with bushes, and then I saw Ewart,[1] with
five or six infantry men about him, slashing right and left at them.
Armour and I dashed up to these half-dozen Frenchmen, who were
trying to escape with one of their standards. I cried to Armour to
'Come on!' and we rode at them. Ewart had finished two of them,
and was in the act of striking a third man who held the Eagle; next
moment I saw Ewart cut him down, and he fell dead. I was just in
time to thwart a bayonet-thrust that was aimed at the gallant sergeant's neck. Armour finished another of them. . . .

We cried out to Ewart, 'Well done, my boy!' and as others had
come up, we spurred on in search of a like success. Here it was
that we came upon two batteries of French guns which had been
sent forward to support the infantry. They were now deserted by
the gunners and had sunk deep in the mud.

We were saluted with a sharp fire of musketry, and again found
ourselves beset by thousands of Frenchmen. We had fallen upon
a second column; they were also Fusiliers. Trumpeter Reeves of
our troop, who rode by my side, sounded a 'Rally', and our men
came swarming up from all sides, some Enniskillens and Royals
being amongst the number. We at once began a furious onslaught on
this obstacle, and soon made an impression; the battalions seemed
to open out for us to pass through, and so it happened that in five
minutes we had cut our way through as many thousands of Frenchmen.

[1] See the next piece.

We had now reached the bottom of the slope. There the ground was slippery with deep mud. Urging each other on, we dashed towards the batteries on the ridge above, which had worked such havoc on our ranks. The ground was very difficult, and especially where we crossed the edge of a ploughed field, so that our horses sank to the knees as we struggled on. My brave Rattler was becoming quite exhausted, but we dashed ever onwards.

At this moment Colonel Hamilton rode up to us crying, 'Charge! charge the guns!' and went off like the wind up the hill towards the terrible battery that had made such deadly work among the Highlanders. It was the last we saw of our colonel, poor fellow! His body was found with both arms cut off. His pockets had been rifled. . . .

Then we got among the guns, and we had our revenge. Such slaughtering! We sabred the gunners, lamed the horses, and cut their traces and harness. I can hear the Frenchmen yet crying *'Diable!'* when I struck at them, and the long-drawn hiss through their teeth as my sword went home. Fifteen of their guns could not be fired again that day. The artillery drivers sat on their horses weeping aloud as we went among them; they were mere boys, we thought.

Rattler lost her temper and bit and tore at everything that came in her way. She seemed to have got new strength. I had lost the plume of my bearskin just as we went through the second infantry column; a shot had carried it away. The French infantry were rushing past us in disorder on their way to the rear.

One of the most noted individual acts of bravery was performed by Sergeant Charles Ewart of the Scots Greys, who captured the Eagle of the 45th French Regiment. Its banner proudly displayed the names of Austerlitz, Jena, Friedland, Essling and Wagram, where the 45th had gained distinction. In a letter dated August 16th, 1815, Ewart, who was commissioned for his conduct, described the action.

It was in the first charge I took the Eagle from the enemy; he and I had a hard contest for it; he thrust for my groin — I parried it off, and I cut him through the head; after which I was attacked by one of their Lancers, who threw his lance at me, but missed the mark by my throwing it off with my sword by my right side; then

I cut him from the chin upwards, which cut went through his teeth. Next I was attacked by a foot soldier, who, after firing at me, charged me with his bayonet; but he very soon lost the combat, for I parried it, and cut him down through the head; so that finished the contest for the Eagle. After which I presumed to follow my comrades, Eagle and all, but was stopped by the General saying to me, 'You brave fellow, take that to the rear; you have done enough until you get quit of it', which I was obliged to do, but with great reluctance. I retired to a height, and stood there for upwards of an hour, which gave me a general view of the field, but I cannot express the sight I beheld; the bodies of my brave comrades were lying so thick upon the field that it was scarcely possible to pass, and horses innumerable. I took the Eagle into Brussels, amidst the acclamations of thousands of the spectators that saw it.

Another Eagle, this time from the French 105th Regiment, was captured by Captain Kennedy Clark and Corporal Francis Stiles of the 1st, or Royal, Regiment of Dragoons. Clark, who afterwards became Lieut.-General Sir Alexander Clark-Kennedy, described the encounter.

When my squadron (the centre one) of the Royal Dragoons had advanced 200 or 300 yards beyond the second hedge, and the first line of French infantry had been broke, I perceived, a little to my left, an enemy's 'Eagle' amongst the infantry, with which the bearer was making every exertion to get off towards the rear of the column. I immediately rode to the place calling out to 'Secure the colour!' and at the same time, my horse reaching it, I ran my sword into the officer's right side, who carried the 'Eagle', who staggered and fell forwards but I do not think he reached the ground, on account of the pressure of his companions. I immediately called out a second time 'Secure the colour; it belongs to me.' This was addressed to some men who were behind me at the time the officer was in the act of falling. As he fell with the 'Eagle' a little to the left, I was not able to catch the standard so as to hold it. Corporal Stiles and some other men rushed up to my assistance, and the standard was in an instant in the corporal's possession, it falling across him as he came up on my left, before it reached the ground.

In a letter written to the Colonel of his regiment after the battle, Lieutenant-Colonel Isaac Blake Clarke of the 2nd Royal North British Dragoons (Scots Greys) had this comment to make:

The impetuosity of the Brigade was so great that, in my opinion, it advanced too far, which was the cause of our tremendous loss; but Valour, not Prudence, seemed alone to animate every breast. In our crippled state and not being able to muster more than 100 effectives, I again formed in the valley we had so lately occupied, when we were soon joined by our friends, the Royals and Enniskillens, who suffered equally with ourselves. While waiting for orders in the valley, the shot and shells fell in showers about us, but we here sustained no loss.

BRUSSELS, GHENT AND ANTWERP
DURING THE BATTLE

Brussels during June 18th was described by Miss Elizabeth Ord, stepdaughter of Mr Thomas Creevey, to her brother William in Florence.

It was passed in a sort of stupid state of despair, now and then enlivened by reports spread to create confusion, that French Dragoons were actually in the Town, Waggons, Baggage, &c. &c. were overturned in the fright, the road was blocked up, and the infamous villains who had raised the cry (composed of stragglers of all nations) plundered everything at their leisure, and above half the Officers of the Army have lost everything they had; those who were left to guard taking fright and galloping off in every direction, and assuring every one the French were at their heels. Every hour brought the name of some Officer either killed or wounded, that the fighting was desperate, &c. &c. Mr. Creevey every time he went out returned with a more dismal face, till at last we sat looking at each other without venturing to ask any questions.

Again at night Major Hamilton arrived having just walked from the field of Battle, leading a horse with two balls in it, and his poor Genl.[1] on it severely wounded, and himself slightly so in the head and foot. His account was that never was there such fighting from the Duke down to the Drummer, but he feared from the Prussians not being yet in action when he left the field, and the immense superiority in numbers, particularly in cavalry, of the French, that things would not end well, and that, as in case Brussels could not be kept, we must make up our minds what to do, and that if we determined to go, he wd. press a carriage &c &c.. Our manner of passing the night I leave you to guess — Anne and I never took off our cloaths; not having slept much for the two nights before, this was spent in trying to decide what we ought to do, there being great danger in either determination.

[1] Andrew Hamilton, who later married Miss Anne Ord, was A.D.C. to Major-General Sir Edward Barnes.

On June 18th Mrs Caroline Capel wrote to her mother from the Château de Walcheuse, some three miles from Brussels at Laeken. She and her family had been in residence barely a week.

The Horrors of that night [17th–18th] are not to be forgot — The very Elements conspired to make it gloomy — For the rain and darkness and wind were frightfull and our court yard was filled during the night with poor wounded drenched soldiers and horses seeking for refuge and assistance which you may imagine we administered as well as we were able — There were some of the Brunswickers whom we had heard march the night before — The next day [18th] was passed in various alarming reports. Capel obliged to leave us and spend it in Bruxelles, trying every means to get a conveyance for us in case Lord W was defeated, the report of which reached us, and that the French were in the Town. 2 hours before Capel's return, I had the horror of *fancying* the Gates were shut and he was detained — At last however he appeared, not a Horse to be had for any sum. The Mayor had put them all in requisition for the Military — 1 man had paid 10 guineas for a pair of Horses to go the first stage to Antwerp, the same difficulty in obtaining a barge; by the greatest interest and acquaintance with the Mayor he got the promise of an order for one, for which we were to pay 20 guineas; 25 was all we could procure any where for all the Banks were shut up — In this situation, uncertain about the Barge, or the means of getting to it except on Foot, and without any of our baggage, we determined, if every thing failed, to get back into Bruxelles anyhow — For a House in a Wood, without any neighbours or means of assistance in the case of a party of French stragglers coming up, was not to be borne.

François René de Chateaubriand, author of René, Atala, Le Génie du Christianisme, *and* Les Martyrs, *was with King Louis XVIII in Ghent as Minister of the Interior. He recalls that on June 18th he went out by the Brussels Gate at about noon and took a walk along the road.*

I had with me Caesar's *Commentaries*,[1] and I was walking slowly, deep in my book. I had already gone more than two miles from the town when I thought I heard a dull rumbling. I stopped, looked

---

[1] Julius Caesar's *De Bello Gallico* and *De Bello Civili*.

up at the sky which was heavy with clouds, and debated whether
to go on or to return towards Ghent in case of a storm. I listened,
but could hear nothing except the call of a waterfowl in the reeds
and the sound of a village clock striking. I continued on my way
and had not taken thirty steps before the rumbling began again,
lasting sometimes a moment, sometimes a longer time, and sounding at irregular intervals. So distant was it that sometimes one
could pick it up only as an air tremor that was transmitted to the
soil of this immense plain. These detonations, which were smaller,
less vibrant, less co-ordinated than those of a thunderstorm, sug-
gested a battle. I found myself standing near a poplar which had
been planted at the corner of a hop field. I crossed the road and
leant against the tree trunk, with my face turned towards Brussels.
A southerly wind had sprung up and now carried the sound of
artillery fire more distinctly. This great but still unnamed battle,
the echoes of which I was listening to under a poplar and of which
the village clock had just struck the unknown funeral notes, was
the battle of Waterloo!

No traveller appeared on the scene. A few women in the fields,
peacefully hoeing rows of vegetables, seemed oblivious of the
sound that I could hear. Then a courier came in sight. I left the
foot of my tree and stood in the middle of the road, stopped the
courier and questioned him. He was in the Duc de Berry's[1] service
and had come from Alost. 'Bonaparte entered Brussels yesterday
(June 17th) after a bloody battle. The battle must have started
again today (June 18th). It is believed that the Allies have been
decisively beaten and that they have ordered a retreat.'

The courier went on his way and I hurried after him. I was overtaken by the carriage of a merchant who was fleeing with his family,
and he confirmed the courier's report. Confusion reigned in Ghent
when I re-entered the town. The gates were being shut, and only
the wickets were ajar. Ill-armed citizens and a few depot troops
stood on guard. I made my way to the King.

Monsieur[2] had just arrived by a detour, having left Brussels on
the strength of a false report that Bonaparte was about to make his
entry, and that a first battle lost afforded no hope of winning a
second. It was said that as the Prussians had not been in line, the
English had been crushed. At this news the *sauve qui peut* became

[1] The King's nephew, Charles Ferdinand, who was assassinated at the opera
in 1820.
[2] The King's brother, the Count of Artois, afterwards King Charles X.

general. Those who had the means departed. I, who am used to owning nothing, was all the time ready and fit. I wanted Madame de Chateaubriand[1] to leave before me. She is a staunch Bonapartist, but she does not like the sound of cannon-fire. She was unwilling to leave me.

In Ghent, at midnight on the 17th, Baron Marie Antoine de Reiset, with the French King at the Hôtel de Hanes, Rue des Champs, wrote in his journal:

Alarm is spreading. It is really terrible to find oneself in such a situation and to do nothing. This immobile anxiety is the worst thing we have to endure, and one is torn between a desire to see the good cause prevail and the fear of seeing the French defeated, however misguided they may be. His Majesty summoned the council this evening in order to decide on measures to be adopted. The sang-froid of the King, who does not go back on his word in tragic circumstances, is a source of amazement and admiration to everyone.

As events become increasingly disquieting, he seems to view them with growing clear-sightedness and calm. 'Let those who are afraid depart,' he was heard to say. 'For myself, I shall not leave here unless forced to do so by the march of events!'

I have just learnt that a number of people decided this evening to leave Ghent and hurriedly set off towards Nimeguen. But the Minister of War had issued such precise orders that no post horse was allowed out, and, to their great disappointment, all the people who had no horses of their own were obliged to give up their journey.

[Twenty-three hours later de Reiset again wrote in his journal.]

This evening the King's carriages have been harnessed up, and they will wait like this all night, ready to move immediately should the news take a turn for the worse. All day we have been without news. The King, who has so far managed to conceal his anxiety under a mask of serenity, has become more and more agitated. He no longer hides his feelings, and his growing concern appears to have given him back the use of his legs, for he paces anxiously up

---

[1] In 1792 Chateaubriand had married Céleste Buisson de la Vigne at St Malo.

and down the drawing-room, can almost get up from his chair unaided, and is constantly going to the window, in the belief, every time he hears the slightest sound, that a courier has arrived with dispatches. His Majesty has declared that he will not go to bed.

On June 17th Miss Charlotte Waldie, with her sister and brother, left Brussels and travelled to Antwerp, where they found rooms in the Hôtel du Grand Laboureur in the Place Meir.

The morning — the eventful morning of Sunday, the 18th of June — rose, darkened by clouds and mists, and driving rain. Amongst the rest of the fugitives, our friends, the Hon. Mr. and Mrs. H., arrived about seven o'clock, and, after considerable difficulty and delay, succeeded in obtaining a wretched little hole in a private house, with a miserable pallet bed, and destitute of all other furniture; but they were too glad to find shelter, and too thankful to get into a place of safety, to complain of these inconveniences; and overcome with fatigue, they went immediately to bed. It was not without considerable difficulty and danger that their carriage had got out of the choked-up streets of Brussels, and made its way to Malines, where they had been, for a time, refused shelter. At length, the golden arguments Mr. H. used, obtained for them admittance into a room filled with people of all sexes, ages, countries, and ranks — French Princes and foreign Counts, and English Barons, and Right Honourable ladies and gentlemen, together with a considerable mixture of less dignified beings, were all lying together, outstretched upon the tables, the chairs, and the floor; some groaning, and some complaining, and many snoring, and almost all of them completely drenched with rain. The water streamed from Mr. H.'s clothes, who had driven his own carriage. In this situation, they, too, lay down and slept, while their horses rested; and then, at break of day, pursued their flight. A hundred Napoleons had been vainly offered for a pair of horses but a few hours after we left Brussels, and the scene of panic and confusion which it presented on Saturday evening surpassed all conception. The certainty of the defeat of the Prussians; of their retreat; and of the retreat of the British army, prepared the people to expect the worst. Aggravated reports of disaster and dismay continually succeeded to each other: the despair and lamentations of the Belgians, the anxiety of the English to learn the fate of their friends who had been in the battle the preceding day; the dreadful spectacle of the waggon loads of wounded coming in, and the terrified fugitives flying out in momentary expectation of the arrival of the French: — the streets, the roads, the canals covered with boats, carriages, waggons, horses, and crowds of unfortunate people, flying from this scene of horror and danger, formed altogether a combination of tumult, terror, and misery which cannot be described. Numbers, even of ladies, unable to procure any means of conveyance, set off on foot, and walked in the dark, beneath the pelting storm, to Malines; and the distress of the crowds who now filled Antwerp, it is utterly impossible to conceive. We were, however, soon inexpressibly relieved, by hearing that there had been no engagement of any consequence the preceding day; that the British army had fallen back seven miles in order to take up a position more favourable for the cavalry, and for communications with the Prussians; that they were now about nine miles from Brussels; and that a general and, most probably, decisive action would inevitably take place to-day.

Although it continued to rain, we set out, for to sit still in the house was impossible, and after passing through several streets, we went into the cathedral, where high mass was performing.

. . . In the course of our wanderings we met many people whom we knew, and had much conversation with many whom we did not know. At this momentous crisis, one feeling actuated every heart — one thought engaged every tongue — one common interest bound together every human being. All ranks were confounded; all distinctions levelled; all common forms neglected. Gentlemen and servants; lords and common soldiers; British and foreigners, were all upon an equality — elbowing each other without ceremony, and addressing each other without apology. Ladies accosted men they had never before seen with eager questions without hesitation; strangers conversed together like friends, and English reserve seemed no longer to exist. From morning till night the great Place de Maire was completely filled with people, standing under umbrellas, and eagerly watching for news of the battle; so closely packed was this anxious crowd, that, when viewed from the hotel windows, nothing could be seen but one compact mass of umbrellas. As the day advanced, the consternation became greater. The number of terrified fugitives from Brussels, upon whose faces were marked the deepest anxiety and distress, and who thronged into the town on horseback and on foot, increased the general dismay, while long rows of carriages lined the streets, filled with people who could find no place of shelter.

Troops from the Hanseatic towns[1] marched in to strengthen the garrison of the city in case of a siege. Long trains of artillery, ammunition, military stores, and supplies of all sorts incessantly poured in, and there seemed to be no end of the heavy waggons that rolled through the streets. Reports more and more gloomy reached our ears; every hour only served to add to the general despondency.

[1] Hamburg, Bremen, Lübeck, Cologne.

PHASE THREE: PRODIGAL CAVALRY
CHARGES

As soon as d'Erlon had rallied the least mauled of his regiments, he was ordered by Ney to storm the farm buildings of La Haye Sainte as quickly as possible. One brigade only was sent forward for this task, and although strongly supported by artillery fire, was driven off by the defenders, who had just been reinforced by a Hanoverian battalion. At this juncture Ney seriously misinterpreted the departure of some British wounded, several groups of French prisoners, and some empty ammunition waggons, all of which he glimpsed through the thick smoke of battle. With the object of hastening what he took to be a crumbling of Wellington's centre, he summoned some 5,000 horsemen to accelerate the incipient 'retreat'. The time was towards four o'clock.

For over an hour they charged with superb *élan*, and with unshaken fortitude fifteen infantry battalions repulsed them. Ney brought up still more cuirassiers and subjected the already decimated squares to the French cavalry's most prodigal, most persistent efforts. The squares remained unbroken. It was not the cavalry swords that wrought havoc among the allied infantry; rather was it the fact that whenever Ney's cavalry force retired down the slope to prepare for a fresh attack, the French gunners fired round-shot into the serried squares with terrible effect. As for the British gunners, having sent their horses to the rear, they were ordered to fire until the cavalry were upon them, then to take refuge in the nearest square. Their guns would be captured for a moment, but the French made no attempt to spike or otherwise damage them and had no horses with which to draw the pieces away.

For the second time that day Lord Uxbridge unleashed a cavalry counterattack. Dragoons, hussars, lancers and carabiniers, 5,000 of them, hurtled against the outnumbered French horsemen and drove them back in disorder. The French reformed. Again they charged up the mud-churned slopes. Again the grapeshot holed the ranks. For a while the situation became so desperate that some British officers believed that all was lost. Then the second onslaught wavered and failed.

Time was running out for Napoleon if he was to defeat Wellington before the Prussians came in. Indeed, they had already begun to press his right flank. As early as one o'clock troops had been seen six miles away to the north-east, on the heights of Chapelle St Lambert. After some disbelief, these had been identified as Prussians, and an order sent to Grouchy urging him to lose not an instant in joining the Emperor and thus helping to crush the foe. When Grouchy received this order nearly six hours later, it was too late for him to do much, and he had already refused to accede to the pleas of his subordinate commanders to march to the sound of the guns, finding Thielmann's corps quite enough trouble for one day.

By four o'clock Bülow's corps, with Blücher well to the fore and urging on his men to haste so that he should not break his promise to Wellington,[1] had come close and were exchanging shots with French outposts. Napoleon realised that he must use Lobau's corps, not to reinforce Ney in the centre but to resist the Prussian onslaught. Lobau, faced by superior forces, attacked before the full strength of Bülow could deploy, and at first he drove them back. The Prussians did not press, but turned instead against Plancenoit, thereby threatening Lobau's right. Between five and six Lobau's men were driven back. Plancenoit was in danger. A division of the Young Guard occupied the village, only to be forced out soon afterwards. Then Napoleon summoned two battalions of the Old Guard to add weight to a counterattack, and their bayonet charge recaptured Plancenoit, drove back the enemy nearly half a mile, and overran several batteries. For a time Napoleon believed that Bülow had shot his bolt, that his own right flank was secure. In fact the other two Prussian corps were drawing near, having left later than Bülow and travelled even more slowly. Wellington had expected Prussian aid to make itself felt in the battle by mid-morning.[2] After all, Wavre was only thirteen miles from Mont St Jean. Thielmann would have had less distance to march, but Bülow was sent first because he had not been engaged at Ligny. His men did not set out until two hours past daybreak, and were then delayed by a fire in Wavre and by crossing the path of another corps: an illustration of faulty staffwork. Gneisenau was still doubtful as to whether Wellington would fight, and not until he heard the cannonade did he allow himself to be convinced and his suspicions to be overridden.

Meanwhile, Ney's front had been reinforced by Kellermann's two cavalry divisions and the Heavy Cavalry of the Guard. The Marshal, already angry and frustrated, launched sixty squadrons — 9,000 horsemen — on a front of less than 1,000 yards between Hougoumont and La Haye Sainte, and supported by one battery only. The butchery was appalling. Some British squares had to repulse a dozen assaults. Ney,

---

[1] Blücher later wrote that in spite of the pain he suffered as a result of his fall at Ligny, he would have had himself fastened to his horse rather than miss the battle.

[2] While visiting the battlefield several years later, Wellington said to Sir John Jones, the distinguished Engineer: 'I first saw the Prussian vedettes about half-past two; and never in my life did I observe a movement with such intense interest. The time they occupied in approaching seemed interminable; both they and my watch seemed to have stuck fast.'

astride his fourth horse of the day, led charge upon charge, but such were the ramparts of dead horses that movement was severely hampered. Again he had to admit failure and withdraw. Next he brought up 6,000 infantry, but too late. The columns were mauled by gunfire, attacked by the infantry brigades of Halkett and Duplat, and gave way into retreat.

A little after three o'clock the 52nd, who had been in reserve in front of Merbe Braine, marched eastwards just after the first attack by French cavalry against the allied squares. Ensign William Leeke described what took place.

Immediately on descending the slope of the position towards the enemy, the regiment, almost concealed by the tall rye, which was then for the first time trampled down, formed two squares. I remember we were not far from the north-eastern point of the Hougoumont inclosure, and on the narrow white road which, passing within 100 yards of that point, crosses the interval between the British and French positions in the direction of La Belle Alliance. . . . The old officers, who had served during the whole of the Peninsula war, stated that they were never exposed to such a cannonade as that which the 52nd squares had to undergo on this occasion for two hours and a half, from the French artillery planted about half a mile in their front. Our own artillery, on, or just under the crest of our position, were also firing over our heads the whole time, either at the enemy's troops or at their guns. Some shrapnel-shells[1] burst short, and wounded some of the 52nd men; but the firing of these shells was discontinued, on our sending notice of what they were doing to the artillery above us.

In the right square of the 52nd, and I suppose it was the same in all the squares of our brigade [Adam's], there was one incessant roar of round-shot and shells passing over or close to us on either flank; occasionally they made gaps in the square. The only interval that occurred in the cannonade was when we were charged by the French cavalry, for they, of course, could not fire on our squares for fear of injuring their own squadrons, so that the charges of cavalry were a great relief to us all I believe; at least, I know they were so to me.

The standing to be cannonaded, and having nothing else to do, is about the most unpleasant thing that can happen to soldiers in

[1] Invented by Lieut.-General Henry Shrapnel (1761–1842). His shell was first used successfully in 1804.

an engagement. I frequently tried to follow, with my eye, the course of the balls from our own guns, which were firing over us. It is much more easy to see a round-shot passing away from you over your head, than to catch sight of one coming through the air towards you, though this also occurs occasionally. I speak of shot fired from six, eight, nine, or twelve-pounder guns. . . .

My position in the right square was in the rear of the centre of the front face. . . . After we had been stationed for more than an hour so far down in front of the British position, a gleam of sunshine, falling on them, particularly attracted my attention to some brass guns in our front which appeared to be placed lower down the French slope, and nearer to us, than the others; I distinctly saw the French artilleryman go through the whole process of spunging out one of the guns and reloading it; I could see that it was pointed at our square, and when it was discharged I caught sight of the ball, which appeared to be in a direct line for me. I thought, Shall I move? No! I gathered myself up, and stood firm, with the colour in my right hand.[1] I do not exactly know the rapidity with which cannon-balls fly, but I think that two seconds elapsed from the time that I saw this shot leave the gun until it struck the front face of the square. It did not strike the four men in rear of whom I was standing, but the four poor fellows on their right. It was fired at some elevation, and struck the front man about the knees, and coming to the ground under the feet of the rear man of the four, whom it most severely wounded, it rose and, passing within an inch or two of the colour pole, went over the rear face of the square without doing further injury. The two men in the first and second rank fell outward, I fear they did not survive long; the two others fell within the square. The rear man made a considerable outcry on being wounded, but on one of the officers saying kindly to him, 'O man, don't make a noise', he instantly recollected himself, and was quiet.

We owe to Sergeant William Lawrence of the 40th Regiment another account of these cavalry onslaughts.

Still nothing daunted, they formed again, and this time ascended at us; but of the two, they met with a worse reception than before,

[1] Leeke said that the colours of the 52nd, having been through the Peninsular War, were 'little more than bare poles'.

for we instantly threw ourselves into three squares with our artillery in the centre; and the word having been given not to fire at the men, who wore armour [cuirassiers], but at the horses, which was obeyed to the very letter, as soon as they arrived at close quarters we opened a deadly fire, and very few of them wholly escaped. They managed certainly at first to capture our guns, but they were again recovered by the fire of our three squares; and it was a most laughable sight to see these Guards in their chimney-armour trying to run away after their horses had been shot from under them, being able to make very little progress, and many of them being taken prisoners by those of our light companies who were out skirmishing. I think this quite settled Buonaparte's Bodyguards, for we saw no more of them, they not having expected this signal defeat.

That affair, however, had only passed off a very few minutes before their infantry advanced and we had again to form line ready to meet them. We in our usual style let the infantry get well within our musket-shot before the order was given to fire, so that our volley proved to be of fearful success: and then immediately charging them we gave them a good start back again, but not without loss on our side as well as on theirs. And no sooner had they disappeared than another charge of cavalry was made, so that we again had to throw ourselves into square on our old ground. These cavalry had no doubt expected to appear amongst us before we could accomplish this, but fortunately they were mistaken, and our persistent fire soon turned them. We did not lose a single inch of ground the whole day, though after these successive charges our numbers were fearfully thinned; and even during the short interval between each charge the enemy's cannon had been doing some mischief among our ranks besides.

The men in their tired state were beginning to despair, but the officers cheered them on continually throughout the day with the cry of 'Keep your ground, my men!' It is a mystery to me how it was accomplished, for at last so few were left that there were scarcely enough to form square.

About four o'clock I was ordered to the colours. This, although I was used to warfare as much as any, was a job I did not at all like; but still I went as boldly to work as I could. There had been before me that day fourteen sergeants already killed and wounded while in charge of these colours, with officers in proportion, and the staff and colours were almost cut to pieces.

K

*Ensign Gronow of the 1st Foot Guards relates how, at about four
o'clock, the enemy's artillery in front suddenly ceased firing and
large masses of French cavalry were seen to advance.*

Not a man present who survived could have forgotten in after
life the awful grandeur of that charge. You perceived at a distance
what appeared to be an overwhelming, long moving line, which,
ever advancing, glittered like a stormy wave of the sea when it
catches the sunlight. On came the mounted host until they got
near enough, whilst the very earth seemed to vibrate beneath their
thundering tramp. One might suppose that nothing could have
resisted the shock of this terrible moving mass. They were the
famous cuirassiers, almost all old soldiers, who had distinguished
themselves on most of the battle-fields of Europe. In an almost
incredibly short period they were within twenty yards of us, shouting '*Vive l'Empereur!*' The word of command, 'Prepare to receive
cavalry', had been given, every man in the front ranks knelt, and
a wall bristling with steel, held together by steady hands, presented
itself to the infuriated cuirassiers.

I should observe that just before this charge the duke entered
by one of the angles of the square, accompanied only by one aide-
de-camp; all the rest of his staff being either killed or wounded.
Our Commander-in-Chief, as far as I could judge, appeared perfectly composed; but looked very thoughtful and pale.

. . . The charge of the French cavalry was gallantly executed;
but our well-directed fire brought men and horses down, and ere
long the utmost confusion arose in their ranks. The officers were
exceedingly brave, and by their gestures and fearless bearing did
all in their power to encourage their men to form again and renew
the attack. The duke sat unmoved, mounted on his favourite
charger. I recollect his asking Colonel Stanhope[1] what o'clock it
was, upon which Stanhope took out his watch, and said it was
twenty minutes past four. The duke replied, 'The battle is mine;
and if the Prussians arrive soon, there will be an end of the
war.'

. . . Again and again various cavalry regiments, heavy dragoons,
lancers, hussars, carabineers of the Guard, endeavoured to break
our walls of steel. The enemy's cavalry had to advance over ground
which was so heavy that they could not reach us except at a trot;

[1] The Hon. James Hamilton Stanhope, 1st Foot Guards, was a half-brother
to Lady Hester.

they therefore came upon us in a much more compact mass than they probably would have done if the ground had been more favourable. When they got within ten or fifteen yards they discharged their carbines, to the cry of '*Vive l'Empereur!*' but their fire produced little effect, as is generally the case with the fire of cavalry. Our men had orders not to fire unless they could do so on a near mass; the object being to economise our ammunition, and not to waste it on scattered soldiers. The result was that when the cavalry had discharged their carbines, and were still far off, we occasionally stood face to face, looking at each other inactively, not knowing what the next move might be.

. . . When we received cavalry, the order was to fire low so that on the first discharge of musketry, the ground was strewed with the fallen horses and their riders, which impeded the advance of those behind them, and broke the shock of the charge. It was pitiable to witness the agony of the poor horses, which really seemed conscious of the dangers that surrounded them: we often saw a poor wounded animal raise its head, as if looking for its rider to afford him aid. . . .

During the battle our squares presented a shocking sight. Inside we were nearly suffocated by the smoke and smell from burnt cartridges. It was impossible to move a yard without treading upon a wounded comrade, or upon the bodies of the dead; and the loud groans of the wounded and dying was most appalling.

At four o'clock our square was a perfect hospital, being full of dead, dying, and mutilated soldiers. The charges of cavalry were in appearance very formidable, but in reality a great relief, as the artillery could no longer fire on us: the very earth shook under the enormous mass of men and horses. I shall never forget the strange noise our bullets made against the breastplates of Kellermann's and Milhaud's[1] cuirassiers, six or seven thousand in number, who attacked us with great fury. I can only compare it, with a somewhat homely simile, to the noise of a violent hail-storm beating upon panes of glass.

The artillery did great execution, but our musketry did not at first seem to kill many men; though it brought down a large number of horses, and created indescribable confusion. The horses of the first rank of cuirassiers, in spite of all the efforts of their riders, came to a stand-still, shaking and covered with foam, at about

[1] Edouard-Jean-Baptiste, Comte Milhaud (1766–1833), commanded the 4th Cavalry Corps of cuirassiers.

twenty yards' distance from our squares, and generally resisted all attempts to force them to charge the line of serried steel.

In writing to friends in Axminster on July 8th, Private John Lewis described how the 95th Regiment faced a charge by cuirassiers.

I do not know what the English newspapers say about the battle; but, thank God, I am living, and was an eye-witness to the beginning of the battle — to the ending of it; but my pen cannot explain to you, nor twenty sheets of paper would not contain, what I could say about it; for, thank God, I had my strength and health more on the days we was engaged than I had in my life: so what I am going to tell you is the real truth. But I think my brother Tom, as he is such a scholar, if he was to look in the newspapers, he might see what officers was killed and wounded of the 95th Regiment: we have but six companies in the country, and after the battle we were only 255 privates; 2 colonels, 1 major, 15 officers, 11 serjeants, and 1 bugler, were killed: my first-rank man was wounded by part of a shell through his foot, and he dropt as we was advancing; I covered the next man I saw, and had not walked twenty steps before a musket-shot came sideways and took his nose clean off; and then I covered another man, which was the third; just after that, the man that stood next to me on my left hand had his left arm shot off by a nine-pound shot, just above his elbow, and he turned round and caught hold of me with his right hand, and the blood run all over my trousers; we was advancing, and he dropt directly. After this, was ordered to extend in front of all our large guns, and small arms was firing at the British lines in our rear, and I declare to God, with our guns and the French guns firing over our heads, my pen cannot explain any thing like it; it was not 400 yards from the French lines to our British lines, and we was about 150 yards in front of ours, so we was about 250 yards from the French, and sometimes not 100 yards; so I leave you to judge if I had not a narrow escape of my life.

As I just said, we now extended in front; Boney's Imperial Horse Guards,[1] all clothed in armour, made a charge at us; we saw them coming, and we all closed in and formed a square just as they came within ten yards of us, and they found they could do no good with us; they fired with their carbines on us, and came to

[1] These should be cuirassiers.

the right-about directly, and at that moment the man on my right hand was shot through the body, and the blood run out at his belly and back like a pig stuck in the throat; he dropt on his side; I spoke to him; he just said, 'Lewis, I'm done!' and died directly. All this time we kept up a constant fire at the Imperial Guards as they retreated, but they often came to the right-about and fired; and as I was loading my rifle, one of their shots came and struck my rifle, not two inches above my left hand, as I was ramming down the ball with my right hand, and broke the stock, and bent the barrel in such a manner that I could not get the ball down; just at that time we extended again, and my rifle was no use to me; a nine-pound shot came and cut the serjeant of our company right in two; he was not above three file from me, so I threw down my rifle and went and took his rifle, as it was not hurt at the time.

Captain Samuel Rudyard, of Major William Lloyd's nine-pounder battery, Royal Artillery, had his guns in support of the 3rd Division, and never moved from the downtrodden cornfield until the battle closed. He gives an impression of how the guns were fought and defended throughout the day.

My horses, ammunition waggons, were in rear of our Guns under cover of a little hollow between us and our Squares of Infantry. The forge cart, artificers' stores, and such like were in the rear of all out of fire. When ammunition was to be replenished, a Subaltern conducted such waggons as could be spared. They were supplied from the depot in the wood, and returned without delay. The ground we occupied was much furrowed up by the recoil of our Guns and the grazing of the shot, and many holes from the bursting of shells buried in the ground. As horses were killed or rendered unserviceable, the harness was removed and placed on the waggons, or elsewhere. Our men's knapsacks were neatly packed on the front and rear of our limbers and waggons, that they might do their work more easily. Every *Gun*, every carriage, spokes carried from wheels, all were struck in many places.

The Cuirassiers and Cavalry might have charged through the Battery as often as six or seven times, driving us into the Squares, under our Guns, waggons, some defending themselves. In general, a Squadron or two came up the slope on our immediate front, and on their moving off at the appearance of our Cavalry charging, we took advantage to send destruction after them, and when advancing on our fire I have seen four or five men and horses piled upon each other like cards, the men not having even been displaced from the saddle, the effect of canister.

The Duke and his Staff were frequently in our rear under the heaviest fire, also the Prince of Orange.

PHASE FOUR: THE FRENCH CAPTURE
LA HAYE SAINTE

WHILE one French division regained possession of Papelotte Farm, Marshal Ney, his enthusiasm still matching his courage and wild vigour, led the wreckage of d'Erlon's corps into a renewed assault on La Haye Sainte. The dogged garrison, who had only three or four rounds left from the sixty they had taken into action that morning — to replenish their stock had proved impossible — had to withdraw to the garden after a furious struggle; but even this became untenable before long, and Major Baring told his men to make their way singly to the main Allied positions behind. Out of four hundred defenders, no more than forty-two were effective at the end.

The capture of La Haye Sainte brought great advantage to the French, because Wellington's troops in the centre were now exposed to close-range musketry. What is more, Ney brought up a battery of horse artillery at three hundred yards' range, and installed infantry much closer still in the sand-pit whence the 95th had been evicted. The Allied centre was dangerously shaken, the soldiers were exhausted, and several formations began to give way under pressure. 'We were in peril,' wrote a senior staff officer; 'at every moment the issue of the battle became more doubtful.'

Ney saw the wavering and asked Napoleon for more troops, having in hand none with whom to drive home the success just gained. The Emperor, his cavalry ruined, his observation post now a target for Prussian round-shot, did not consider the moment right for reinforcing Ney. He was wrong. Had he been prepared to raise the stakes a little by committing his fourteen battalions of the Old and Middle Guard, this added force must have turned the scales and snatched victory. Wellington's reserves were almost exhausted, the centre of the line between Halkett and Kempt was almost bare of troops, and a counter-attack by Ompteda's battalions of the King's German Legion had been halted and the leading files massacred by predatory cuirassiers. Yet Napoleon refused waspishly: '*Des troupes? Où voulez-vous que j'en prenne? Voulez-vous que j'en fasse?*' And when he did change his mind, it was already too late. Wellington had a half-hour of grace in which to reorganise his defence line. Calmly he ordered up the Brunswickers and sent for all the German troops and any available guns. The gap was filled by these and a Belgian–Dutch division. And Zieten's much delayed corps at last arrived on the left flank, thereby releasing men to strengthen the centre. The great crisis of Waterloo had passed.

Major George Baring, defending La Haye Sainte with a battalion of the King's German Legion, describes the day's fighting.

As day broke on the 18th of June, we sought out every possible means of putting the place in a state of defence, but the burned gate of the barn presented the greatest difficulties. With this employment, and cooking some veal which we found in the place, the morning was past until after eleven o'clock, when the attack commenced against the left wing.

Every man now repaired to his post, and I betook myself to the orchard, where the first attack was to be expected: the farm lies in a hollow, so that a small elevation of the ground immediately in front of the orchard, concealed the approach of the enemy.

Shortly after noon, some skirmishers commenced the attack. I made the men lie down, and forbade all firing until the enemy were quite near. The first shot broke the bridle of my horse close to my hand, and the second killed Major [Adolphus] Bösewiel, who was standing near me. The enemy did not stop long skirmishing, but immediately advanced over the height, with two close columns, one of which attacked the buildings, and the other threw itself in mass into the orchard, shewing the greatest contempt for our fire. It was not possible for our small disjointed numbers fully to withstand this furious attack of such a superior force, and we retired upon the barn, in a more united position, in order to continue the defence: my horse's leg was broken, and I was obliged to take that of the adjutant.

Colonel von Klencke now came to our assistance with the Lüneburg battalion. We immediately recommenced the attack, and had already made the enemy give way, when I perceived a strong line of cuirassiers form in front of the orchard; at the same time Captain Meyer came to me and reported that the enemy had surrounded the rear garden, and it was not possible to hold it longer. I gave him orders to fall back into the buildings, and assist in their defence. Convinced of the great danger which threatened us from the cuirassiers, in consequence of the weak hedge, so easy to break through, I called out to my men, who were mixed with the newly arrived Hanoverians, — to assemble round me, as I intended retiring into the barn. The number of the battalion which had come to our assistance exceeded, by many degrees, that of my men, and as, at the same time, the enemy's infantry gained the garden, — the skirmishers having been driven out by a column attack, — the former, seeing the cuirassiers in the open field, imagined that their only chance of safety lay in gaining the main position of the army. My voice, unknown to them, and also not sufficiently penetrating, was, notwithstanding all my exertions, unequal to halt and collect my men together; already overtaken by the cavalry, we fell in with the enemy's infantry, who had surrounded the garden, and to whose fire the men were exposed in retiring to the main position. In this effort a part succeeded. Notwithstanding this misfortune, the farmhouse itself was still defended by Lieutenants George Graeme and [Thomas] Carey, and Ensign [George] Franck. The English dragoon guards now came up, — beat back the cuirassiers, — fell upon the infantry, who had already suffered much, and nearly cut them to pieces.

In this first attack I lost a considerable number of men, besides three officers killed, and six wounded; on my requisition for support, Captains [Frederick] von Gilsa and [G.B.] Marschalck were sent to me, with their companies of the 1st light battalion; to these, and a part of my own battalion, I gave the defence of the garden, leaving the buildings to the three officers who had already so bravely defended them: the orchard I did not again occupy.

About half an hour's respite was now given us by the enemy, and we employed the time in preparing ourselves against a new attack; this followed in the same force as before; namely, from two sides by two close columns, which, with the greatest rapidity, nearly surrounded us, and, despising danger, fought with a degree of courage which I had never before witnessed in Frenchmen. Favored by their advancing in masses, every bullet of ours hit, and seldom were the effects limited to one assailant; this did not, however, prevent them from throwing themselves against the walls, and endeavouring to wrest the arms from the hands of my men, through the loop-holes; many lives were sacrificed to the defence of the doors and gates; the most obstinate contest was carried on where the gate was wanting, and where the enemy seemed determined to enter. On this spot seventeen Frenchmen already lay dead, and their bodies served as a protection to those who pressed after them to the same spot.

Meantime four lines of French cavalry had formed on the right

front of the farm: the first cuirassiers, second lancers, third dragoons, and fourth hussars, and it was clear to me that their intention was to attack the squares of our division in position, in order
by destroying them to break the whole line. This was a critical
moment, for what would be our fate if they succeeded! As they
marched upon the position by the farm, I brought all the fire possible to bear upon them; many men and horses were overthrown,
but they were not discouraged. Without in the least troubling themselves about our fire, they advanced with the greatest intrepidity,
and attacked the infantry. All this I could see, and confess freely
that now and then I felt some apprehension. The manner in which
this cavalry was received and beaten back by our squares, is too
well known to require mention here.

. . . When the cavalry retired, the infantry gave up also their
fruitless attack, and fell back, accompanied by our shouts, and
derision. Our loss, on this occasion, was not so great as at first;
however, my horse was again shot under me, and as my servant, be-
lieving me dead, had gone away with my other horse, I procured
one of those that were running about.

Our first care was to make good the injury which had been sustained; my greatest anxiety was respecting the ammunition, which,
I found, in consequence of the continued fire, had been reduced
more than one half. I immediately sent an officer back with this
account, and requested ammunition, which was promised. About
an hour had thus passed when I discovered the enemy's columns
again advancing on the farm; I sent another officer back to the
position with this intelligence, and repeated the request for ammunition.

Our small position was soon again attacked with the same fury,
and defended with the same courage as before. Captain von
Wurmb was sent to my assistance with the skirmishers of the fifth
line battalion, and I placed them in the court; but welcome as this
reinforcement was, it could not compensate for the want of ammunition, which every moment increased, so that after half an
hour more of uninterrupted fighting, I sent off an officer with the
same request.

This was as fruitless as the other two applications; however, two
hundred Nassau troops were sent me. The principal contest was
now carried on at the open entrance to the barn; at length the
enemy, not being able to succeed by open force, resorted to the
expedient of setting the place on fire, and soon a thick smoke was

seen rising from the barn! Our alarm was now extreme, for although there was water in the court, all means of drawing it, and carrying it were wanting, — every vessel having been broken up. Luckily the Nassau troops carried large field cooking kettles; I tore a kettle from the back of one of the men; several officers followed my example, and filling the kettles with water, they carried them, facing almost certain death, to the fire. The men did the same, and soon not one of the Nassauers was left with his kettle, and the fire was thus luckily extinguished; — but alas! with the blood of many a brave man! Many of the men, although covered with wounds, could not be brought to retire. 'So long as our officers fight, and we can stand,' was their constant reply, 'we will not stir from the spot.'

. . . This attack may have lasted about an hour and a half, when the French, tired from their fruitless efforts, again fell back. Our joy may be well imagined. With every new attack I became more convinced of the importance of holding the post. With every attack also, the weight of the responsibility that devolved upon me increased. This responsibility is never greater than when an officer is thus left to himself, and suddenly obliged to make a decision upon which, perhaps, his own as well as the life and honor of those under him, — nay even more important results, — may depend. In battles, as is well known, trifles, apparently of little importance, have often incalculable influence.

What must have been my feelings, therefore, when, on counting the cartridges, I found that, on an average, there was not more than from three to four each! The men made nothing of the diminished physical strength which their excessive exertions had caused, and immediately filled up the holes that had been made in the walls by the enemy's guns, but they could not remain insensible to the position in which they were placed by the want of ammunition, and made the most reasonable remonstrances to me on the subject. These were not wanting to make me renew the most urgent representations, and finally to report specifically that I was not capable of sustaining another attack in the present condition. All was in vain! With what uneasiness did I now see two enemy columns again in march against us! At this moment I would have blessed the ball that came to deprive me of life. — But more than life was at stake, and the extraordinary danger required extraordinary exertion and firmness. On my exhortations to courage and economy of the ammunition, I received one unanimous reply:

'No man will desert you, — we will fight and die with you!' — No pen, not even that of one who has experienced such moments, can describe the feeling which this excited in me; nothing can be compared with it! — Never had I felt myself so elevated: — but never also placed in so painful a position, where honor contended with a feeling for the safety of the men who had given me such an unbounded proof of their confidence.

The enemy gave me no time for thought; they were already close by our weak walls, and now, irritated by the opposition which they had experienced, attacked with renewed fury. The contest commenced at the barn, which they again succeeded in setting on fire. It was extinguished, luckily, in the same manner as before. Every shot that was now fired, increased my uneasiness and anxiety. I sent again to the rear with the positive statement that I must and would leave the place if no ammunition was sent me. This was also without effect.

Our fire gradually diminished, and in the same proportion did our perplexity increase; already I heard many voices calling out for ammunition, adding:— 'We will readily stand by you, but we must have the means of defending ourselves!' Even the officers, who, during the whole day, had shewn the greatest courage, represented to me the impossibility of retaining the post under such circumstances. The enemy, who too soon observed our wants, now boldly broke in one of the doors; however, as only a few could come in at a time, these were instantly bayonetted, and the rear hesitated to follow. They now mounted the roof and walls, from which my unfortunate men were certain marks; at the same time they pressed in through the open barn, which could no longer be defended. Inexpressibly painful as the decision was to me of giving up the place, my feeling of duty as a man overcame that of honor, and I gave the order to retire through the house into the garden.[1]

Lieutenant George Drummond Graeme of the 2nd Light Battalion, King's German Legion, wrote thus about the fighting for La Haye Sainte.

In the first attack I perceived *no* French Cavalry on the British left of the farm of La Haye Sainte. I was favourably situated, and

[1] Baring was promoted to Lieut.-Colonel, made a Companion of the Order of the Bath, and received from the King of the Netherlands the Wilhelm's Order (4th Class).

think I must have seen them had there been any, being placed with a section of our Rifles behind the *abatis* across the high road a little in front of the great gate of the farm, afterwards with about a dozen men on top of the '*piggery?*' (there was a calf in it!)

The [French] Infantry came down in heavy columns with a line of skirmishers as thick almost as an advancing line of our troops. When close upon us we entered the farm, and closed the gates, and poured a constant fire on their Columns as they passed us, and even until they were up on the crest of the British position, when they were repulsed and broken by the British line, and repassed us like a flock of sheep, followed by the Life Guards, who came down the hollow road or sandpits, pursuing some French Cuirassiers (who, I presume, had been separated from their Regiment in the rear or to the right of our farm). A party of our men sallied out and pursued in the crowd a considerable way up towards Belle Alliance. None passed *through* our *abatis*, as we afterwards returned, and I placed my men behind it as before.

The ground was literally covered with French killed and wounded, even to the astonishment of my oldest soldiers, who said they had never witnessed such a sight. The French wounded were calling out '*Vive l'Empereur*', and I saw a poor fellow, lying with both his legs shattered, trying to destroy himself with his own sword, which I ordered my servant to take from him.

. . . The French came down obliquely towards the farm in the first attack, over the fields as well as down the high road. A large Column was all day in the rear [?front] of the farm, and trying to get possession of the barn, the door of which was open towards our right. They never tried to escalade, and we kept them off the great gate by firing from the piggery (where I was placed most of the day), although the *abatis* served them for cover, unfortunately.

We had no loopholes excepting three great apertures, which we made with difficulty when we were told in the morning that we were to defend the farm. Our Pioneers had been sent to Hougoumont the evening before. We had no scaffolding, nor means of making any, having burnt the carts, &c. Our loopholes, if they may be thus termed, were on a level with the road on the outside, and later in the day the Enemy got possession of the one near the pond, and fired in upon us. This they also did during the first attack on the roadside.

. . . I may add that the barn was filled with straw, and it was a fortunate circumstance that it was all carried off by the different troops during the night, the French repeatedly having tried during the attack to set it on fire. Lieut. Carey, in spite of the Enemy's fire, went out, and with his men poured water on the flames.

[*Towards half past six that evening the defenders' ammunition began to run very low, and the French, having forced their way into the stables and then been prevented from entering the yard, clambered on to the roof of the stables and picked off the Germans of the Legion. Major Baring ordered the surviving defenders to withdraw through a passage into the garden. Lieutenant Graeme wrote an account of this withdrawal.*]

We all had to pass through a narrow passage. We wanted to halt the men and make one more charge, but it was impossible; the fellows were firing down the passage. An Officer of our Company called to me, 'Take care', but I was too busy stopping the men, and answered, 'Never mind, let the blackguard fire.' He was about five yards off, and levelling his piece just at me, when this Officer stabbed him in the mouth and out through his neck; he fell immediately.

But now they flocked in; this Officer got two shots, and ran into a room, where he lay behind a bed all the time they had possession of the house; sometimes the room was full of them, and some wounded soldiers of ours who lay there and cried out 'pardon' were shot, the monsters saying, 'Take that for the fine defence you have made.'

An Officer and four men came in first; the Officer got me by the collar, and said to his men, '*C'est ce coquin.*' Immediately the fellows had their bayonets down, and made a dead stick at me, which I parried off with my sword, the Officer always running about and then coming to me again and shaking me by the collar; but they all looked so frightened and pale as ashes, I thought, 'You shan't keep me', and I bolted through the lobby; they fired two shots after me, and cried out '*Coquin*', but did not follow me.

I rejoined the remnant of the Regiment, when we were immediately charged by Cuirassiers. All the Army was formed in squares. We hastily got our men into a hollow, and peppered them so, I believe they found the cuirass not thick enough for rifles.

When Sir John Byng's brigade was sent to help the defenders of Hougoumont, the Duke ordered the Brunswick troops and other regiments, including the 14th Foot, to fill the gap left between the brigades commanded by Halkett and Kempt. Ensign Keppel recalled that one of Lord Hill's aides-de-camp brought orders for the 14th to advance.

We marched in columns of companies. Emerging from the ravine we came upon an open valley, bounded on all sides by low hills. The hill on our front was fringed by the enemy's cannon, and we advanced to our new position amid a shower of shot and shells. . . .

We halted and formed square in the middle of the plain. As we were performing this movement, a bugler of the 51st, who had been out with skirmishers, and had mistaken our square for his own, exclaimed, 'Here I am again, safe enough.' The words were scarcely out of his mouth, when a round shot took off his head and spattered the whole battalion with his brains, the colours and the ensigns in charge of them coming in for an extra share. One of them, Charles Fraser, a fine gentleman in speech and manner, raised a laugh by drawling out, 'How extremely disgusting!' A second shot carried off six of the men's bayonets, a third broke the breastbone of a Lance-Sergeant (Robinson), whose piteous cries were anything but encouraging to his youthful comrades. The soldier's belief that 'every bullet has its billet' was strengthened by another shot striking Ensign [Alfred] Cooper, the shortest man in the regiment and in the very centre of the square. These casualties were the affair of a second.

We were now ordered to lie down. Our square, hardly large enough to hold us when standing upright, was too small for us in a recumbent position. Our men lay packed together like herrings in a barrel. Not finding a vacant spot, I seated myself on a drum. Behind me was the Colonel's charger, which, with his head pressed against mine, was mumbling my epaulette, while I patted his cheek. Suddenly my drum capsized and I was thrown prostrate, with the feeling of a blow on the right cheek. I put my hand to my head, thinking half my face was shot away, but the skin was not even abraded. A piece of shell had struck the horse on the nose exactly between my hand and my head, and killed him instantly. The blow I received was from the embossed crown on the horse's bit.

The French artillerymen had now brought us so completely within range, that if we had continued much longer in this exposed situation I should probably not have lived to tell my tale. We soon received the order to seek the shelter of a neighbouring hill. . . .

Lieut.-Colonel Ludwig von Reiche relates how, at two o'clock that
afternoon, Zieten's 1st Corps, of which he was Chief of Staff,
marched out of its bivouac at Bierges near Wavre.

Our march to the battlefield was extremely difficult. Sunken
lanes cut through deep ravines had to be negotiated; almost im-
penetrable forest grew on each side, so that there was no question
of avoiding the road, and progress was very slow, all the more so
because in many places men and horses could get through only
one at a time. The column became very split up and wherever the
ground allowed it, the heads of the columns had to halt so as to
give time for the detachments to collect themselves again.

. . . Amid the repeated hold-ups on the march I hurried forward
to discover the state of the battle and assess how best the 1st Army
Corps could participate.

As I came out of the wood on to the plateau of Ohain, I could
see the battle in full swing before me. To the right, in the direction
of Mont St Jean, was Wellington's army; and to the left, beyond
Frichermont towards Plancenoit, the Prussian army (the 2nd and
4th Army Corps[1]) under Blücher's personal command.

. . . When I reached the battlefield I found myself next to the
English army and I headed there straightaway to report that our
corps was approaching. The first people I came on were the
Nassau troops forming the left wing of the English army, and it
was not long before I met our General von Müffling, attached to
Wellington's Headquarters. From him I learnt that the Duke
was anxiously awaiting our arrival and had repeatedly declared
that time was running very short, and that if we did not arrive soon
he would have to retreat. Müffling added that the Duke had already
strengthened his centre at the expense of his left wing, and it was
therefore urgent that Zieten should link up with that wing; and I
was to direct the corps accordingly.

With these instructions I hurried back to the column and having
decided not to waste time by first looking for General Zieten, who
was further back, I gave the advance-guard the appropriate direction in the light of Müffling's instructions; and then hurried forward again to await the corps.

On returning to the battlefield I found that the situation had
deteriorated. The Nassau ranks had given way and their guns were
already moving back. I did my best to prevent anything worse hap-

[1] Commanded by Pirch I and Bülow.

pening, and assured them over and over again that the 1st Prussian Army Corps must arrive at any minute. I was hurrying back towards the corps in order to report to General Zieten, when Captain von Scharnhorst, now a lieutenant-general and Inspector of Artillery but at that time on Prince Blücher's staff, dashed up to me, shouting that the 1st Army Corps must push on immediately to Blücher beyond Frichermont, because things were beginning to go badly there. I pointed out to him what had been arranged with Müffling, and emphasised that Wellington was relying implicitly on our arrival. But von Scharnhorst would not listen, and said that this was Blücher's order and he would hold me responsible for the consequences if it was not carried out.

Never in my life have I found myself in such a difficult situation. On the one hand Blücher's order . . . and the thought that our troops were perhaps in danger there and could not hold out any longer. On the other hand the certainty that Wellington was counting on our arrival. I was nearly in despair,[1] all the more so as the head of the advance-guard was just arriving and wanted to know where to march next. General Zieten himself was not in sight,[2] and General Steinmetz,[3] who commanded the advance-guard, came up to the halted troops at this very moment, stormed at me in his usual violent manner, and insisted upon an advance. He was scarcely willing to listen to how things stood. My embarrassment increased not a little when General Steinmetz let the head of the column resume its march and himself went past the point where the road to Frichermont branches off.

As I was unwilling to make any decision and, moreover, had no means of knowing what General Zieten would decide, be it for Blücher or for Wellington, I allowed the head of the column to go back to the fork for Frichermont.[4] As this took place in view of the Nassau troops, it had never crossed my mind that this apparent withdrawal could be misunderstood and could make a bad impression, as was in fact the case for a minute or two.

Fortunately General Zieten came up at this critical moment. I hurried over to him and when I had given my report, he issued

---

[1] I had quite decided, if any mishap occurred as a result of my action, to seek death on the battlefield. To survive would have been for me a fearful torment [Reiche].

[2] I was not prepared to hunt for him along the column in the sunken road so as to obtain orders, for I was afraid of missing him [Reiche].

[3] Karl Friedrich Franciscus von Steinmetz (1768–1837), a Hessian.

[4] All the more permissible, as the brigade had become very split up on the bad road and still had not quite collected any of its battalions [Reiche].

orders for the march to be directed without fail towards the English army. Nobody could have been more pleased than I was.

At about three o'clock Sir Augustus Frazer galloped up to 'G' Troop, Royal Horse Artillery, and shouted to Captain Mercer, 'Left limber up, and as fast as you can.'

The words were scarcely uttered when my gallant troop stood as desired in column of subdivisions, left in front, pointing towards the main ridge. 'At a gallop, march!' and away we flew, as steadily and compactly as if at a review. I rode with Frazer, whose face was as black as a chimney-sweep's from the smoke, and the jacket-sleeve of his right arm torn open by a musket-ball or case-shot, which had merely grazed his flesh. As we went along, he told me that the enemy had assembled an enormous mass of heavy cavalry in front of the point to which he was leading us (about one-third of the distance between Hougoumont and the Charleroi road), and that in all probability we should immediately be charged on gaining our position. 'The Duke's orders, however, are positive,' he added, 'that in the event of their persevering and charging home, you do not expose your men, but retire with them into the adjacent squares of infantry.' As he spoke, we were ascending the reverse slope of the main position. We breathed a new atmosphere — the air was suffocatingly hot, resembling that issuing from an oven. We were enveloped in thick smoke, and, *malgré* the incessant roar of cannon and musketry, could distinctly hear around us a mysterious humming noise, like that which one hears of a summer's evening proceeding from myriads of black beetles; cannon-shot, too, ploughed the ground in all directions, and so thick was the hail of balls and bullets that it seemed dangerous to extend the arm lest it should be torn off.

In spite of the serious situation in which we were, I could not help being somewhat amused at the astonishment expressed by our kind-hearted surgeon (Hitchins),[1] who heard for the first time this sort of music. He was close to me as we ascended the slope, and, hearing this infernal *carillon* about his ears, began staring round in the wildest and most comic manner imaginable, twisting himself from side to side, exclaiming, 'My God, Mercer, what *is* that?

[1] Richard Hichins, an assistant-surgeon in the Ordnance Medical Department.

What *is* all this noise? How curious! — how very curious!'And then when a cannon-shot rushed hissing past, '*There! — there!* What *is* it all?' It was with great difficulty that I persuaded him to retire: for a time he insisted on remaining near me, and it was only by pointing out how important it was to us, in case of being wounded, that he should keep himself safe to be able to assist us, that I prevailed on him to withdraw.

Amidst this storm we gained the summit of the ridge, strange to say, without a casualty; and Sir Augustus, pointing out our position between two squares of Brunswick infantry, left us, with injunctions to remember the Duke's order, and to economise our ammunition. The Brunswickers were falling fast — the shot every moment making great gaps in their squares, which the officers and sergeants were actively employed in filling up by pushing their men together, and sometimes thumping them ere they could make them move. These were the very boys whom I had but yesterday seen throwing away their arms, and fleeing, panic-stricken, from the very sound of our horses' feet. Today they fled not bodily, to be sure, but spiritually, for their senses seemed to have left them. There they stood, with recovered arms, like so many logs, or rather like the very wooden figures which I had seen them practising at in their cantonments. Every moment I feared they would again throw down their arms and flee; but their officers and sergeants behaved nobly, not only keeping them together, but managing to keep their squares closed in spite of the carnage made amongst them.

To have sought refuge amongst men in such a state were madness — the very moment our men ran from their guns, I was convinced, would be the signal for their disbanding. We had better then, fall at our posts than in such a situation. Our coming up seemed to reanimate them, and all their eyes were directed to us— indeed, it was providential, for, had we not arrived as we did, I scarcely think there is a doubt of what would have been their fate. Our first gun had scarcely gained the interval between their squares, when I saw through the smoke the leading squadrons of the advancing column coming on at a brisk trot, and already not more than one hundred yards distant, if so much, for I don't think we could have seen so far. I immediately ordered the line to be formed for action — *case-shot!* and the leading gun was unlimbered and commenced firing almost as soon as the word was given: for activity and intelligence our men were unrivalled.

The very first round, I saw, brought down several men and horses. They continued, however, to advance. I glanced at the Brunswickers, and that glance told me it would not do; they had opened a fire from their front faces, but both squares appeared too unsteady, and I resolved to say nothing about the Duke's order, and take our chance — a resolve that was strengthened by the effect of the remaining guns as they rapidly succeeded in coming to action, making terrible slaughter, and in an instant covering the ground with men and horses. Still they persevered in approaching us (the first round had brought them to a walk), though slowly, and it did seem they would ride over us. We were a little below the level of the ground on which they moved — having in front of us a bank of about a foot and a half or two feet high, along the top of which ran a narrow road — and this gave more effect to our case-shot, all of which almost must have taken effect, for the carnage was frightful. I suppose this state of things occupied but a few seconds, when I observed symptoms of hesitation, and in a twinkling, at the instant I thought it was all over with us, they turned to either flank and filed away rapidly to the rear.

Retreat of the mass, however, was not so easy. Many facing about and trying to force their way through the body of the column, that part next to us became a complete mob, into which we kept a steady fire of case-shot from our six pieces. The effect is hardly conceivable, and to paint this scene of slaughter and confusion impossible. Every discharge was followed by the fall of numbers, whilst the survivors struggled with each other, and I actually saw them using the pommels of their swords to fight their way out of the *mêlée*. Some, rendered desperate at finding themselves thus pent up at the muzzles of our guns, as it were, and others carried away by their horses, maddened with wounds, dashed through our intervals — few thinking of using their swords, but pushing furiously onward, intent only on saving themselves. At last the rear of the column, wheeling about, opened a passage, and the whole swept at a much more rapid pace than they had advanced, nor stopped until the swell of the ground covered them from our fire. We then ceased firing; but as they were still not far off, for we saw the tops of their caps, having reloaded, we stood ready to receive them should they renew the attack.

PHASE FIVE: THE GUARD ATTACKS

AT about seven o'clock Napoleon took forward the last reserve which had spent the day near Rossomme and entrusted it to Marshal Ney. Six battalions of the Middle Guard formed square and advanced for the ultimate assault, followed by part of the Old Guard. In review order, accompanied by firing guns but ill-supported by cavalry, the Guard hastened up the slope to the west of the Brussels road. A French officer deserted and gave warning of the imminent attack. Against Halkett's brigade they came, and upon Maitland's Guards brigade arrayed along the ridge between Hougoumont and La Haye Sainte. In the past the entry into a battle of these renowned veterans had so often heralded a victory, but not this time.

After desperate fighting and some dangerous moments, the French right wing was repulsed by Halkett's musketry and by grapeshot salvoes. In the centre the British Guards were called to their feet by Wellington, fired a devastating volley, and then advanced until their opponents broke into a downhill retreat. Two French battalions emerged from the smoke on Maitland's flank, only to be shattered by the fire of the 52nd who came over the ridge, wheeled parallel to the French left flank, and shooting with deadly effect, sent the *chasseurs* reeling back.

Now was heard the death-knell verdict, *'La garde recule'*. Now did the French divisions down in the hollow halt their tardy advance to support, and become infected and dejected by the sight of the retreating last hope: the Imperial Guard. Now Wellington unleashed his last reserve, the cavalry brigades of Vandeleur and Vivian. Down into the valley they charged with exultation, fell upon the disordered *grognards* and cuirassiers, and turned the enemy's centre into a panicky mob beyond discipline and control. Behind the horsemen Wellington's whole line advanced in support, but they met almost no resistance, only the débris of an army.

Zieten's corps now penetrated between d'Erlon and Lobau. At La Belle Alliance Vivian, Vandeleur and the Prussian cavalry converged, and they had then to charge the last stand of the Old Guard by the *chaussée*: three squares under Cambronne which resisted for a while and covered Napoleon's retreat. The Young Guard, fighting resolutely in the cemetery or from house to house, upstairs, downstairs, with thatched roofs blazing about them, held out in Plancenoit till nightfall, and thereby thwarted the Prussian bid to cut off the French army from retreat.

Lieutenant Edward Macready of the 30th Foot saw two French guns unlimber within seventy yards of his position and then proceed to inflict terrible damage upon the regimental square, the first discharge of grapeshot killing seven men in the centre.

We would willingly have charged these guns, but, had we deployed, the cavalry that flanked them would have made an example of us.

The *vivida vis animi* — the glow which fires one upon entering into action — had ceased. It was now to be seen which side had most bottom, and would stand killing longest. The Duke visited us frequently at this momentous period; he was coolness personified. As he crossed the rear face of our square a shell fell amongst our grenadiers, and he checked his horse to see its effect. Some men were blown to pieces by the explosion, and he merely stirred the rein of his charger, apparently as little concerned at their fate as at his own danger. No leader ever possessed so fully the confidence of his soldiery, 'but none did love him'; — wherever he appeared, a murmur of 'Silence — stand to your front — here's the Duke!' was heard through the columns, and then all was steady as on a parade. His aides-de-camp, Colonels Canning and Gordon, fell near our square, and the former died within it.[1] As he came near us late in the evening, Halkett rode out to him and represented our weak state, begging his Grace to afford us a little support. 'It's impossible, Halkett,' said he. And our General replied, 'If so, sir, you may depend on the brigade to a man!' Our colours were ordered to the rear. This measure has been reprobated by many, but I know I never in my life felt such joy, or looked on danger with so light a heart, as when I saw our dear old rags in safety.

. . . It was near seven o'clock, and our front had sustained three attacks from fresh troops, when the Imperial Guard was seen ascending our position in as correct order as at a review. As they rose step by step before us, and crossed the ridge, their red epaulettes and cross-belts put on over their blue great-coats, gave them

---

[1] Charles Fox Canning died, holding the hand of a fellow aide-de-camp and propped up by knapsacks, while the Earl of March listened to his last requests.

a gigantic appearance, which was increased by their high hairy caps and long red feathers, which waved with the nod of their heads as they kept time to a drum in the centre of their column. 'Now for a clawing,' I muttered, and I confess, when I saw the imposing advance of these men, and thought of the character they had gained, I looked for nothing but a bayonet in my body, and I half breathed a confident sort of wish that it might not touch my vitals.

While we were moving up the slope, Halkett, as well as the noise permitted us to hear him, addressed us and said, 'My boys, you have done everything I could have wished, and more than I could expect, but much remains to be done; at this moment we have nothing for it but a charge.' Our brave fellows replied by three cheers. The enemy halted, carried arms about 40 paces from us, and fired a volley. We returned it, and giving our 'Hurrah!' brought down the bayonets. Our surprise was inexpressible, when, pushing through the clearing smoke, we saw the back of the Imperial Grenadiers; we halted and stared at each other as if mistrusting our eyesight. Some 9-pounders from the rear of our right poured in the grape amongst them, and the slaughter was dreadful. In no part of the field did I see carcases so heaped upon each other.

. . . There was a hedge to our rear, to which it was deemed expedient to move us, I suppose, for shelter from the guns. We faced about by word of command, and stepped off in perfect order. As we descended the declivity the fire thickened tremendously, and the cries from men struck down, as well as from the numerous wounded on all sides of us, who thought themselves abandoned, were terrible. An extraordinary number of men and officers of both regiments went down almost in no time. [Lieutenant Edmund] Prendergast of ours was shattered to pieces by a shell; [Captain Alexander] McNab killed by grape-shot, and [Ensigns] James and Bullen lost all their legs by round-shot during this retreat, or in the cannonade immediately preceding it. As I recovered my feet from a tumble, a friend knocked up against me, seized me by the stock, and almost choked me, screaming, (half maddened by his five wounds and the sad scene going on,) 'Is it deep, Mac, is it deep?' At this instant we found ourselves commingled with the 33rd and 69th Regiments; all order was lost, and the column (now a mere mob,) passed the hedge at an accelerated pace. (I imagine the 33rd and 69th must have received a similar order to ourselves, and that the two bodies clashed from bad leading on one or both parts, the officers, from the nature of our formation, being inoperative within the squares.)

The exertions of the officers, added to the glorious struggling of lots of the men to halt and face about, were rendered of no avail by the irresistible pressure, and as many, cursing and crying with rage and shame, seized individuals to halt them, they were themselves jammed up against them and hurried on with the current, literally for many yards not touching the ground. At this infernal crisis some one hurra'd, — we all joined, and every creature halted, faced about, and retraced his steps to the hedge. Here Major Chambers ordered our light company to dash out as far as they dare, and under cover of their fire (reinforced as they soon were by [Lieutenant John] Roe's company,) the brigade got into a four deep formation, the 33rd and 69th soon afterwards taking ground to their right and front, and some of their men under (I think) Mr [Lieutenant Charles William] Ingle, joining our skirmishers. I cannot conceive what the enemy were about during our confusion. Fifty cuirassiers would have annihilated our brigade; they must, however, have been quick about it, for terrible as this occurrence was, I suppose five minutes would have included it all from first to last. The officers did wonders, but the shout alone saved us. I never could learn who raised it. . . .

While things were looking badly some Brunswickers had marched up to our left. They gave way once bodily just as they reached the crashing line of fire, but were rallied, and afterwards stood well.

Ensign William Leeke of the 52nd takes up his story again.

It was now getting on for seven o'clock. The 52nd formed line four deep, the right wing being in the front line, the left wing having closed up upon it. The regiment stood about forty paces below the crest of the position, so that it was nearly or quite out of fire. The roar of round-shot still continued, many only just clearing our heads — others, striking the top of the position and bounding over us — others, again, almost spent and rolling down gently towards us. One of these, when we were standing in line, came rolling down like a cricket-ball, so slowly that I was putting out my foot to stop it, when my colour-serjeant quickly begged me not to do so, and told me it might have seriously injured my foot. Exactly in front of me, when standing in line, lay, at a distance of two yards, a dead tortoise-shell kitten. It had probably been frightened out of Hougoumont, which was the nearest house to us, and about a quarter of a mile off. The circumstance led me to think of my friends at home.

Bounding our view, about forty paces in our front, was a bank not quite three feet high; there was a stunted hedge on it away to the right of our centre, but not so to the left. Under this bank and hedge lay some twenty of our badly and mortally wounded men, covered by their blankets, which some of the poor fellows had got out from their knapsacks. . . .

In front of our left company were several killed and wounded horses; some of the latter were lying, some standing, but some of both were eating the trodden down wheat or rye, notwithstanding that their legs were shot off, or that they were otherwise badly wounded. I observed a brigade of artillery, coming from our left, pass over the bank into action in a very cool and gallant style. In doing this, some of the guns went over the legs of the wounded horses — the wounded *men* were out of their way. . . . There was a peculiar smell at this time, arising from a mingling of the smell of the wheat trodden flat down with the smell of gunpowder.

Half an hour, or perhaps three-quarters of an hour, had elapsed after our return to the position, when a French cuirassier officer came galloping up the slope and down the bank in our front, near to Sir John Colborne, crying 'Vive le Roi!' He was a chef d'escadron, and took that opportunity of escaping from the French left wing, that he might shew his loyalty to Louis XVIII. He told Sir John Colborne that the French Imperial Guard were about to advance, and would be led by the Emperor. I think the officer of cuirassiers was sent, under the charge of a serjeant, to the Duke of Wellington.

Soon after this, when it was nearly eight o'clock, the Duke rode across our front from the left of the line quite alone, and spoke to Sir John Colborne, as they were both sitting on their horses observing the enemy. The Duke's dress consisted of a blue surtout coat, white kerseymere pantaloons, and Hessian boots. He wore a sword with a waist-belt, but no sash, and had a small extended telescope in his right hand. He rode a chestnut horse [Copenhagen]. He rode across our front within fifteen paces of our centre, so that I had a complete view of him. . . .

We heard what the officer of cuirassiers had said to Sir John

Colborne about the attack of the Imperial Guard, and not long after we heard them advancing with continued shouts of '*Vive l'Empereur*' away to our left front. The drummers were beating the '*pas de charge*', which sounded, as well as I recollect, very much like this, 'the rum dum, the rum dum, the rummadum dummadum, dum, dum', then '*Vive l'Empereur.*' This was repeated again and again.

Colonel Octave Levasseur remembered how one of the Emperor's aides-de-camp, General Dejean,[1] *came up to Marshal Ney.*

'*Monsieur le Maréchal,*' he said. '*Vive l'Empereur! Voilà Grouchy!*' The Marshal at once ordered me to go right along the line and announce that Grouchy had arrived. I set off at a gallop and, with my hat raised on the point of my sabre, rode down the line, shouting: '*Vive l'Empereur! Soldats, voilà Grouchy!*' The sudden shout was taken up by a thousand voices. The exaltation of the troops reached fever pitch and they all shouted: '*En avant! En avant! Vive l'Empereur!*' I had scarcely reached the far end of our line when I heard cannon fire behind us. Enthusiasm gave way to a profound silence, to amazement, to anxiety. The plain was covered with our vehicles and with the multitude of non-combattants who always follow the army. The cannonade went on and drew closer. Officers and soldiers got mixed up with the non-combattants.

In utter consternation I rode up to the Marshal, who forbade me to go and find out the cause of this panic. I went next to General ——, who said to me: '*Voyez! Ce sont les Prussiens!*' I turned back to look for Marshal Ney, but could not find him.

Our army was by this time nothing better than a disorganised mass, in which every regiment was involved. At this critical moment there was no longer any command. Everyone was speechless in the face of a danger which no one could define. Up came Drouot and called out: '*Formez le carré!*' I then saw the Emperor go past me, followed by his staff. When he came opposite his Guard, he said: '*Qu'on me suive!*' and he moved off in front along the road which was swept by a hundred enemy guns.

One hundred and fifty bandsmen now marched down at the head of the Guard, playing the triumphant marches of the Car-

[1] Pierre-François-Marie-Auguste, Comte Dejean (1780–1845).

rousel as they went. Soon the road was covered by the Guard marching by platoons in the wake of the Emperor. Bullets and grapeshot left the road strewn with dead and wounded.

Marshal Ney afterwards addressed the following account of his experiences that evening to Joseph Fouché, Duke of Otranto, who had become President of the Provisional Government in Paris:

About seven o'clock in the evening, after the most frightful carnage which I have ever seen, General Labedoyère[1] came to me with a message from the Emperor that Marshal Grouchy had arrived on our right, and attacked the left of the English and Prussians united. This General Officer, in riding along the lines, spread this information among the soldiers, whose courage and devotion remained unshaken, and who gave new proofs of both at that moment, despite their fatigue. Immediately afterwards, what was my astonishment, nay indignation, when I learned that, far from Marshal Grouchy having arrived, as the whole army had been assured, between forty and fifty thousand Prussians had attacked our extreme right and forced it to retire!

Whether the Emperor was misled as to the time at which the Marshal could support him, or whether Grouchy's advance was held up by the enemy's efforts, the fact remains that at the moment when we were told of his arrival, he was only at Wavre on the Dyle, which to us was the same as if he had been a hundred leagues from the battlefield.

A short time afterwards I saw four regiments of the Middle Guard, led by Napoleon, march in. With these men he wished to renew the attack and break through the enemy's centre. He ordered me to lead them forward. Generals, officers and soldiers all displayed the greatest gallantry; but they were too weak to hold out for long against the opposing forces, and the hopes which this attack had momentarily kindled were soon renounced. General Friant[2] was struck by a ball at my side, and my own horse was killed and fell on top of me.

The brave men who return from this terrible battle will, I trust, do me justice by saying that they saw me on foot and sword in

[1] Charles de La Bedoyère (1786–1815) was aide-de-camp to Napoleon. He was shot for having, at Grenoble, welcomed the Emperor on his return from Elba.
[2] Louis, Comte Friant (1758–1829) commanded two regiments of Grenadiers in the Imperial Guard.

hand throughout the evening, and that I was one of the last to quit the scene of carnage, at a time when retreat could no longer be prevented. At the same time the Prussians continued their offensive movements, and our right wing pulled back, while the English in their turn advanced. We still had four squares of the Old Guard to cover our retreat. These brave grenadiers, the élite of the army, yielded ground foot by foot until, overwhelmed by sheer numbers, they were almost annihilated.

Napoleon had become so pressed by the Prussian advance that he determined, too late, to play his final stake: the precious Imperial Guard. Only a short time before this Wellington had ordered Maitland's 1st Brigade of Guards to take ground to its left and form line four deep. One officer of the 1st Foot Guards who found himself with his company in the centre of the line was Captain Harry Weyland Powell, who narrates what happened.

This brought the Brigade precisely on the spot the Emperor had chosen for his attack. There ran along this part of the position a cart road, on one side of which was a ditch and bank, in and under which the Brigade sheltered themselves during the cannonade, which might have lasted three-quarters of an hour. Without the protection of this bank every creature must have perished.

The Emperor probably calculated on this effect, for suddenly the firing ceased, and as the smoke cleared away a most superb sight opened on us. A close Column of Grenadiers (about seventies in front) of la Moyenne Guard, about 6,000 strong, led, as we have since heard, by Marshal Ney, were seen ascending the rise *au pas de charge* shouting '*Vive l'Empereur.*' They continued to advance till within fifty or sixty paces of our front, when the Brigade were ordered to stand up. Whether it was from the sudden and unexpected appearance of a Corps so near them, which must have seemed as starting out of the ground, or the tremendously heavy fire we threw into them, *La Garde*, who had never before failed in an attack, *suddenly* stopped. Those who, from a distance and more on the flank, could see the affair, tell us that the effect of our fire seemed to force the head of the Column bodily back.

In less than a minute above 300 were down. They now wavered, and several of the rear divisions began to draw out as if to deploy, whilst some of the men in their rear beginning to fire over the heads of those in front was so evident a proof of their confusion, that Lord Saltoun . . . holloaed out, '*Now's the time, my boys.*' Immediately the Brigade sprang forward. La Garde turned and gave us little opportunity of trying the steel. We charged down the hill till we had passed the end of the orchard of Hougoumont, when our right flank became exposed to another heavy Column (as we afterwards understood of the Chasseurs of the Garde) who were advancing in support of the former Column. This circumstance, besides that our charge was isolated, obliged the Brigade to retire towards their original position.

Opportunely, Sir F. Adam's Light Brigade had in the meantime come round the knoll between the position and Hougoumont, when we had been ordered to take ground on our left, and were advancing under the hedge and blind line along the northern side of the orchard at Hougoumont. As soon therefore as we had uncovered their front we halted and fronted.

The two Brigades now returned to the charge which the Chasseurs did not wait for, and we continued our forward movement till we got to the bottom of the valley between the positions. Here our Brigade halted to restore its order by calling out the covering Sergeants and forming Companies. As soon as the Column was formed we proceeded towards the *chaussée* [to Charleroi], where we found nearly sixty pieces of Artillery jammed together and deserted. Whilst we were halted in the valley the Light Troops and Cavalry had passed us and gone in pursuit.

Captain Horace Churchill, 1st Foot Guards, has described his experiences as Lord Hill's aide-de-camp when Napoleon's Imperial Guard attacked with cavalry in a column on the left flank and the grenadiers of the Guard on the right.

They advanced most steadily up to our line in one great mass — halted and commenced firing; our troops were literally mowed down; the fire was so great, nothing could stand. Our guns were moved close up to the flank of their column, *foudroyer* with grape into it. Lord Hill moved a column, our *élite*, round the flank. I brought up six squadrons of cavalry, and we made a general charge. The cuirassiers of the Imperial Guard had their ranks much thinned by our artillery, and went about; we with the cavalry pursued them, leaving the French infantry steady on our flank.

Marshal Ney was with their retreating cavalry and I was within 20 paces of him; I could not get six of our cavalry to follow me or we must have taken him; he was alone with about six orderlies. I hollaed out to our rascals, but nothing could get them to face him. Our cavalry then gave way and we were obliged to gallop. The enemy ran down about 20 of his guns and fired *such* a shower of grape! the infantry then opened upon us, and the French cuirassiers came clean into us. I was on my old brown horse; a grape-shot went through his body, and a round shot struck my hat at the same moment; he fell dead. I was a good deal stunned and could not get from under my horse. The French cuirassiers rode over me, but did not wound me. I lay there till they were licked back; they again rode by me; one of their cuirassiers was killed passing me — I seized his immense horse, and with some difficulty got upon him. I rode off, and hardly was I clear of them when a round shot struck my horse on the head and killed him on the spot. An officer of the 13th Dragoons dismounted one of his men and gave me his horse: this was shot in the leg about half an hour after. The enemy was now beat back; Bonaparte had led his own Guards and been beaten. . . .

Never was such devotion witnessed as that of the French cuirassiers. I could not help exclaiming when the *mêlée* was going on. 'By God! those fellows deserve Bonaparte, they fight so nobly for him.' I had rather have fallen that day as a British infantry-man, or as a French cuirassier, than die ten years hence in my bed. I did my best to be killed, but Fortune protected me: I was struck by a ball on the side of my thigh, which did not even bleed me; one also struck me on the back of my shoulder, which I did not know of till after the action was over.

Captain John Kincaid of the 95th Rifles paints the scene as he recalled it years afterwards.

For the two or three succeeding hours there was no variety with us, but one continued blaze of musketry. The smoke hung so thick about, that, although not more than eighty yards asunder, we could only distinguish each other by the flashes of the pieces. . . .

I shall never forget the scene which the field of battle presented about seven in the evening. I felt weary and worn out, less from fatigue than anxiety. Our division, which had stood upwards of five thousand men at the commencement of the battle, had gradually dwindled down into a solitary line of skirmishers. The twenty-seventh Regiment were lying literally dead, in square, a few yards behind us. My horse had received another shot through the leg, and one through the flap of the saddle, which lodged in his body, sending him a step beyond the pension-list. The smoke still hung so thick about us that we could see nothing. I walked a little way to each flank, to endeavour to get a glimpse of what was going on; but nothing met my eye except the mangled remains of men and horses, and I was obliged to return to my post as wise as I went.

I had never yet heard of a battle in which every body was killed; but this seemed likely to be an exception, as all were going by turns. We got excessively impatient under the tame similitude of the latter part of the process, and burned with desire to have a last thrust at our respective *vis-à-vis*; for, however desperate our affairs were, we had still the satisfaction of seeing that theirs were worse. Sir John Lambert continued to stand as our support, at the head of three good old regiments, one dead (the twenty-seventh) and two living ones, and we took the liberty of soliciting him to aid our views; but the Duke's orders on that head were so very particular that the gallant general had no choice.

Presently a cheer, which we knew to be British, commenced far to the right, and made every one prick up his ears; — it was Lord Wellington's long-wished-for orders to advance; it gradually approached, growing louder as it drew near; — we took it up by instinct, charged through the hedge down upon the old knoll, sending our adversaries flying at the point of the bayonet. Lord Wellington galloped up to us at the instant, and our men began to cheer him; but he called out, 'No cheering, my lads, but forward, and complete your victory!'

Sergeant Robertson tells how the battle ended for the 92nd Regiment.

It was now seven o'clock and by this time there was no officer in the regiment but the commanding officer (whose horse had been shot), the adjutant, and a very few sergeants. I had charge of two companies, and was ordered to pay particular attention to any signal or movement I might see in front, for which purpose I was furnished with a spy-glass. In a short time one of our skirmishers came running in, and called to me to look at the French lines, as something extraordinary was going on. On the enemy's right I saw that a cross fire had been commenced, and that troops in the same dress had turned the extremity of their line and were advancing rapidly. I immediately informed the adjutant, who said that perhaps it was a mutiny in the French army, and that we had better form our companies close so as to be ready to march to any point. At this instant an aide-de-camp came galloping down our rear, and calling out, 'The day is our own — the Prussians have arrived.' All eyes were now turned to the right to look for the signal to charge which was to be given by the Duke of Wellington. Nothing could stop our men, and it was only by force that the non-commissioned officers could keep them from dashing into the French lines. No language can express how the British army felt at this time; their joy was truly ecstatic.

By this time the aide-de-camp had returned to the Duke who was standing in the stirrups with his hat elevated above his head. Every eye was fixed upon him, and all were waiting with impatience to make a finish of such a hard day's work. At last he gave three waves with his hat and the loud three cheers that followed the signal were the heartiest that had been given that day. On seeing this, we leapt over the hedge that had been such a protection to us during the engagement and in a few minutes we were among the French lines. Nothing was used now but the bayonet, for, after the volley we gave them, we set off at full speed, and did not take time to load.[1] All was now destruction and confusion. The French at length ran off throwing away knapsacks, firelocks, and every thing that was cumbersome, or that could impede their flight.

Major-General Sir John Ormsby Vandeleur's brigade of cavalry, consisting of the 11th, 12th and 16th Light Dragoons, was now ordered to descend into the plain and pursue the enemy. One officer who rode with the 16th was Captain William Tomkinson, who explains what happened.

We were led into the plain by our general betwixt the road to Charleroi and the Observatory,[2] and had to open out and pass over

---

[1] Captain William Clayton, Royal Regt. of Horse Guards, wrote in 1834: 'When at the close the British Infantry advanced in line to the charge, it very much resembled the curvature of the surf on the shore.' [B.M. Add. MSS. 34, 703.]

[2] The observatory stood about 1,000 yards west of Caillou and the Charleroi road. It reached up some 60 feet, had three platforms, and was a fixed point for a trigonometrical survey.

many killed and wounded. In retiring from the last attack the enemy had made considerable haste to the rear, and not until we were lineable with the Observatory did we receive any fire or perceive any intention of stopping us. They were in complete deroute and confusion. On the top of a small hill they at length opened a couple of guns and fired a few round shot. We continued to advance in a trot, and on coming closer to these guns, they fired once with grape, which fell about fifty yards short of the brigade, and did not the least damage.

The Observatory was situated at the edge of a wood, and as from the line we were moving on we must leave this in our rear, I sent Sergeant-Major Greaves of my troop to see if the enemy had any force in the wood. He returned and caught us, saying they had none, when I rode on before the brigade to an eminence (which we were ascending) to see what force the enemy had in our front. From this point I saw a body of infantry with a squadron of cuirassiers formed in the valley, close to a by-road which ran at right angles to the point we were moving on. The infantry were about 1,000 in column, with about three companies formed behind a hedge, which ran alongside of the road in question. I rode back and told General Vandeleur that the enemy had the force I have named, and that the left of the 16th and right of the 11th would (as they were then advancing) come in contact with it; that the 12th had nothing in their front, and if ordered to proceed on to the front and bring forward their right, they would get in their rear and make a considerable number of prisoners.

He took no notice, except saying, *Where are they?* and in a minute the brigade was on the top of the rising ground, in a gallop the instant they saw the enemy, and proceeded to the charge. The enemy's infantry behind the hedge gave us a volley, and being close at them, and the hedge nothing more than some scattered bushes without a ditch, we made a rush and went into their column with the companies which were stationed in their front, they running away to the square for shelter. We completely succeeded, many of their infantry immediately throwing down their arms and crowding together for safety. Many, too, ran away up the next rising ground.

We were riding in all directions at parties attempting to make their escape, and in many instances had to cut down men who had taken up their arms after having in the first instance laid them down. From the appearance of the enemy lying together for safety, they

M

were some yards in height, calling out, from the injury of one pressing upon another, and from the horses stamping upon them (on their legs). I had ridden after a man who took up his musket and fired at one of our men, and on his running to his comrades, my horse trod on them. (He had only one eye, and trod the heavier from not seeing them.)

. . . After some little delay in seeing they all surrendered, we proceeded in pursuit of the enemy's other scattered troops. It was nearly dark at the time we made the charge, and when we moved from the spot it was quite so. (It was a light night.)

Another account, this time of the charge of Sir Hussey Vivian's brigade that evening, comes from a letter written by Private John Marshall, 10th Hussars.

Our brigade was then formed into three lines, each regiment comprising its own line, which was the 10th, 18th, and a regiment of the German Legion Hussars, my own regiment forming the first line. The General then came in front of the line, and spoke in the following manner:— 'Tenth,' he said, 'you know what you are going to do, and you also know what is expected of you, and I am well assured it will be done; I therefore shall say no more, only wish you success;' and with that he gave orders for us to advance.[1] I am not ashamed to say, that, well knowing what we were going to do, I offered up a prayer to the Almighty, that for the sake of my children and the partner of my bosom he would protect me, and give me strength and courage to overcome all that might oppose me, and with a firm mind I went, leaving all that was dear to me to the mercy of that great Ruler, who has so often in the midst of peril and danger protected me.

After advancing about one hundred yards we struck into a charge, as fast as our horses could go, keeping up a loud and continual cheering, and soon we were amongst the Imperial Guards of France. The 18th Hussars also charging, as soon as we got amongst them; which so galled them, that we slew and overthrew them like so many children, although they rode in armour, and carried lances ten feet long: but so briskly did our lads lay the English steel about them, that they threw off their armour and

---

[1] Vivian wrote: 'To the 18th I said, "Eighteenth, my lads, you will, I know, follow me." On which Sergeant-Major Jeffs, who was near me, answered: "Yes, General; to hell, if you will lead us." '

pikes, and those that could get away flew in all directions. But still we had not done, for there were two great solid squares of infantry, who had hurt us much, whilst we were advancing, with their fire, and still continued to do so, whilst we were forming again: in short they were all around us. We therefore formed as well as we could, and at them we went, in spite of their fixed bayonets. We got into their columns, and, like birds, they fell to the ground. Thus they were thrown into confusion, for it seemed like wild-fire amongst their troops that the Guards were beaten, and, panic-struck, they flew in all directions. But we had done our part, and left those to pursue who had seen the onset.

We took sixteen guns at our charge, and many prisoners: but it was so dark, we could not see any longer, and at length we assem-bled what few men we had got left of the regiment, and the General of Brigade formed us in close columns, so that we might all hear him, and he addressed us in the following manner: 'Now, Tenth,' he said, 'you have not disappointed me; you were just what I thought you were. You was the first regiment that broke their lines, and to you it is that we are indebted for turning the fate of the day; and depend upon it that your Prince shall know it; for nothing but the bravery and good discipline of the regiment could have com-pleted such a work.'

Three days after the battle, when the 10th Hussars, commanded by Lord Robert Manners, bivouacked at Merbes Ste Marie near the Sambre, Captain Thomas Taylor wrote a long letter to his family.

. . . The Duke was in the hottest fire as usual — and a Hanover-ian Regt. giving way, he headed and cheered them back himself. I am happy to say he saw our charge and said 'Well done 10th & 18th'. The Guards too saw us coming down & cheered in high style — it must have been a beautiful sight — but I had not time to look at it, being anxious to restrain the men & keep them in Line. I only remember that the French going over the rising ground above us struck me as the gayest looking Army I ever saw — what with cuirasses, Helmets, furcaps, Lances & Flags and variety of Uniforms. The *hurry skurry* was the funniest thing — as we were coming up, down went a party of Lancers; a party of the 23rd checked them, then came our right squadron on the Lancers, drove them back — then came a body of heavy Dns on our right squadron, then our centre squadron on them, & away they went. Then we soon came on the square which the right squadron charged — and I hear broke completely. I went with mine to the left of the square & Lord Robert was with us — we were among Infantry — Imperial Guard, blue with large fur caps, who were throwing down their arms — & themselves roaring *pardon*, on the knees many of them. On top of the hill a party of Infantry formed & with Cavalry behind them commenced a sharp fire — we checked to form a little, about 35 paces from them — then Lord Robert gave a hurra, and at them we went. They turned directly Horse & foot in most complete flight — Infantry throwing themselves down, Cavalry off their horses.

Soon we came to a deep hollow — on the opposite side a steep knowl — with a square of Infantry very well formed. A party of the 18th dashed down the hollow, up the hill & at the square in most gallant style — but as I foresaw were checked & turned by their fire. Lord R. & I rallied a party to be able to support them if charged in turn — for I decline the honor of charging square unnecessarily, tho' one could not but admire the Gallantry of the thing — then the rest of the Light Cavalry coming up we retired, collecting our men, our business being done. Poor little Chopin [Taylor's horse] who had gone through the deep ground with a strength & activity that surprises me was quite done, & could barely make a walk back, as if he had entered into the spirit of the thing. Thinking [we] might advance again I was going to change but did not on finding that our job was over, tho' even then a shell was thrown & burst near us, by the retiring Guns. It was then moonlight & no bad picture. We met a number of Prisoners in charge of the 11th — at last we formed on the hill & saw the line of retreat of the French by things they set fire to. A Regt. of Prussian Cavalry passed now in pursuit. The moon & field of Battle put me in mind of Miss Holforth,[1] & the men seeking their Regts. calling out 18th, 10th, 2nd Germans &c. of Walter Scott in the Lay of the last Minstrel.[2]

---

[1] Miss Margaret Holford (1778–1852) was a friend of Southey and her writings included *Wallace, or The Flight of Falkirk. A Metrical Romance* (1809), *Poems* (1811) and *Margaret of Anjou*. She married in 1826 Septimus Hodson, Chaplain to the Prince of Wales and Rector of Thrapston.

[2] Taylor was probably thinking of these lines from Canto Fifth:

> And frequent, on the darkening plain,
> Loud hello, whoop, or whistle ran,
> As bands, their stragglers to regain,
> Gave the shrill watchword of their clan.

Genl. [Sir Colquhoun] Grant of the other Hussar Brigade told us he had four Horses shot under him that day. His Brigade suffered much more than ours — as they were very much exposed to cannonade. General Vivian manoeuvred us beautifully. The manner in which he led the Column down always keeping under cover of the Hill, when the ground allowed it, was excellent. The only miracle to me is that we suffered so little, for I believe our Regiment after all has only 10 men & 2 officers killed outright. I mean on the spot; and about 35 men & 6 officers wounded. A good many more horses. We are getting strong again by men coming up, who have had Horses shot &c. To me who saw the ground about, struck perpetually with shot, it does seem very odd, but it was the ground that took off the effect of shot, much from its being deep mud, from the rain — & trampling of Horse & foot, so that often shot did not rise and shells buried & exploded upward, sending up the mud like a fountain. I had mud thrown over me in this way often.

Ensign William Leeke relates that about three quarters of an hour after his battalion had halted at Rossomme, the first column of the Prussians who were to take up the pursuit arrived.

As they marched round the column of the 52nd from Planchenoit into the Charleroi road, they broke into slow time, and their bands played 'God save the King'. A mounted officer, who rode up the bank, and passed along the flank of the column, which was lying down, pulled up and asked me in French 'if that was an English colour'; (I still kept it in my possession, to give some poor tired fellow a little rest before he was placed sentry over it.) On my replying that it was, he let go of his bridle, and taking hold of the colour with both hands, pressed it to his bosom, and patted me on the back, exclaiming, '*Brave Anglais.*'

IN THE HOUR OF VICTORY AND DEFEAT

AT a quarter past nine Blücher and Wellington met and congratulated each other outside La Belle Alliance inn, a symbolic name which the Prussian commander-in-chief would have liked to bestow upon the day's victory. Describing the encounter twenty-five years later, Wellington said: 'We were both on horseback; but he embraced me, exclaiming, *Mein lieber kamerad*, and then *Quelle affaire!* which was pretty much all he knew of French.'[1] Darkness was serving not only to exacerbate the confusion in the French army but also to cause British and Prussian forces inadvertently to clash, with slight loss; several disastrous encounters were narrowly avoided. Wellington halted his troops by La Belle Alliance and Rossomme, and accepted Blücher's offer to undertake the pursuit with his tired but comparatively fresh soldiers 'as long as they had a man and a horse able to stand'.

While Wellington rode back the five miles to his headquarters in Waterloo, after which he chose to name the battle won that day, and while the British and allied regiments bivouacked for the night among the corpses of men and horses, the ardent Prussians under Gneisenau's spurring leadership conducted a relentless nocturnal hunt by moonlight. Napoleon had hoped to rally the fragments of his beaten *Armée du Nord* at Genappe, but after several vain attempts he realised that to restore order was out of the question and to gain some respite by organising resistance to stem the Prussian pursuit was quite impossible, so choked with waggons, guns and panicky troops was the village street and the bridge over the steep-banked Dyle. The Emperor himself took an hour to thread his way through the ghastly confusion, and no sooner had he stepped into his campaign carriage, which had just been re-covered among a host of abandoned vehicles, than Prussian cavalry clattered close and he had to jump out and on to his horse again and hasten south towards Charleroi with a few of his trusted staff and a small escort of lancers. At Charleroi the chaos was no less, but the imperial party extricated itself soon after five, and reached Philippeville four hours later.

As for the Prussians, they pressed the French so hard that they could not rally. Many were cut down or captured in the moonlight. Blücher,

---

[1] Writing on June 8th, 1816, to William Mudford, who was planning a history of the battle, the Duke denied that the scene occurred at La Belle Alliance: 'It happens that the meeting took place after ten at night, at the village of Genappe.'

exhausted and 'trembling in every limb', and Bülow's corps did not go further than Genappe, but Gneisenau and his 4,000, eager to avenge Jena, kept ten times that number of Frenchmen on the run, so that the divisions which had fought so tenaciously all day dissolved into a rabble of fugitives, many throwing away musket and knapsack as they went. Just south of Frasnes even the eager Gneisenau, who later told his wife 'it was the finest night of my life', had to admit that his vanguard was worn out and much reduced in size, so much so that he called off the pursuit. Over two hundred guns and a thousand vehicles fell into allied hands, but not one more flag or eagle, for all the disordered rout.

The butcher's bill indicates the ferocity of the struggle. Whereas the Prussian losses numbered 7,000, British dead and wounded exceeded 15,000 in number. Out of sixty-three British commanding officers (infantry, cavalry, artillery), no less than eleven were killed and twenty-four wounded, several of them mortally. Almost half the 840 infantry officers engaged at Quatre Bras and Waterloo were killed or wounded, and just over one third of those holding commissions in the cavalry. Regiments in which the fighting tore particularly severe gaps were the Royal Scots (thirty-one out of thirty-seven officers), the 27th Foot (sixteen out of nineteen), the 73rd Highlanders (twenty-two out of twenty-six), and the Cameron Highlanders, the last-mentioned losing thirty-two officers, over half the sergeants, and 260 out of 684 rank and file. As for the French, they suffered some 25,000 casualties, and a further 8,000 men were taken prisoner.

Lieutenant-General Jean-Martin, Baron Petit, who, when Napoleon abdicated in 1814, had received his farewell kiss at Fontainebleau, now commanded the 1st Regiment of Grenadiers à pied *in the Guards. He takes up the story after General Cambronne has been wounded and when the army begins to retreat before superior numbers. Petit writes in the third person.*

The Emperor galloped back and placed himself inside the square of the 1st Battalion of the 1st Regiment of Grenadiers. The whole army was in the most appalling disorder. Infantry, cavalry, artillery — everybody was fleeing in all directions. Soon no unit retained any order except the two squares formed by this regiment's two battalions posted to right and left of the main road. On orders from the Emperor, their commander, General Petit, had the *grenadière* sounded to rally those guardsmen who had been caught up in the torrent of fugitives. The enemy was close at our heels, and, fearing that he might penetrate the squares, we were obliged to fire at the men who were being pursued and who threw themselves wildly at the squares. This was one evil we had to incur in order to avoid a greater one.

It was now almost dark. The Emperor himself gave the order for us to leave our positions, which were no longer tenable, being entirely outflanked to left and to right. The two squares withdrew in good order, the 1st Battalion across country, the second along the road. A halt had to be made every few minutes so as to maintain the lines of the squares and to give time for the *tirailleurs* and the fugitives to catch up.

Half a league outside Genappe the two squares found themselves reunited on the main road and they marched along it in column by sections. In this way we picked up all that remained of the other regiments of the Guard. The enemy was following us, but without causing us much worry. Not until panic seized the soldiers of the artillery train, who cut the traces of their horses and overturned the guns and ammunition waggons, using these to barricade and clutter up the road, did the enemy open heavy fire on the left of the column. Little damage was done considering the volume of fire, but it greatly increased the chaos which was already, so to speak, at its height.

In these circumstances it was no longer possible to get what remained of the Guard through the town, but we did succeed in making our way to the left of the road and town.

Colonel Levasseur had become separated from Marshal Ney, to whom he was aide-de-camp.

It was dark. Despairing of finding my Marshal, I rejoined the column which could scarcely move forward and which was not being pursued by the enemy. What was my astonishment, on reaching Genappe, to see this town encumbered with vehicles that it was impossible to walk upright in the streets and the infantry were obliged to crawl under the waggons in order to get through. The cavalry were able to bypass the town. When I got beyond the square I stood across the street, drew my sword and shouted: '*De par l'Empereur, on ne passe pas!*' A hussar officer, in the belief that I had received orders to act in this way, stood beside me and together we barred the route. Then we heard all the officers and soldiers shouting: 'This way, the 25th, the 12th, the 8th! &c.' They were all trying to rally, and we spent the whole night amid shouts of this kind. Several generals and other individuals tried to force their way past, but I said: '*On ne passe pas!*' and they stayed.

Captain Pierre Robinaux of the 2nd Regiment of the Line, which had fought earlier in the day for the Château de Hougoumont, says that he could not see clearly what the rest of the French troops were doing, had received no orders, and was worried by the fact that he could hear the cannonade only at a distance. With another captain he went forward some three hundred yards to reconnoitre.

What did we see? Our troops in full retreat at every point. We at once told the general, who gave the command: 'Columns in retreat!' just as soon as he had ascertained the situation. He warned us to maintain absolute silence and good order. The whole affair did not last long. We were shot at occasionally from the rear, and several frightened soldiers, looking behind them, saw our Polish lancers, mistook them for English cavalry, and shouted: 'We are lost!' The rumour spread down the column and soon we were thrown into complete disorder. Each man thought only of his own safety. It was impossible to rally the scattered troops. The cavalry followed the example of the infantry, and I saw dragoons galloping off and knocking down the wretched foot-soldiers, even riding over their bodies. This happened to me once. Furious at this disorder, and exhausted with running, I realized that we had been hurrying across the plain without being pursued at all, so I kept shouting in a loud voice: 'Halt! We must rally. Nobody is after us.'

Seeing that my efforts were futile, I armed myself with a musket, fixed the bayonet, and faced up to several dragoons, taking aim at them. In a firm tone of voice I shouted to them that no one was following us and that the first man to cross the line would get a bullet through him. Eventually I prevailed upon them to stop and I managed so well that I collected a dozen cavalrymen and about sixty foot-soldiers. I said to them: 'Follow me. I will be responsible for leading you across the Sambre without any trouble.' They took me on, and I did my utmost not to let them down. I set off for a place I knew called Pont-sur-Sambre. We marched all night and on the 19th arrived there at six o'clock in the morning. We crossed the river without difficulty, whereas at Charleroi things were pitiful. The approaches to the town, the streets, and the bridge were jammed with every sort of vehicle. It was a second Leipzig.[1] Once over the river we took up positions on high ground to wait for the remnants of the army; but seeing nothing except scattered groups of soldiers on the plain, I decided to move on with my little column, which was in fairly good order. In this way we marched through the day.

Major M. Lemonnier-Delafosse, aide-de-camp to General Foy, who had been wounded in the shoulder, has left a vivid account of his experiences during that night of defeat and flight.

Picture to yourself 40,000 men on a single road and halted in great masses. No one could follow this route without danger, so the generals who had collected near the hedge at Hougoumont set off across the fields. Only General Foy stayed with his three hundred soldiers who had been gleaned on this field of battle, and he marched off at their head, leaving me as a look-out.

. . . It was pitch dark by this time, and as I could do no good in the post to which he had assigned me, I rejoined the General, who kept his handful of men together as best he could. Just then I heard someone demanding a horse for Marshal Ney, who, dismounted and on foot, had fallen into the mire. Major Schmidt of the Red Lancers obtained one, and the Marshal rode off on it.

We had to withdraw from the battlefield without getting caught up with the fugitives. The General wanted to retreat in proper military fashion. Seeing three fires on the horizon, gleaming like beacons, he asked me where I thought they were. 'The first is at Genappe, the second at the Bois de Bossu, by the farm of Quatre Bras, and the third at Gosselies.'

'Very well, we will march on the second. Let nothing stop us. Lead the column and don't lose the direction mark.' Such were his orders.

After all the bustle and ceaseless noise of a long day's fighting,

[1] On October 19th, the morning after the Battle of Leipzig, Napoleon took leave of the King of Saxony and then escaped through a garden, having failed to force a passage through the confusion of men and guns and baggage that blocked the gates of the town. Some 36,000 men and 100 guns, besides several hundred waggons, had still to be extricated; the men could move only in single file through the motionless mass of carriages and guns. Owing to some artillerymen being seized with panic, the bridge over the Elster was prematurely blown up, thereby cutting off the retreat of thousands of unwounded soldiers and four generals, who were captured.

how impressive the silence of the night seemed! Only our marching feet broke it. All of a sudden there came a shout of '*Qui
vive?*'

'France!'

'Kellermann!'

'Foy!'

'It's you, is it, General?'

We were on a slope leading down to a hamlet. From the front
of the column General Foy summoned me and said: 'Kellermann
knows this area. His cavalry have ridden over it in daylight. We
will follow him.'

'And your orders?'

During this conversation we left the hamlet with Kellermann
and his officers. However, they headed for the first fire, at Genappe,
and this led us to the main road which the General had rightly
wished to avoid. A short gallop confirmed me of the wisdom of
this. I also realized just how disorganised an army in full flight can
be.

Moving straight through woods and across fields, we came to
the back of the Bois de Bossu, and here our battalion halted. 'Go
to Quatre Bras Farm,' said the General, 'and report that I am here.
The Emperor or Soult must be there. Ask for orders, and remember
that I shall be awaiting your return and the fate of these men depends upon how exact you are.'

The farm stood on the far side of the main road, which was still
crammed by the fleeing army. In spite of being on horseback I was
caught up by the flood of men and it took me *a quarter of an hour*
to get through. Eventually I reached the farm and found General
Lobau[1] and his staff in occupation. His 6th Corps must be bivouacked nearby. Everything was quiet. I asked for the chief of staff.
He was asleep! Then I noticed some horses, unsaddled and in
their stables, just as if they were in a garrison, so I called out in
amazement: 'What on earth are you doing here? The whole army
is in flight.'

'Nonsense!' replied an aide-de-camp. 'Our army corps is here,
we have halted, and we intend to support the retreat.'

The poor fellows, thinking themselves secure and now without
a guide, were quite oblivious of the fact that they had the farm to
themselves and that their corps had been swept away by the flood

---

[1] Georges Mouton, Comte de Lobau (1770–1838). Lobau is an island on the
Danube below Vienna; French troops crossed there in 1809.

of refugees. A sudden outburst of firing woke them up, but as they had received no orders from their commander who, like us, could have done with some, I left the farm and, once more struggling to make headway against the tide, I rejoined my General. Tired of waiting for me, he had come hurrying forward with his three hundred men, but the moment the current touched them they were caught up in it and left us on our own, *alone!*

[*Next day, after sleeping in Marchienne for a few hours, Foy and his companions reached Beaumont.*]

We led General Foy to a good looking house and asked the lady there for something with which to make him some soup. 'Alas, gentlemen! This is the tenth general who has come to my house since daybreak. I have nothing left! You must go and hunt around.'

Unable to give the General any refreshment, I persuaded him to remove his coat so that we could examine his wound, which had not been dressed since the previous evening. The bullet, after piercing the thick bullion of his left epaulette, had passed round the shoulder without breaking anything. Though not a surgeon, I managed the dressing, and for this the lady of the house provided some linen.

One of those who became most involved in the débâcle of retreat was Monsieur Fleury de Chaboulon, Secretary to the Emperor and to the Cabinet. When Bülow's corps broke through the French right flank he was at Headquarters in the farm of Le Caillou.

An aide-de-camp came from the Grand Marshal to warn the Duke of Bassano[1] that the Prussians were approaching. As the Duke had received orders from the Emperor to stay put, he was unwilling to leave, and we resigned ourselves to await events. Enemy dragoons soon captured the little wood which screened the farm, and then came at our men with sabres. Our guard repulsed them with fire, but the Prussians returned to the attack in greater strength and obliged us, despite the Duke of Bassano's stoical conduct, to retire very smartly. The imperial carriages, drawn by strong horses, took us rapidly out of reach of the enemy's pursuit,

[1] Hugues-Bernard Maret (1763–1839) had been made Duke of Bassano in 1809. A former diplomat, he had been Minister for Foreign Affairs and was now *Secrétaire d'État.*

but the Duke was not so fortunate and his badly harnessed carriage was fired on several times. In the end he was compelled to escape on foot and take refuge in my vehicle.

The cease-fire and hurried retreat of what remained of the army only served to emphasise the fateful outcome of the battle. We made enquiries for the Emperor here, there and everywhere, but no one could set our anxious minds at rest. Some assured us that he had been taken prisoner, others that he had been killed. Hoping to put an end to the anxieties weighing upon us, I took the horse ridden by the man in charge of our carriages and horses, and set off back towards Mont St Jean, followed by a first groom named Chauvin who had come with Napoleon from Elba. I importuned a host of officers with questions, but all in vain. Then I met a page, young Gudin, who assured me that the Emperor must have left the battlefield. I pushed forward, only to be stopped by two cuirassiers with raised sabres. 'Where are you going?' they asked. 'I am going to find the Emperor.' 'You are lying. You are a royalist and are on your way to join the English!' I do not know how this incident would have ended had not a senior officer of the Guard, a heaven-sent emissary, recognised me and come to my rescue. He declared that the Emperor, whom he had escorted for a long time, must be away in front, so I rode off and found the Duke of Bassano again.

The certainty that the Emperor was safe and sound momentarily allayed our grief, but it soon regained all its force. Only someone not of French blood could have witnessed our appalling catastrophe without weeping. The army itself, having recovered from its first impressions, forgot the dangers still threatening it and dwelt sadly on the future. Its steps were dejected, its expression was one of consternation, and its painful contemplation was unbroken by any word or groan. One would have said that the army was escorting a funeral, was watching the obsequies of its glory and those of the nation.

The capture and pillage of the army's baggage had momentarily halted the enemy's pursuit, but at Quatre Bras he caught up with us and fell upon our vehicles. At the head of the convoy went the treasure, and behind it our carriage. Five other carriages immediately behind us were attacked and sabred, but by a miracle ours managed to escape. . . . The Prussians, in savage pursuit, treated the wretches whom they overtook with unparalleled barbarity. Except for a few imperturbable veterans, most of the soldiers had thrown away their weapons and now found themselves defenceless. They were nonetheless massacred without mercy.

. . . We continued our retreat towards Charleroi. The further we advanced, the more difficult it became. Those who were in front of us blocked the road, either as a means of stopping the enemy or else from motives of treachery, and we had constantly to break down the barricades. During one halt I heard shouts and wailing at the roadside and on going over I found that the noise came from a ditch into which two huge waggonloads of wounded had overturned. These poor fellows, buried higgledy-piggledy under the upturned waggons, were imploring passers-by to help them, but so far their weak voices, drowned by the noise of passing ammunition carts, had gone unheard. We all set to work and managed to drag them from their tomb. Some of them were still breathing, but the majority had been stifled to death. Their joy moved us to tears, but it was short-lived, because we had to leave them.

Still pursued and harassed by the enemy, we reached Charleroi. Here we found such congestion, such disorder, that we had to abandon our carriage and our luggage. The secret portfolio of the Cabinet was taken by the keeper of the portfolio; the other important documents were torn up.[1] We left only some reports and unimportant letters. The Duke of Bassano and I were already making our way forward on foot when I spotted several grooms leading some of the Emperor's horses. I ordered them to be brought to us. Such was the Duke's respect for everything that concerned Napoleon that he hesitated to take advantage of this piece of good fortune, but I was able to overcome his scruples, very luckily for him, as the Prussians had caught up with us, and the sound of firing made it clear that fighting was in progress only a few yards away.

By chance we took the road to Philippeville, and there learned, with a joy we scarcely thought ourselves capable of feeling any longer, that the Emperor was in the town. We hurried to him. When he saw me he graciously held out his hand. I covered it with my tears. The Emperor himself was unable to contain his emotion, and a large tear betrayed the struggle going on inside him.

---

[1] In a letter dated June 25th, the Duc de Bassano wrote: 'The papers were not allowed to be burnt in my carriage, as it was caught among the artillery trains, but they were all torn up one after the other and thrown in the mud in such a way that the enemy would not have been able even to pick up the bits.'

On June 19th the Emperor wrote to his brother, King Joseph, in Paris:

All is not lost. I suppose that, when I reassemble my forces, I shall have 150,000 men. The *fédérés* and National Guards (such of them as are fit to fight) will provide 100,000 men, and the regimental depots a further 50,000. Thus I shall have 300,000 soldiers ready immediately to bring against the enemy. I shall use carriage-horses to drag the guns; raise 100,000 men by conscription; arm them with muskets taken from Royalists and from National Guards unfit for service; organize a mass levy in Dauphiné, the district of Lyons, Burgundy, Lorraine, Champagne; and overwhelm the enemy. But people must help me, not deafen me with advice. I am just leaving for Laon. I am sure to find someone there. I have heard nothing of Grouchy. If he has not been captured, as I rather fear, that will give me 50,000 men within three days — plenty to keep the enemy occupied, and to allow time for Paris and France to do their duty. The Austrians are slow marchers; the Prussians fear the peasantry and dare not advance too far. There is still time to retrieve the situation.

A Prussian lieutenant named Julius, having been captured by the French, spent the night in a village east of Beaumont as a prisoner of war, and next morning was caught up in the throng of fugitives from the battlefield.

The things I witnessed exceeded anything I had expected, and were beyond belief. Had I not actually seen it all, I should have considered it impossible for a disciplined army — an army such as the French was — to melt away to such an extent. Not only the main road, as far as one could see in either direction, but also every side road and footpath was covered with soldiers of every rank, of every arm of the service, in the most complete and utter confusion. Generals, officers, wounded men — and these included some who had just had limbs amputated: everybody walked or rode in disorder. The entire army had disintegrated. There was no longer anyone to give orders, or anyone to obey. Each man appeared bent on nothing but saving his own skin. Like a turbulent forest stream this chaotic mass surged around the waggon in which I was sitting with several companions in misfortune. Jostled by the crowd, hampered by the bottomless lane, this waggon could hardly be dragged forward. Moreover, all round us rang out wild threats uttered by those who went past — threats of 'Overturn it!' 'Why should we drag prisoners any further?' 'Massacre them!' 'Cut them down!'

The few *gendarmes* beside us tried very hard to protect us, but how long would their efforts prevail? We really expected to be murdered at any moment. Very occasionally someone would shout to us: '*Sauvez-vous!* We are lost! Thank God we shall have peace at long last! We shall be going home!' Several times the cry came up from the rear: 'He's coming! The enemy's coming! *Sauve qui peut!*' and then everyone ran in desperate haste. Some threw down their weapons, others their knapsacks, and they took refuge in the corn or behind hedges, until the reassuring shout of: 'No, no, it's all right! They're our own men!' calmed down the panic.

A single cavalry regiment could have taken many thousands of prisoners here, because there was no question of offering resistance or of sticking together. Along this road I saw no guns at all, though near Beaumont a solitary cannon lay abandoned. Even in Beaumont there were no longer any regular authorities, as they had all fled.

[Julius escaped and soon found his regiment.]

Assistant Commissary Alexander Dallas, who had served in the Peninsula and later took Holy Orders, describes what he saw in Waterloo that evening.

As I was approaching the village of Waterloo, I perceived, to my great sorrow, my own kind General Alten,[1] supported on each side by an officer, on a horse led by a sergeant. As I drew my horse's rein, the General perceived me, and beckoned to me to come near, while he halted to receive me; he had been wounded in two places, and was suffering much at the time. I never shall forget his words. 'Mr. Dallas, my brave fellows are famished for thirst and support, where are the spirits you promised to send them?' I could have wept as I answered, telling him of the miscarriage of my arrangements. 'Well, well,' he said, 'make haste to give them help; I know you will do what you can.' I promised earnestly to do this, and set spurs to my horse.

[1] Lieut.-General Charles Count Alten commanded the Third Division.

What could I do? I greatly feared that my young officer had run away in panic, which indeed turned out to be the case. As I rode through Waterloo, I saw a storekeeper sitting by the side of the road, with a loaded cart, on which there was what I recognised to be a Commissariat barrel of rum. I rode up to him and asked to what officer he belonged, and where he was, and what he was waiting there for. He answered my questions, and told me that a Commissariat clerk had left him there, and desired him to remain till he came again. 'How long had he waited?' 'Full five hours.' I had no doubt that his employer had partaken of the panic, and ran away; and though I had nothing to do with the division to which he belonged, I thought it my duty to take possession of this barrel; and so I desired the storekeeper to come with me, and I would bear him harmless. As the progress of this horse and cart was slow, I happened to see a Corporal of one of the regiments of our division, who was going to the front, into whose charge I gave the storekeeper and the load, and desired him to bring it safely to the division, while I cantered on.

The road to Nivelles diverges to the right at Mont St Jean, and at that time, all along the right of that road was occupied by a thick wood of fir-trees. In this a part of our reserve had been stationed, which the French, having discovered, they made it the mark for a field battery, and were constantly firing cannon shot into it. Our reserve had been removed, which the enemy did not know; and at the time I came to Mont St Jean, cannon shot were constantly passing over the road, and some falling short, tore up the road itself. . . .

. . . One of these difficulties was that painful thirst and need of support of which the General spoke; and while I was looking on at the charges on the squares, I saw my cart of spirits coming down the rising ground. It had hardly turned the crest of the hill, when a stray shot struck the poor storekeeper, and wounded him, though not seriously. The Corporal brought the cart down to the rear of the square, and I told an officer that I had brought him this by a special order from the General. The barrel was rolled into the centre amidst a shout from the men, who opened rank to admit it, and I left it in charge of the officer, requesting him to get at the contents and distribute the spirits. A Sergeant took the cart back to the poor storekeeper, and laid him on it, and took him to the rear.

It was not long after this that the final charge took place and the
N

Prussians appeared on the left. In galloping upon the hard road, under the cannon shot, my horse had cast a hind shoe, which was a very serious loss to me at that time; but this became more serious when, by the cranking of one of his fore shoes, I felt that he was likely to lose a second, and presently as I was returning to Mont St Jean, I lost that shoe also; so that I was mounted on a wearied horse, after a hard day's work, with two tender feet, to carry me over hard ground. The rain now began to set in with very determined downfall, which was a merciful blessing to the wounded on the field.

I had the happiness of seeing the Duke of Wellington and his staff quietly riding into Waterloo; and it has always been a feeling of rejoicing to me that I was able to salute him on the evening of his great victory.

Dr. John Hume, who was Deputy-Inspector of the Medical Department and surgeon to Wellington, has left an account of his visit to the Duke early on the morrow of the battle.

I came back from the field of Waterloo with Sir Alexander Gordon, whose leg I was obliged to amputate on the field late in the evening. He died rather unexpectedly in my arms about half-past three in the morning of the 19th. I was hesitating about disturbing the Duke, when Sir Charles Broke-Vere[1] came. He wished to take his orders about the movement of the troops. I went upstairs and tapped gently at the door, when he told me to come in. He had as usual taken off his clothes, but had not washed himself. As I entered, he sat up in bed, his face covered with the dust and sweat of the previous day, and extended his hand to me, which I took and held in mine, whilst I told him of Gordon's death, and of such of the casualties as had come to my knowledge. He was much affected. I felt the tears dropping fast upon my hand, and looking towards him, saw them chasing one another in furrows over his dusty cheeks. He brushed them suddenly away with his left hand, and said to me in a voice tremulous with emotion, 'Well, thank God, I don't know what it is to lose a battle; but certainly nothing can be more painful than to gain one with the loss of so many of one's friends.'

[1] Lieut.-Colonel Sir Charles Broke was an Assistant Quartermaster-General. He took the additional surname of Vere in 1822.

On the 19th Wellington found time to write a short letter to his brother William Wellesley-Pole:

You'll see the account of our Desperate Battle and victory over Boney!!

It was the most desperate business I ever was in; I never took so much trouble about any Battle; & never was so near being beat.

Our loss is immense particularly in that best of all instruments British Infantry. I never saw the Infantry behave so well.

At about eleven o'clock on the 19th Thomas Creevey went out into the streets of Brussels and heard a report that the Duke of Wellington had arrived in the capital.

I went from curiosity to see whether there was any appearance of him or any of his staff at his residence[1] in the Park. As I approached, I saw people collected in the street about the house; and when I got amongst them, the first thing I saw was the Duke upstairs alone at his window. Upon his recognising me, he immediately beckoned to me with his finger to come up.

I met Lord Arthur Hill[2] in the ante-room below, who, after shaking hands and congratulation, told me I could not go up to the Duke, as he was then occupied in writing his dispatch; but as I had been invited, I of course proceeded. The first thing I did, of course, was to put out my hand and congratulate him upon his victory. He made a variety of observations in his short, natural, blunt way, but with the greatest gravity all the time, and without the least approach to anything like triumph or joy. — 'It has been a damned serious business,' he said. 'Blücher and I have lost 30,000 men. It has been a damned nice thing — the nearest run thing you ever saw in your life. Blücher lost 14,000 on Friday night, and got so damnably licked I could not find him on Saturday morning; so I was obliged to fall back to keep up my communications with him.' — Then, as he walked about, he praised greatly those Guards who kept the farm (meaning Hugomont) against the repeated attacks of the French; and then he praised all our troops, uttering repeated expressions of astonishment at our men's courage. He repeated so often its being *so nice a thing — so nearly run a thing,*

[1] Now Number 54, Rue Royale.
[2] Captain Hill was an extra aide-de-camp to Wellington.

that I asked him if the French had fought better than he had ever seen them do before. — 'No,' he said, 'they have always fought the same since I first saw them at Vimeiro.'[1] Then he said: 'By God! I don't think it would have done if I had not been there.'

Immediately after the battle Prince Blücher wrote to his wife:

The enemy's superiority of numbers obliged me to give way on the 17th; but on the 18th, in conjunction with my friend Wellington, I put an end at once to Buonaparte's dancing. His army is completely routed, and the whole of his artillery, baggage, caissons, and equipages are in my hands; the insignia of all the various orders he had worn are just brought me, having been found in his carriage, in a casket. I had two horses killed under me yesterday. It will soon be over with Buonaparte.

And in another letter, dated from Gosselies on June 25th, he had this to say:

I have recovered from my fall, but I have again had a horse wounded. I believe now that we shall have no considerable battles in the near future, perhaps not at all. The victory is the most complete that ever was gained. Napoleon escaped in the night, without either hat or sword. I send both sword and hat to-day to the King [of Prussia]. His most magnificently embroidered state mantle and his carriage are in my hands, as also his perspective glass, with which he observed us during the battle. His jewels and all his valuables are the booty of our troops. Of his equipage he has nothing left.

Major Harry Smith of the 95th, who had sent his Spanish wife Juana back to Brussels for safety, rode across the battlefield early on the 19th.

At daylight I was on horseback, with a heart of gratitude as became me, and anxious to let my wife know I was all right. I took a party of each Regiment of my Division with me, and went back

---

[1] The battle of Vimeiro, north of Lisbon, was fought on August 21st, 1808.

to the field; for I was now established as Assistant Quartermaster-General.

I had been over many a field of battle, but with the exception of one spot at New Orleans,[1] and the breach of Badajos,[2] I had never seen anything to be compared with what I saw. At Waterloo the *whole* field from right to left was a mass of dead bodies. In one spot, to the right of La Haye Sainte, the French Cuirassiers were literally piled on each other; many soldiers not wounded lying under their horses; others, fearfully wounded, occasionally with their horses struggling upon their wounded bodies. The sight was sickening, and I had no means or power to assist them. Imperative duty compelled me to the field of my comrades, where I had plenty to do to assist many who had been left out all night; some had been believed to be dead, but the spark of life had returned. All over the field you saw officers, and as many soldiers as were permitted to leave the ranks, leaning and weeping over some dead or dying brother or comrade. The battle was fought on a Sunday, the 18th June, and I repeated to myself a verse from the Psalms of that day — 91st Psalm, 7th verse: 'A thousand shall fall beside thee, and ten thousand at thy right hand, but it shall not come nigh thee.' I blessed Almighty God our Duke was spared, and galloped to my General [Sir John Lambert], whom I found with some breakfast awaiting my arrival.

[1] On January 8th, 1815, a British force was defeated by the Americans.
[2] In Spain, April 6th, 1812.

HOW THE NEWS REACHED BELGIUM,
FRANCE AND BRITAIN

In Antwerp Miss Charlotte Waldie learnt from five wounded and wildly excited Highland soldiers that a courier had just brought news of a complete Allied victory.

To the last hour of my life, never shall I forget the sensations of that moment. Scarcely daring to credit the extent of this wonderful, this transporting news, I did, however, believe that the English had gained the victory.

. . . In the mean time the Highlanders, regardless of their wounds, their fatigues, their dangers, and their sufferings, kept throwing up their Highland bonnets into the air, and continually vociferating, — 'Boney's beat! Boney's beat! hurrah! hurrah! Boney's beat!' Their tumultuous joy attracted round them a number of old Flemish women, who were extremely curious to know the cause of this uproar, and kept gabbling to the soldiers in their own tongue. One of them, more eager than the rest, seized one of the men by his coat pulling at it, and making the most ludicrous gestures imaginable to induce him to attend to her; while the Highlander, quite forgetting in his transport that the old woman did not understand Scotch, kept vociferating that 'Boney was beat, and rinning away ta his ain country as fast as he could gang.' At any other time, the old Flemish woman, holding the soldier fast, shrugging up her shoulders, and making these absurd grimaces, and the Highlander roaring to her in broad Scotch would have presented a most laughable scene — 'Hout, ye auld gowk,' cried the good-humoured soldier, 'dinna ye ken that Boney's beat —what, are ye deef? — dare say the wife — I say Boney's beat, woman!'

A boy named Labretonnière, who was studying mathematics at the Lycée Louis-le-Grand, shared a room with his friend Hippolyte Lemercier in the Hôtel d'Anjou, Rue Serpente, near where the

Boulevard St Michel crosses the Boulevard St Germain. Every morning they and other students used to go and read the newspapers and drink in the nearby Café des Pyrénées.

Confidence in French arms stood very high; it seemed to us that the superb army which Paris had just seen march out, so full of ardour, must be invincible. Thus it was with less surprise than joy that we heard the news of the first success gained over the Allies, outside the walls of Charleroi on June 15th. At last the fight was on!

Very early one Sunday morning, while I was still dozing, I thought I heard several loud explosions. I woke up and listened carefully. 'Hippolyte!' I shouted excitedly to my friend who was asleep near me. 'Do you hear it?' 'What?' he said, waking up.

'The gun is firing from the Invalides. It must be a great victory!' We got up at once and ran off to make enquiries. The gun was certainly celebrating the victory the Emperor had gained over the Prussians at Ligny on June 16th. Wild with joy we went to the Café des Pyrénées to read the bulletin. There every eye shone with pride. The Invalides gun had stirred in our youthful hearts memories of the triumphs which had rocked our childhood. We were intoxicated with pride. And it was the 18th! and the Waterloo cannon was booming at that very instant!

To lessen the effect of this victory, the Royalists spread the most exaggerated rumours. I recall the enthusiasm with which one student named Rousseau from Grenoble came to tell me that Wellington had been captured, Blücher killed, etc., etc. Eventually a short bulletin appeared in the *Moniteur*,[1] announcing very briefly the battle of Ligny.

However, two days had elapsed, and in this interval no further news of our Flanders army had been published. It was said in undertones that we had suffered a defeat, but this seemed to us an impossibility. Eventually, on June 21st, as I was going down into the courtyard of the Hôtel d'Anjou, I saw nearly all the students who lived there talking heatedly and in a state of great excitement. 'Have you heard the news?' they asked me. 'We are assured that the army has been destroyed and that the Emperor arrived in Paris this morning.'

In such circumstances we always repaired to the café to obtain the latest news. There you could read consternation on every face.

[1] *Le Moniteur Universel*, founded in 1789, was the official newspaper of the French Government.

However, a few people were trying to raise the downcast morale of the others. They pointed out that this was perhaps no more than a Royalist trick and that the situation could not possibly be so desperate that the Emperor had thus abandoned his army. No doubt they forgot Egypt, Moscow and Leipzig.

In order to ascertain more quickly what really to believe, I went and stood in front of the Elysée, which Napoleon had chosen as his summer residence. There I saw movement which dispelled any doubts I might have had as to whether the Master had arrived. The palace courtyard was full of horses covered in sweat and dust; aides-de-camp kept on coming in, and looked to be utterly worn out. Several cavalry soldiers of the Imperial Guard were sitting gloomily on a bench by the gate, while the tethered horses waited in the yard. One of the horsemen had his face bandaged with a black scarf. The whole scene betokened shame and grief.

General Paul Thiébault, a veteran of Austerlitz and Vimeiro and a former governor first of Salamanca and then of Hamburg, tells in his memoirs of June in Paris.

My division was to be collected and encamped near Montrouge, where my headquarters would be established, together with those of the Count of Valence. . . . As the troops were not to begin arriving before the 20th, I had continued to sleep at my own house [Rue Caumartin], merely going to Montrouge two or three times with the Count to make sure that everything required by the troops would be ready. On the morning of the 20th I was making arrangements to go and instal myself there, when I heard someone striding through my dining-room and drawing-room, the doors of which were open, and I beheld Captain Viennet coming to the threshold of my bedroom; with a distraught expression on his face and in a highly melodramatic manner he halted at the sight of me, threw up his arms, and cried in a voice of terror, 'All is lost!' walking about the while like a man who has lost his reason. . . . It was thus that I heard of the disaster at Waterloo and the return of Napoleon to Paris.

. . . In moments of misfortune it is always what we dread most that seems most probable, and, in spite of myself, my anxiety turned upon the line which the Chamber of Deputies would take. I went, therefore, to the lobby of the House. . . . Everything was in a state of tumult and buzz, men going in and out, disappearing and reappearing, talking to people of all kinds, who, like the deputies themselves, looked as if they had been bitten by tarantulas. At that moment all disunion, any change of authority, might be fatal. . . . And yet when I left the Chamber I could no longer doubt that this was the melancholy spectacle which the majority meant to give us. From the Chamber I went to the Ministry of War to find out what was to become of the first corps of reserve. I learnt that the troops which were to compose it were receiving fresh orders, that our appointments were regarded as null and void, and that our part was over before it had begun. I hastened to inform the Count of Valence of this.

Next morning at nine o'clock I was at the Elysée. The thought that the foreigner was advancing on the heels of our soldiers to defile France a second time with his presence kindled in me a sort of patriotic frenzy, and took me back almost involuntarily towards the man in whom, to my eyes, the sole hope of safety was embodied. . . . On entering the palace, I was struck by the solitude which prevailed. The gallery was deserted; not more than a dozen or fifteen people were in the room to which it led. I had scarcely entered when a door opened, just near where I stood. Napoleon appeared.

I took two steps towards him and, bowing more deeply than usual, I said, 'Allow me, sir, to lay at your feet the expression of a devotion no less profound than respectful.' 'It is France of which we must think at this moment,' he replied. 'More than ever,' I rejoined, 'it is in your person that one must show pity for her.' He looked hard at me and must have seen my emotion, for he turned his eyes away, and passed on to someone else. I withdrew, and these were the last words I ever exchanged with that extraordinary man.

As soon as Comte Lavallette heard that the Emperor had arrived in Paris, he hurried to the Elysée to see him.

He sent for me to his study, and directly he caught sight of me he came to meet me, laughing like an epileptic, a terrifying laugh. 'Oh, my God!' he said, looking up at the sky, and then he walked two or three times round the room. This spasm of feeling lasted a very short time. Then he recovered his self-possession and asked me what was happening at the Chamber of Deputies. I did not feel it my duty to conceal from him that exasperation was at its height, and that the majority seemed determined to demand his abdication, or to proclaim it if he did not send it in. 'What!' he exclaimed. 'And if they take no action, the enemy will be at the gates within a week. Alas!' he added, 'I have accustomed them to such great victories; they cannot endure one day of misfortune! What is to become of this poor France? I have done what I could for her.' And he sighed deeply.

In December 1831 Mr Julian Young, son of the famous actor Charles Mayne Young, took up residence as sub-chaplain at Hampton Court Palace and called on Mrs Edmund Boehm, whose husband, a very wealthy Russian merchant, had left her a widow. She told Young about the night when the news of Waterloo brought to a sudden end her assembly at No. 16, St James's Square, now the East India and Sports Club.

That dreadful night! Mr. Boehm had spared no cost to render it the most brilliant party of the season; but all to no purpose. Never did a party, promising so much, terminate so disastrously! All our trouble, anxiety, and expense were utterly thrown away in consequence of — what shall I say? Well, I must say it — the unseasonable declaration of the Waterloo victory! Of course, one was very glad to think one had beaten those horrid French, and all that sort of thing; but still, I always shall think it would have been far better if Henry Percy had waited quietly till the morning, instead of bursting in upon us, as he did, in such indecent haste; and even if he had told the Prince alone, it would have been better; for I have no doubt his Royal Highness would have shown consideration enough for my feelings not to have published the news till the next morning.

. . . After dinner was over, and the ladies had gone upstairs, and the gentlemen had joined them, the ball guests began to arrive. They came with unusual punctuality, out of deference to the Regent's presence. After a proper interval, I walked up to the Prince, and asked if it was his Royal Highness's pleasure that the ball should open. The first quadrille was in the act of forming, and the Prince was walking up to the dais on which his seat was placed, when I saw every one without the slightest sense of decorum rushing to the windows, which had been left wide open because of the excessive sultriness of the weather. The music ceased and the dance was stopped; for we heard nothing but the vociferous shouts of an enormous mob, who had just entered the Square, and were running by the side of a post-chaise and four, out of whose windows were hanging three nasty French eagles. In a second the door of the carriage was flung open, and, without waiting for the steps to be let down, out sprang Henry Percy[1]— such a dusty figure! — with a flag in each hand, pushing aside every one who happened to be in his way, darting up stairs, into the ball-room, stepping hastily up to the Regent, dropping on one knee, laying the flags at his feet, and pronouncing the words 'Victory, Sir! Victory!' The Prince Regent, greatly overcome, went into an adjoining room to read the despatches; after a while he returned, said a few sad words to us, sent for his carriage, and left the house. The royal brothers soon followed suit; and in less than twenty minutes there was not a soul left in the ballroom but poor dear Mr Boehm and myself. Such a scene of excitement, anxiety, and confusion never was witnessed before or since, I do believe! Even the band had gone, not only without uttering a word of apology, but even without taking a mouthful to eat. The splendid supper which had been provided for our guests stood in the dining-room untouched. Ladies of the highest rank, who had not ordered their carriages till four o'clock a.m., rushed away, like maniacs, in their muslins and satin shoes, across the Square; some accompanied by gentlemen, others without escort of any kind; all impatient to learn the fate of those dear to them; many jumping into the first stray hackney-coaches they fell in with, and hurrying on to the Foreign Office or Horse Guards, eager to get a sight of the List of Killed and Wounded.

Mrs Melesina Trench wrote to her husband Richard on June 23rd from London:

We are all in triumph and tears of a dear-bought victory. The Prince was at dinner at Mrs. Boehm's when the news was brought to him. Ministers and all wept in triumph among the bottles and glasses. The Regent fell into a sort of womanish hysteric. Water

[1] Major Percy had been sent home with the Duke of Wellington's dispatch, which he carried in a purple handkerchief given to him by a partner at the Duchess of Richmond's ball.

was flung in his face. No, that would never do. Wine was tried
with better success, and he drowned his feelings in an ocean of
claret. They seem to have been a little disturbed in their natural
course, for he called Jekyll, and said, 'Lady Gertrude Sloan's
brother is killed.[1] Take my carriage and tell her so.' Jekyll ex-
postulated that Lady Gertrude was gone to bed — just ready to be
confined, and the surprise might be fatal, if the news was announced
in that way at that hour. The Regent persisted, and at last said,
'Well, go to Lord Carlisle's; for some of them *must* know it', which
Jekyll also resisted.

An advocate named James Simpson recorded how the news of Water-
loo reached Edinburgh, preceded by tidings that Wellington had
been obliged to retreat from Quatre Bras. The first news met him
as he was entering the outer hall of the Courts of Law.

The unwonted words were passing from mouth to mouth —
'Wellington is defeated! He has retreated to a place called Waterloo! The game is up! The hero of a hundred fights quails before
the eagles of Napoleon! The Prussian army is annihilated!'
    . . . 'No! No!' said one more sanguine reasoner of the long
robe, 'we shall have news of a victory yet; and, as it must be near
at hand, one way or the other, I should be more delighted than
surprised if the castle guns should wake us to-morrow morning.'
Another barrister, quite as patriotic, but less sanguine, would
cheerfully pay a guinea for every gun fired for a victory, to any
one who would take very easy odds. The bet was taken, the taker
patriotically wishing to win, the offerer still more patriotically
wishing to lose.
    The business of the morning had scarcely proceeded two hours
when a gentleman rushed into the great hall, and almost breathless
shouted 'Victory!' He was mobbed. 'How had the news come?'
'By express from the Lord Provost of Edinburgh, then in London.
The French completely routed, at *the* place called Waterloo, by
one grand bayonet charge of the whole British army!'
    . . . The bearer of the glad tidings was soon in the Court where
the judges were sitting; the cheers of the Outer Hall were suspended

---

[1] Lady Gertrude, third daughter of the 5th Earl of Carlisle, had married in
June, 1806. One of her brothers, Frederick Howard, a major in the 10th Hussars,
was killed at Waterloo.

only to be renewed in the Inner. Further law proceedings were out of the question; adjournment was ruled; and judges, advocates, agents, and officers were speedily in the streets, already crowded by their excited and exulting townsmen. Nobody could stay at home. The schools were let loose. Business was suspended, and a holiday voted by acclamation. Everybody shook hands with everybody; and as the Lord Provost's brief express, got by heart by the whole population, could not be made longer or more particular than it was, the most restless were perforce obliged to wait, with what patience they might, for the dawn of the next day. The sun of that morning saw no 'sluggard slumbering 'neath his beams.' The streets were crowded before the post arrived. The mail-coach was descried approaching, adorned with laurels and flags, the guard waving his hat; and soon it dashed into the town amid cheers that made the welkin ring.

The accounts were now official. All was confirmed; and, as early as seven o'clock, the Castle flag rose, and nineteen twenty-four pounders sounded in the ears and filled the eyes — for the effect was overpowering — of the excited throng. Need we say that the *nineteen guineas* were joyfully paid by the loser? or need we add, that the winner handed them over to the fund, speedily commenced, for the wounded, and the widows and families of the slain?

Newspapers, with the despatches, including the list of the casualties, so far as known, were snatched from the post-office. They were common property, and the holder of each, whether he willed it or no, was elevated on the nearest vacant steps to read out the accounts, *pro bono publico*; and many who had relatives in the battle trembled as they listened to the names of the killed and wounded; and a fearful catalogue it was.

Mrs Harriet Ward, the daughter of Colonel Frank Tidy who commanded the 14th Foot at Waterloo, relates how news of the battle reached her family in England.

My mother anxiously awaited news from the Continent. It came at last, — and in this way; for she, having little intercourse with anyone beyond her children, had scarcely any knowledge of what was passing in the world abroad. My brother and I, standing at the front gate of the cottage garden, were one morning attracted by the sound of music, and the gaudy appearance of the coaches coming down the road, streaming with gilded flags that bore the words —

WELLINGTON!   VICTORY!   WATERLOO!

These words, in printed capitals, caught our eyes. We repeated them with the passing crowd, and then rushed in to my mother.

'There has been a battle,' we said; 'they have been fighting the French, and *we* have beaten them!'

My mother started up, and without bonnet or shawl was proceeding to the post-town, about two miles from where we were residing, when her maid followed her through the gate with these necessary articles. She put them on mechanically, and hastened on her road. She has often said, she knew not how she reached the post-office; but she got there safely, and received two letters, — one from my father, containing but few words. They had gained the victory; he was safe, but his favourite mare had been shot under him. The other was from the Colonel of the regiment, congratulating her on the laurels her husband and his corps had won.

I have been told by a friend of my mother's, who went to visit her on the morning she received that memorable letter, that she was struck by the group collected in the porch of the cottage as she entered it. On a low hall-chair sat my mother, with her little ones gathered round her. My father's letter was in her hand, and she was reading it aloud. A faithful servant, with one of the children in her arms, stood beside her; while we, silent and wondering, gazed and listened earnestly. The golden sun streamed up the garden-walk, and shed its light upon our little group: bees murmured in the jasmined porch, and the perfume of June flowers came floating through the open door.

Letters of congratulation poured in upon the Duke of Wellington. Of these none gushed more fulsomely than the Prince Regent's, written at Carlton House on June 22nd.

I lose not a moment in communicating to you the fulness of my joy and admiration at the unparalleled triumph of your last and greatest achievement. Greatest, my dear Lord, not only in military glory, but in political importance; and not only in this proof of what all believed, that even the consummate skill of the Corsican could not withstand the superior genius of our own hero, but in the now nearly realised expectation, resulting from this victory, that England, under the auspices of her transcendent General, is again destined to rescue the world from tyranny and oppression.

Receive the fullest tribute of my gratitude, as the representative of the Sovereign of this favoured land, whose happiness has no alloy but in the grief we must feel for the loss of the brave who have fallen.

I have now, my dearest Lord, only to add my thanks to the Almighty for having, in His mercy, preserved your life in this most dreadful and sanguinary conflict; and my prayers for His constant protection of your person, and His fullest blessings in the glorious exertions which may yet remain for you to make in the final deliverance of Europe.

I remain, my dear Lord, your most sincere friend,

George, P.R.

CARE OF THE WOUNDED

Already on June 17th Baron Vanderlinden d'Hooghvorst, Mayor of
Brussels, had published the following announcement:

The Mayor of the City of Brussels and Chamberlain to His
Majesty the King of the Netherlands warns the public that the
pressing circumstances in which we find ourselves makes it imperative that people should come to the aid of the army. Accordingly, he invites his fellow citizens to deposit at the Hôtel de Ville
the largest possible amount of bedding, in particular mattresses or
palliasses, bolsters, bed sheets and blankets.

The Mayor of Brussels is confident that those who are well-to-do
will respond to the present appeal, and in this he relies upon their
patriotism and their zeal. They will no doubt come forward to
help the brave men who have just shed their blood in the finest and
most righteous of causes. Though he much regrets doing so, the
Mayor of Brussels would add this warning to well-to-do people:
he will feel himself obliged to billet wounded or sick soldiers on
them if they do not respond to his appeal.

[Later on the same day he made a further announcement:]

The Mayor of Brussels and Chamberlain to His Majesty the
King of the Netherlands warns the public that the large general
hospital of the allied army has today been established in this city.
Anyone who has old linen or lint is requested to deposit it at once
with the priests of the parish to which he or she belongs. The
humanity which has always characterised the people of Brussels
will ensure the success of this appeal made to them.

Present in Waterloo throughout the day was Pierre-Jean Tellier,
sixteen-year-old son of the village schoolmaster. He and his
brother Urbain stayed at home, while the other eight children were
sent to relatives for safety.

Urbain and I went up to the loft, to the very ridgetop of our
house, and took out a tile so as to see the battlefield better. We

could easily distinguish the cannon fire and hear the musketry. During the afternoon many of the villagers went out of doors or to their attic windows to watch the battle. We could see the flashes of the guns and heard quite distinctly the sound of firing, but smoke prevented us from making out the actual fighting. Mama was very frightened.

At about three o'clock wounded soldiers began to come along the path from Mont St Jean. They could not use the paved road as this was congested with ammunition and ambulance waggons, the latter laden with seriously wounded men, and ration carts, etc. Little by little the number of wounded increased. Most of them came to our house, asking for a drink to quench their thirst with. To prevent them from entering, my father stationed me at the corner of the house with a barrel of beer, and being afraid that our supply would soon run out, he diluted it with water. When they had taken a drink, the wounded went on their way towards Brussels, hurrying to put the battlefield behind them. Between three and four we heard shouts of ' *Sauve qui peut.*'

Around seven o'clock some soldiers under the command of a sergeant arrived with an officer. They carried him on a door which had no doubt been wrenched off some building in Mont St Jean. The sergeant asked me: 'My lad, is there room here for a wounded officer?' I went in to ask my father, and he ran outside, saying, 'I expect so. I expect so.' The wounded man was lifted through a window into the room to the left of the hall and laid on a mattress. He had been mortally wounded by a case-shot bullet which had pierced the right side of his chest. It was Major Devilliers of the Belgian Regiment of Hussars. He died on the Tuesday morning. Papa made an inventory of the major's effects, and the sergeant promised to send these to the widow.

We heard the cannon and musket fire without a break from half past eleven until half past eight in the evening. About an hour later an officer came to see the wounded man; and I heard him remark: 'We have had the good fortune to drive the French back towards Genappe.'

Mr Pryse Lockhart Gordon, whose health had been poor for the past two years, had come to Brussels in the autumn of 1814 with his

o

wife, and had taken a house in the Park. He was at home almost all day on June 18th.

Before the evening had closed, great numbers of wounded soldiers and officers of the British army had arrived; and many of the former dropped down in the streets from loss of blood and exhaustion. I had picked up, close to my door, a serjeant of the Inniskillings and four privates of infantry in this situation, whom we bivouacked in my garden-house. An aide-de-camp of a general officer, completely worn out with fatigue, and a captain of the 33rd, with two officers of the 30th wounded, occupied all the spare apartments in my house. None of their wounds were serious, and I was fortunate enough to procure the aid of my friend Dr Perkins to dress them, and my family became nurses. Various were the accounts and opinions of our guests respecting the issue of the conflict; so that my wife's nerves began to give way, and we made preparations to emigrate should the event of the battle be unfavourable, which, however, I could not allow myself to think was possible.

As we had but little sleep the previous night, we were stepping into bed at rather an earlier hour than usual, when a thundering rap at my door announced a stranger. I looked from the window, and found the visitor to be my friend Colonel Rooke[1] of the Guards in search of his family, whom he had a few days before left under my protection. 'Open your doors and your cellar, my friend,' said the gallant soldier, 'I have glorious news for you!' I flew to the door in my shirt, and had the pleasure of finding him 'hale of limb and lith', but famishing of hunger, and faint with fatigue; for he had been eighteen hours on horseback, during which he had but little refreshment. As soon as he had satisfied the cravings of nature by frequent attacks on a buttock of beef and a flask of my best Bordeaux, he dropped his head on a sofa, and I allowed him to sleep three hours. The colonel was on the staff, in the quarter-master-general's department, and had got a *congé* of a few hours to see his family; but I had sent them off the preceding day to Antwerp.

When the French columns advanced against Picton's division the 1st Battalion of the 95th was engaged, and one of the officers who re-

[1] Lieut.-Colonel Henry Willoughby Rooke, 3rd Regt. Foot Guards.

*ceived a wound was Lieutenant George Simmons. He later wrote
an account of his experiences in several letters to his parents in
Yorkshire.*

I was a little in front of our line, and hearing the word charge, I
looked back at our line, and received a ball, which broke two of
my ribs near the backbone, went through my liver, and lodged in
my breast. I fell senseless in the mud, and some minutes after
found our fellows and the enemy hotly engaged near me. Their
skirmishers were beaten back and the column stopped. Two men
dragged me away to the farm of Mont St Jean a little to the rear.

A good surgeon, a friend of mine [James Robson], instantly
came to examine my wound. My breast was dreadfully swelled.
He made a deep cut under the right pap, and dislodged from the
breast-bone a musket-ball. I was suffocating with the injury my
lungs had sustained. He took a quart of blood from my arm. I now
began to feel my miseries. Sergeant Fairfoot was also here wounded
in the arm. He got me everything he could, and said he would go
and knock some French prisoner off his horse for me in order to get
me off. The balls were riddling the house we were in. Fairfoot was
very anxious to get me away. He went in search of a horse, and
returned with a Frenchman's, and tried to put me on it, but I
fainted, and was carried back to my straw. When I came to myself,
I heard the surgeons say, 'What is the use of torturing him? he
cannot live the night; he is better where he is than to die on horseback.' This admonition made Fairfoot desist, but he got me water
and behaved very kind. The enemy made a very desperate attack,
and it was thought this place would in a few minutes be between
the fire of the parties; under such circumstances we should be
either burnt or shot. Everybody that could crawl left the place. I
asked the hospital sergeant, who was the last person there, if we
were to be left? He durst not answer me. A gallant young friend of
mine, who was badly wounded and dying, crawled near me and
said, 'George, do not swear at the fellow; we shall soon be happy;
we have behaved like Englishmen.'

At this moment Fairfoot entered, and a Rifle Man who gallantly
exposed himself to carry me off the field. Fairfoot said, 'We must
not, nor shall not be murdered, but there is no time to spare.' A
Life Guardsman and he put me on the horse. I was held on by the
legs. Oh what I suffered! I had to ride twelve miles. The motion of
the horse made the blood pump out, and the bones cut the flesh to a

jelly. I made my way to the house I had been billeted on — very respectable people. I arrived about 10 o'clock on that doleful night. The whole family came out to receive me. The good man and his wife were extremely grieved. I had everything possible got for me, a surgeon sent for, a quart of blood taken from me, wrapped up in poultices, and a most excellent nurse.

[*Simmons recovered, rejoined his regiment in the following January, and did not die until 1858, aged seventy-two, though he suffered a good deal from his wounds.*]

One of those wounded at Quatre Bras was Sergeant Edward Costello of the 95th Rifles: a ball struck his trigger finger, tearing it off and turning the trigger aside; a second shot passed through the mess-tin on his knapsack. He made his way back to the capital on foot and in a cart.

On my arrival at Brussels, and going to my quarters, I found it so crowded with Belgian officers and men (some of them quite free from wounds), that I could get no reception. It was about six o'clock in the evening of the 18th. I was entering the large square, and gazing on some hundreds of wounded men who were there stretched out on straw, when an alarm was given that the French were entering the city; in a moment all was in an uproar; the inhabitants running in all directions, closing their doors, and some Belgian troops in the square, in great confusion; loading my rifle, I joined a party of the 81st regiment who remained on duty here during the action. The alarm, however, was occasioned by the appearance of about 1700 or 1800 French prisoners, under escort of some of our dragoons.

The panic over, I partook of a little bread and wine and lay down for the night on some straw in the square; and in spite of the confusion and uproar, occasioned by the continual arrival of waggons loaded with wounded men, I slept soundly. In the morning the scene surpassed all imagination, and baffles description: thousands of wounded French, Belgians, Prussians and English; carts, waggons, and every other attainable vehicle, were continually arriving heaped with sufferers. The wounded were laid, friends and foes indiscriminately, on straw, with avenues between them, in every part of the city, and nearly destitute of surgical attendance. The humane and indefatigable exertions of the fair ladies of Brussels,

however, greatly made up for this deficiency; numbers were busily
employed — some strapping and bandaging wounds, others serving out tea, coffee, soups, and other soothing nourishments; while
many occupied themselves stripping the sufferers of their gory and
saturated garments, and dressing them in clean shirts, and other
habiliments.[1]

One lady I noticed particularly, she was attended by a servant
bearing on his shoulder a kind of pannier, containing warm and
cold refreshments: her age I guessed about eighteen, and the pecu-
liarity of the moment made her appear beyond the common order
of humanity. She moved along with an eye of lightning, glancing
about for those whom she thought most in need of her assistance.

Fanny Burney, Madame D'Arblay, the author of Evelina,
Cecilia *and a celebrated diary, was in Brussels and took a share
in dressing wounds and attending sick beds.*

Humanity could be carried no further; for not alone the Belgians and English were thus nursed and assisted, nor yet the Allies,
but the prisoners also; and this, notwithstanding the greatest apprehension being prevalent that the sufferers, from their multitude,
would bring pestilence into the heart of the city.

The immense quantity of English, Belgians, and Allies, who
were first, of course, conveyed to the hospitals and prepared houses
of Brussels required so much time for carriage and placing, that
although the carts, waggons, and every attainable or seizable
vehicle were unremittingly in motion — now coming, now returning to the field of battle for more, — it was nearly a week, or at
least five or six days, ere the unhappy wounded prisoners, who
were necessarily last served, could be accomodated. And though I
was assured that medical and surgical aid was administered to
them whenever it was possible, the blood that dried upon their
skins and their garments, joined to the dreadful sores occasioned
by this neglect, produced an effect so pestiferous, that, at every new
entry, eau de Cologne, or vinegar, was resorted to by every inhabi-
tant, even amongst the shopkeepers, even amongst the commonest
persons, for averting the menaced contagion.

Even the churches were turned into hospitals, and every house

---

[1] Lady Georgiana Lennox recorded years later: 'We were all employed in
scraping lint, and preparing cherry water for the wounded.'

in Brussels was ordered to receive or find an asylum for some of the sick. . . . We were all at work more or less in making lint. For me, I was about amongst the wounded half the day, the British, s'entend!

When Charles Bell, the surgeon who was afterwards knighted for his discoveries concerning the nervous system, heard the news of Waterloo, he exclaimed to his brother-in-law, John Shaw: 'Johnnie! how can we let this pass? Here is such an occasion of seeing gun-shot wounds come to our very door. Let us go!' They travelled to Brussels without passports, waving surgical instruments at the officials instead. They stayed in the Hôtel d'Angleterre, Rue de la Madeleine, and on July 1st Bell wrote home:

I have just returned from seeing the French wounded received in their hospital. When laid out naked, or almost so, 100 in a row of low beds upon the ground, tho' wounded, low, exhausted, tho' *beaten*, you would still conclude with me that those were fellows capable of marching, unopposed from the west of Europe to the east of Asia. Strong, thick-set, hardy veterans, brave spirits and unsubdued, they cast their wild glance upon you, their black eyes and brown cheeks finely contrasted with their fresh sheets: you would much admire their capacity of adaptation. These fellows are brought from the field after lying many days on the ground, many dying, many in the agony, many miserably racked with pain and spasms, and the fellow next to him mimics him and gives it a tune. 'Ah, ah! vous chantez bien!'

. . . Beside a case which I was visiting to-day, lay a woman wounded with gun-shot — French. It is dreadful to visit these wounded French, the perpetual plaintive cry of 'Pansez, pansez, monsieur docteur, pansez ma cuisse. Ah! je souffre, je souffre beaucoup, beaucoup, beaucoup.' The second Sunday, many not yet dressed.

[On his return to London, Charles Bell wrote to Francis Horner, M.P., as follows:]

After I had been five days engaged in the prosecution of my object, I found that the best cases, that is, the most horrid wounds, left totally without assistance, were to be found in the hospital of the French wounded; this hospital was only forming. They were even then bringing in these poor creatures from the woods. It is impossible to convey to you the picture of human misery continually before my eyes. What was heart-rending in the day was intolerable at night; and I rose and wrote, at four o'clock in the morning, to the chief surgeon, offering to perform the necessary operations upon the French. At six o'clock I took the knife in my hand, and continued incessantly at work till seven in the evening; and so the second and third day.

All the decencies of performing surgical operations were soon neglected. While I amputated one man's thigh, there lay at one time thirteen, all beseeching to be taken next; one full of entreaty, one calling upon me to remember my promise to take him, another execrating. It was a strange thing to feel my clothes stiff with blood, and my arms powerless with the exertion of using the knife! and more extraordinary still, to find my mind calm amidst such variety of suffering; but to give one of these objects access to your feelings was to allow yourself to be unmanned for the performance of a duty. It was less painful to look upon the whole than to contemplate one object.

When I first went round the wards of the wounded prisoners, my sensations were very extraordinary. We had everywhere heard of the manner in which these men had fought — nothing could surpass their devotedness. In a long ward, containing fifty, there was no expression of suffering, no one spoke to his neighbour. There was a resentful, sullen rigidness of face, a fierceness in their dark eyes as they lay half covered in the sheets.

[*Bell made this note in his diary:*]

The force with which the cuirassiers came on is wonderful. Here is an officer wounded; a sword pierced the back and upper part of the thigh, went through the wood-work and leather of the saddle, and entered the horse's body, pinning the man to the horse.

THE ADVANCE ON PARIS

EVEN in the hour of a defeat he would not yet acknowledge, Napoleon planned to gain time for Grouchy to withdraw to Laon, for Rapp's corps and other troops to hasten to Paris from east and west alike, and for Soult to gather between St Quentin, Rheims and Soissons the remnants of the *Armée du Nord* now in retreat from Belgium and scattered over the countryside. The struggle was not to be abandoned. By the defensive strategy of 1814 he would show a front and somehow hold off the confident Allies coming from the east, perhaps wear them out, perhaps create an opportunity for beating them in detail. He himself must first go to Paris to restore confidence and take certain urgent steps.

By a roundabout route he reached the capital on June 21st, after an absence of ten fateful days. Here disappointment awaited his hopes, for he found the Chambers of Peers and Deputies openly hostile, and, in order to forestall any attempt he might make to dissolve them and assume a dictatorship, they declared themselves to be in permanent session. Though public support was still widespread, political backing had been withdrawn, and being unwilling to act in such a way as to risk the unleashing of civil war, the Emperor, faced with the choice of resigning, or being deposed, signed his abdication in favour of his son on June 23rd, and then installed himself in nearby Malmaison. His departure removed the main obstacle to the opening of negotiations between France and the Allied Powers, since many Frenchmen argued that as it was against Napoleon alone that Europe had declared war, only he had stood between France and peace. A Provisional Government was appointed under Fouché's leadership.

Meanwhile the Prussian army, inspired by revengeful memories of French occupation, was advancing ruthlessly through Charleroi and Avesnes, where the surrender of the fortress was hastened by the destructive explosion of a huge powder magazine. On the Prussians marched and rode, from Guise to St Quentin and then to Compiègne, encountering scanty resistance, yet leaving behind them a trail of excess and bitter resentment.

More slowly, because of the need to allow time for the arrival of pontoons and vital stores, Wellington's gentler troops took the more westerly route through Nivelles, Maubeuge, Cambrai, taken by escalade with trifling loss, and Péronne, which was stormed and soon

The last leaders of the Grande Armée

Nicholas Soult, Marshal of France

Emmanuel, Marquis de Grouchy and Marshal of France

surrendered, the garrison being allowed to lay down their arms and return to their homes. The Anglo-Dutch forces entered the outskirts of Paris two days later than did Blücher.

Soult had been vigorous in his efforts to rally the débris of the Waterloo divisions, but he was unable to collect an army to make head against Wellington or Blücher. However, by June 25th he had marched his troops to Soissons where he met Grouchy's force next day coming from Réthel and the valley of the Aisne. Then Soult found himself superseded in command by the Provisional Government, so the chagrined marshal went off to Paris, leaving Grouchy to follow with some 60,000 men. This army, seriously diminished by desertions, was in no state to make a significant stand, and after suffering minor defeats at Compiègne, Senlis, Creil and Villers-Cotterets, and losing several thousand prisoners — Grouchy himself narrowly escaped capture — it could hope to achieve no more than elude the Prussians and reach Paris by devious routes. This it did on June 29th.

At the same time other Allied armies were moving into France. Prince Schwarzenberg's 250,000 troops from Austria, Bavaria, Würtemberg, Saxony and Hesse-Darmstadt had crossed the Rhine near Basel and Mannheim, where the main Russian force of 167,000 men also crossed. A Bavarian corps took Sedan on June 25th and Nancy two days later. By July 7th the Russians had reached Laon and Rheims, but a fortnight elapsed before the Austrians came to Dijon. Far to the south, 60,000 Austrian and Sardinian soldiers from Italy reached Geneva and then spread out towards Besançon, while two other columns headed for Lyons, meeting sharp resistance from Marshal Suchet on the way. Certain fortresses were deliberately bypassed and left in rear of the advancing armies, not being captured until the latter part of July or even August.

Lieutenant Henry Boldero, 14th Foot, wrote to his mother from Le Cateau on June 23rd, heading his letter with the words 'We entered FRANCE *21st dressed out with Laurels.'*

I hope you received a slight notification of the existence and safety of your two sons — we wrote it the day after the great Battle from Nivelles. Since that time we have been marching incessantly in pursuit of the French who are flying in all directions. The remains of Bony's Army consisting of 11,000 men only, passed thro' here the day before yesterday. Nobody knows where he is himself — but the general opinion is that he has concealed himself in the woods — we do not meet with the slightest opposition and it is not expected that we shall have any more fighting. If we continue at this rate my next letter will be dated from Paris. The Chamber of Peers have already sent to the D. of Wellington to say that the gates of the City shall be opened to him immediately on his arrival.

What a glorious Battle! and what a lucky woman you are to have had two sons in it and neither of them touched. Lonsdale had three Horses shot under him in the two days and yet escaped — and I lay under the heaviest canonade that ever was brought to bear in a Battle for seven hours — and yet had the same good fortune — you may depend upon it we are reserved for some more ignoble exit. I suppose Sophy upon the strength of it will trot with her Prayer Book and Cardinal to Church four times a day instead of twice. The French lost 40,000 killed and wounded, one hundred and sixty pieces of canon on the Field. Since that time the Prussians have harassed them incessantly and killed and taken prisoners many thousands more. When once they gave way the slaughter was horrid. The English and Hanoverians destroyed them without mercy or remorse and to crown their discomfiture after we had beaten them a Body of Prussian Cavalry came up quite fresh to make the butchery (more) complete. Thank God! (see how righteous fighting makes me) I never was better in Health or Spirits altho' I have been obliged to make the whole Campaign on Foot. We were engaged two days and to make it more aggreeable in the first I had nothing at all to eat except a Bit of old Cow about as big as my thumb — and on the day of the grand Battle a handful of Pear and a Segar were the extent of my luxuries.

I think my Father will alter now that I cannot do without my bottle of Port and Beef Steak. I took advantage of this day to write to you, it being the first halt we have made for one week. God bless you all.

On June 23rd Wellington wrote from Le Cateau to the Earl of Uxbridge:

I may be wrong, but my opinion is, that we have given Napoleon his death blow; from all I hear his army is totally destroyed, the men are deserting in parties, even the Generals are withdrawing from him. The infantry throw away their arms, and the cavalry and artillery sell their horses to the people of the country and desert to their homes. Allowing for much exaggeration in this account, and knowing that Buonaparte can still collect, in addition to what he had brought back with him, the 5th corps d'armée, under Rapp,[1] which is near Strasbourg, and the 3rd corps, which was at Wavre, during the battle, and has not suffered so much as the others, and probably some troops from La Vendée, I am still of opinion that he can make no head against us, *qu'il n'a qu'à se pendre*. . . .

Blücher wrote to his wife from Compiègne on June 27th:

Here I sit in a room where Marie-Louise celebrated her wedding night. Nothing could be more beautiful, more agreeable than Compiègne. The only pity is that I have to leave again early to-morrow, as I must reach Paris in three days. It is possible and highly likely that Bonaparte will be handed over to me and to Lord Wellington. I shall probably not be able to do better than to have him shot, which would be a service to mankind. In Paris everyone has deserted him and he is hated and scorned. I believe the whole affair will soon be ended, and then I shall hurry home. Farewell. The orderly wants to leave; but for God's sake, I don't get a single letter from you.

Many British soldiers who rode or marched to Paris wrote bitterly about the conduct of the Prussian troops along the route, and Private George Farmer of the 11th Light Dragoons recalled the following:

Up to the present point the British army seemed to have followed a route of its own. Our march of the next day brought us up on the track of the Prussians; and the contrast between our discipline and theirs was curious in the extreme. Our column passed, for example, about noon, a large château, with a village attached; and I and my men were sent, as a matter of course, to protect both. Alas! we came too late. The Prussians had been here before us, and the skill and industry with which they seemed to have carried on the work of devastation I have no language to describe. In the château there was not one article of furniture, from the costly pierglass down to the common coffee-cup, which they had not smashed

---

[1] Jean, Comte Rapp (1772–1821), famous for his prolonged defence of Dantzig and his 22 wounds. He was Napoleon's aide-de-camp for 12 years.

to atoms. The flour-mill, likewise, attached to the mansion, was all gutted, the sacks cut to pieces, and the flour wantonly scattered over the road. Stables, cow-sheds, poultry-houses, and gardens, seemed to have been, with infinite care, rendered useless; and as to living things, there was none — not so much as a half-starved pigeon — to be seen about the premises. In like manner, the village was one wide scene of devastation. Its inhabitants appeared, indeed, to have escaped, for we came upon no human being, nor the corpse of any; but furniture, doors, windows, and here and there roofs, all seemed to have passed through the merciless hands of the spoilers. I never beheld such a specimen of war, conducted in a spirit of ferocious hostility. I was half ashamed of the connexion that subsisted between ourselves and the Prussians, when I looked upon the horrid work which they had perpetrated.

Another who was to comment adversely on the conduct of the Prussian troops, even though he understood their motives, was Gronow of the 1st Guards.

We perceived, on entering France, that our allies the Prussians had committed fearful atrocities on the defenceless inhabitants of the villages and farms which lay in their line of march. Before we left La Belle Alliance, I had already seen the brutality of some of the Prussian infantry, who hacked and cut up, in the most savage manner, all the cows and pigs which were in the farmyards; placing upon their bayonets the still quivering flesh, and roasting it on the coals. On our line of march, whenever we arrived at towns or villages through which the Prussians had passed, we found that every article of furniture in the houses had been destroyed in the most wanton manner: looking-glasses, mahogany bedsteads, pictures, beds and mattresses, had been hacked, cut, half-burned, and scattered about in every direction; and, on the slightest remonstrance of the wretched inhabitants, they were beaten in a most shameful manner, and sometimes shot. It is true that the Prussians owed the French a long debt of vengeance for all the atrocities committed by the French at Berlin; particularly by Davoust's corps after the battle of Jena. The French had behaved so ill that the Prussians had sworn to be revenged, if ever they had the opportunity to visit upon the French the cruelties, the extortion, insults, and hard usage their own capital had suffered; and they kept their word.

In view of the Prussian depredations along the route, a paragraph in
the memoirs of Major-General Baron von Müffling is significant.

On the march to Paris, the Prussian army made longer marches
than the English; and when in the morning I made my daily communications to the Duke, I took the liberty of respectfully calling
his attention to this, and suggesting that it would be better if he
kept the same pace as his ally. He was silent at first, but on my
urging him again to move more rapidly, he said to me: 'Do not
press me on this point, for I tell you, it won't do. If you were
better acquainted with the English army, its composition and
habits, you would say the same. I cannot separate from my tents
and my supplies. My troops must be well kept and well supplied
in camp, if order and discipline are to be maintained. It is better
that I should arrive two days later in Paris, than that discipline
should be relaxed.'

THE OCCUPATION OF PARIS

JUST as Napoleon had been faced with a choice, so Paris had now to choose between a siege and immediate capitulation. Marshal Davout, unflinching as Minister of War and Governor of the capital, was at first resolved to oppose the armies of Wellington and Blücher. Together they did not total much over 120,000; and he had, besides 60,000 troops who had come in with Grouchy or from the Loire and other parts of France, some 30,000 National Guards of doubtful value, a new levy, largely composed of veterans, and numerous guns. But other counsels prevailed, since a short-term success was all that could be hoped for, and renewed fighting must lead to further loss, grief, damage and disaster. Paris, moreover, was scarcely defensible on the southern side, having there no line of fortifications as on the north. So Davout was won over to the side of the peacemakers, and a capitulation was agreed upon.

By the convention signed at St Cloud on July 3rd, the French army was to evacuate Paris within three days and move south of the Loire — a decision which was received with such widespread disfavour that many troops were reluctant to go without fighting, and certain commanders had difficulty in persuading their regiments to obey. Subsequently the army was disbanded with tact and skill. Rather than acknowledge Napoleon II, choose another ruler or proclaim a republic, the Provisional Government recognised Louis XVIII as king. The Allies took possession of the Paris suburbs, where the Prussians at least had been obliged to fight hard; and on July 7th they entered the capital. Next day Louis XVIII was restored to the Tuileries and to his throne.

Wellington, a target for sightseers, would-be historians, visiting celebrities, and old friends, had his work cut out to moderate the Prussians from revengeful acts and to urge upon the Allies a lenient policy towards vanquished France. In this he met favourable response, for whereas Prussia was eager for Alsace and Lorraine, Great Britain and Russia firmly opposed any mutilation of France. Nevertheless, an indemnity of 700 million francs was exacted, and all the art treasures were to be restored to their owners. Whereas in 1814 the Allies had been prepared to believe that they had been fighting Napoleon rather than France, and had granted lenient terms, now they changed their attitude, because the welcome and support given to the returning Emperor showed that the French people had identified themselves with his acts and were accomplices in his crimes.

In November 1815 a second convention was signed, providing for the withdrawal of all foreign troops apart from an army of 150,000 men to be maintained at French expense along the northern and eastern frontiers. Britain, Austria, Prussia and Russia each furnished a contingent of about 30,000, the Bavarians had nearly 10,000, and smaller forces were provided by Denmark, Hanover, Saxony and Würtemberg. The occupation was to last for five years, but was brought to an end after three.

John Cam Hobhouse, Byron's friend and later Lord Broughton, wrote a letter from Paris dated July 3rd:

It was known early this morning that there had been partial actions yesterday at Nanterre, at Sèvres, and upon different points on the right bank of the Seine, between Neuilly and Argenteuil; that Versailles had been retaken, and the bridge of Choisy occupied by the Prussians. The Prussians and English passed the night in entrenching themselves in the wood of Meudon and Versières, and advanced early this morning to the villages of Vanvres and Issy, as in preparation for a general attack of the combined armies on the capital. At eight o'clock the two armies were in face of each other; the French in the plain of Grenelle, and the allies in the plain beneath Meudon. Firing had been heard and seen the whole night from the heights of Chaillot, which were crowded by people with telescopes. A portion of the cavalry of the Guard, which was stationed in the Champ de Mars, rode off at eleven o'clock along the left bank of the Seine, and were the last to take up their positions, which, at twelve o'clock, seemed concluded, and left the two armies in line of battle.

... It was commonly reported early in the afternoon that a general action was on the point of being fought. The throng and the silence, and the eager looks of the multitudes in the gardens and boulevards, the groups collected round, and trailing after two or three straggling dragoons leading their wounded horses, or carrying orders to the headquarters of the square Vendôme; the dead, unsocial solemnity of the heavy patrols parading the streets without music; the doors of the houses and courts all shut; the upper windows opened every now and then, and occupied by female faces, as the clattering horse of a gendarme announced the expectation of intelligence — every appearance of anxiety and apprehension, unusual even since the commencement of the siege, was to be recognised at the first glance for an hour or two after it was known that the two armies were in presence. More than once crowds rushed towards the elevated spots of the gardens and squares at the exclamation of individuals who announced the opening cannonade.

At four o'clock the battle had not begun.

On July 6th Lieutenant Hugh Wray of the 40th Regiment wrote in his diary:

This day appears a day of great joy to the Parisians, who are in great numbers at this moment in our camp, waving white handkerchiefs, flags, and lilies to us all. There are about three hundred carriages, lots of the National Guard, and people of all sorts here waiting the arrival of the King, who passes by here in a couple of hours, on his way to St Denis, which is only half a mile from our camp and three and a half miles from Paris. The French army left Paris this morning, and Lord Wellington and Marshal Blücher entered at the head of our hussars and Prussian guards in triumph.

(5 o'clock) — the King has just passed with all his guards, going at an easy walk. He was received by us in line, and by all the people with loud and frequent shouts of '*vive le Roi! vivent les Bourbons!*'

Ensign William Leeke relates how on the morning of July 7th General Adam's brigade, comprising the 52nd, 71st and 95th, had the honour of entering Paris by the Barrière de l'Etoile. They marched down the centre of the road leading through the Champs Elysées to the Place Quinze and the Tuileries.

A brigade of artillery, with lighted matches, was posted close to the barrier on either side of the chaussée. It was a proud and happy moment, when, with bands and bugles playing, we thus took possession of, and entered, the capital of France. At least I am sure it was the proudest moment of my life, when I found myself riding down the centre of the avenue of the Champs Elysées, bearing in triumph into the enemy's capital that same 52nd regimental colour which I had the honour of carrying to victory on the eventful and glorious day of Waterloo.

The whole brigade halted and piled arms in the Champs Elysées. . . . Before the 52nd band was dismissed, Sir John Colborne ordered it to play 'Vive Henri Quatre', one of the principal royalist tunes, but it did not appear to attract any number of people.

. . . Either the day after we entered Paris, or on the following day, No. 9 and No. 10 companies of the 52nd were ordered to encamp nearer to the Place Louis Quinze, and near to where the quarter-guard already was, close to the wall of the Duke of Wellington's garden. The cords of the officers' tents were close to the short palings, which fenced off about ten feet of garden-ground between them and the wall. My tent was against the little gate in the palings which led to the garden-door, and close up to it, so close that one day, about a week or fortnight after we arrived, I heard somebody floundering about and stumbling over the cords, and, on looking out, found it was the duke himself, who sometimes, but not often, came out that way. He desired that the tent might be moved a few feet forward.

At five o'clock on the evening of July 7th General Maximilien-Sébastian Foy wrote in his journal:

I have seen the Prussians enter; about one division of infantry and one of cavalry. Bad troops who looked tired and wretched. English and Prussian officers fill the city. The tricolour flag is still to be seen. The commanders of the National Guard legions have declared that they will retain our cockade for ever. One hears not a single cry of '*Vive le Roi!*' The people are either indifferent or dissatisfied. Tears came into my eyes when I saw these enemy hordes in our capital. We are told that the Bourbons will come in to-morrow. I pity the King entering Paris in the wake of hostile armies. It strikes me as impossible to maintain authority when it has been established in such a scandalous fashion over a nation imbued with vanity and valour.

At Jargeau on the Loire Colonel Fantin des Odoards made a bitter entry in his journal for July 13th:

I was not fortunate enough to be killed during the brief and fatal campaign which has brought the enemy to Paris, and I have survived in order to witness the funeral of our poor unhappy land. It

P

is worse than death. After the battle of Pavia,[1] Francis the First said: 'All is lost save honour.' We have not even that consolation: all is lost, even honour. Cowardice, incompetence, treachery, apathy — they all contributed to our downfall. How black the future is!

Here I am on the left bank of the Loire, with what remains of my army corps, and before my very eyes the Prussians are holding the right bank to ransom just as they please. It is enough to make one die of shame and grief. But then there is no patriotism left in France. The sacred flame which, to their despair, still animates a small number of soldiers whose hands have been tied and who are without a leader, has been extinguished in every other breast. We are ripe for enslavement.

Labretonnière, the student at the Lycée Louis-le-Grand, was very anxious to watch the march-past of the Anglo-Dutch army.

It was to leave the Bois de Boulogne and go to the Place de la Concorde, there to be inspected by the commanders-in-chief of the new crusade against France. By dint of persevering I remained in the same spot for over three hours, leaning against a tree in the Champs-Elysées. In the course of this very long march-past I saw all that I had still not seen of the uniforms and armour of civilised Europe.

Oh! it was really like being beaten twice over, *bis mori*, to have been beaten by an army as badly turned out as the English army was. One can tolerate being shot at by those fine grenadiers of the Russian and Prussian Guards, who look so masculine and military; to receive sabre cuts from those old hussars from Brandenburg and Silesia, typical of light cavalry. But how could one be a good soldier under that little sugar-loaf with a peak, with the inelegantly cut red jacket, those grey trousers clinging to knock-knees?

I did notice one thing to England's credit: on the 50,000 breasts that I watched go past, I saw no ribbons,[2] none of that jewelry which bedecks the armies of the rest of Europe. Only at rare intervals did I see a medal hanging from a violet ribbon on some

[1] In 1525 Francis I of France was defeated at Pavia and taken captive to Madrid. He and Charles of Spain had been rival claimants to the throne of the Holy Roman Empire, and Charles V had been elected. His repeated attempts to destroy the imperial power all failed.
[2] A Waterloo medal was issued in 1816, but veterans of earlier campaigns had to wait till 1848 for the Military General Service Medal.

officer's breast. Love of country, the glory of old Albion — that is what has to suffice for British troops to make them fight with such admirable courage.

A paragraph written by Captain Mercer bears out Labretonnière's observations about the appearance of the British contingents:

Our infantry — indeed our whole army — appeared in the same clothes in which they had marched, slept, and fought for months. The colour had faded to a dusky brick-dust hue; their coats, originally not very smartly made, had acquired by constant wearing that loose, easy set so characteristic of old clothes, comfortable to the wearer, but not calculated to add grace to his appearance. *Par surcroît de laideur*, their cap is perhaps the meanest, ugliest thing ever invented. From all these causes it arose that our infantry appeared to the utmost disadvantage — dirty, shabby, mean, and very small.

Frances, Lady Shelley, arrived in Paris during the second half of July with her husband, who had known the Duke of Wellington for many years. She and the Duke had several conversations. After one meeting she wrote:

Those who accuse him of a lack of feeling — and some there are who state as much — have not seen him as I have, his eye glistening, and his voice broken, as he spoke of the losses sustained at Waterloo. 'I hope to God,' he said one day, 'that I have fought my last battle. It is a bad thing to be always fighting. While in the thick of it I am too much occupied to feel anything; but it is wretched just after. It is quite impossible to think of glory. Both mind and feelings are exhausted. I am wretched even at the moment of victory, and I always say that, next to a battle lost, the greatest misery is a battle gained. Not only do you lose those dear friends with whom you have been living, but you are forced to leave the wounded behind you. To be sure, one tried to do the best for them, but how little that is! At such moments every feeling in your breast is deadened. I am now just beginning to regain my natural spirits, but I never wish for any more fighting.'
I quote the Duke's words just as they were spoken.

Some of the clergymen attached to the Army at this period come in for rough handling in the memoirs and diaries, but the Rev. Charles Frith, who had distinguished himself in the Peninsula, was a notable exception; and Lieutenant-Colonel Charles Cadell of the 28th Regiment gives an example of his conduct.

We were so fortunate as to have again attached to our division (the fifth) our excellent chaplain, the Rev. Charles Frith. On the Sunday after our arrival at Clichy, the division paraded for divine service, the first time since the battle of the 18th, in the park of the chateau (Sir James Kempt's quarters), when Mr. Frith gave us an impressive discourse. The text, as well as I can recollect, was — 'Go to your tents and rejoice, and return thanks to the Lord for the mercies he has granted you.'

The beautiful manner in which he dwelt on the battle, and the sad and sudden loss of friends and comrades, drew tears from many; and when he wound up with the sad pangs it would cause at home, to the widows and orphans, the parents and friends of those that had fallen, concluding with the text, 'Go to your tents and rejoice, and return thanks to the Lord for the mercies he has granted you,' there was hardly a dry eye in the whole division, and it had an excellent effect on the men.

Napoleon surrenders his sword to Captain Maitland on board the *Bellerophon* (*New York Public Library Print Collection*)

The end. A German cartoon ridiculing Napoleon on St. Helena
(*New York Public Library Print Collection*)

NAPOLEON TAKES LEAVE OF EUROPE

On June 29th a column sent by Blücher to capture Napoleon dead or alive had been thwarted by Marshal Davout, who had ordered the Seine bridge nearest to Malmaison to be blown up, and by Fouché, who had directed the ex-Emperor to leave for Rochefort, which he did early that same day in a yellow calèche, just ahead of the Prussians. On reaching the coast he hoped to escape to America, and he got as far as embarking on July 8th in a French frigate and sailing to Aix, there to await a favourable wind; but when such a wind did blow, Napoleon found himself unable to elude the vigilance of the British Navy, so he put himself in touch with Captain Frederick Maitland of H.M.S. *Bellerophon*, who commanded the blockading squadron, and was informed that he would not be permitted to cross the Atlantic. Instead he surrendered to Maitland, threw himself on the protection of the Prince Regent, and on July 15th went on board the *Bellerophon*, which had fought on the First of June, at the Nile and Trafalgar. He hoped to become an exiled guest, but the Allies were determined never again to let him disturb the peace of Europe; so on reaching Torbay Napoleon was transferred to another ship of the line, H.M.S. *Northumberland*, for the journey to St Helena, which remote island had meanwhile been selected as his place of captivity. He landed there on October 17th.

On July 13th Napoleon in Rochefort addressed this letter to the Prince Regent:

Royal Highness, Exposed to the factions which divide my country, and to the enmity of the greatest Powers of Europe, I have terminated my political career, and I come, like Themistocles,[1] to throw myself on the hospitality of the British people. I place myself under the protection of their laws, which I claim from Your Royal Highness as the greatest, the most constant and the most generous of my enemies.

---

[1] In about 471 B.C. the Athenian statesman and soldier was banished from Athens, withdrew to Argos, only to be accused of treason and obliged to flee. He was eventually granted protection by King Ataxerxes.

*Captain Frederick Maitland, R.N., relates how Napoleon Bonaparte
came on board the* Bellerophon *soon after six o'clock on July 15th.*

On coming on board the *Bellerophon,* he was received without
any of the honours generally paid to persons of high rank; the
guard was drawn out on the break of the poop, but did not present
arms. His Majesty's Government had merely given directions,
in the event of his being captured, for his being removed into any
one of his Majesty's ships that might fall in with him; but no
instructions had been given as to the light in which he was to be
viewed. As it is not customary, however, on board a British ship
of war, to pay any such honours before the colours are hoisted at
eight o'clock in the morning, or after sunset, I made the early hour
an excuse for withholding them upon this occasion.

Buonaparte's dress was an olive-coloured great coat over a green
uniform, with scarlet cape and cuffs, green lapels turned back and
edged with scarlet, skirts hooked back with bugle horns embroidered in gold, plain sugar-loaf buttons and gold epaulettes; being
the uniform of the Chasseur à Cheval of the Imperial Guard. He
wore the star, or grand cross of the Legion of Honour, and the
small cross of that order; the Iron Crown; and the Union, appended
to the button-hole of his left lapel. He had on a small cocked hat,
with a tri-coloured cockade; plain gold-hilted sword, military
boots, and white waistcoat and breeches. The following day he
appeared in shoes, with gold buckles, and silk stockings — the
dress he always wore afterwards, while with me.

On leaving the *Epervier* [a French brig of war], he was cheered
by her ship's company as long as the boat was within hearing;
and Mr. Andrew Mott [the First Lieutenant] informed me that
most of the officers and men had tears in their eyes.

General Bertrand came first up the ship's side, and said to me,
'The Emperor is in the boat.' He then ascended, and, when he
came on the quarter-deck, pulled off his hat, and, addressing me
in a firm tone of voice, said, 'I am come to throw myself on the
protection of your Prince and laws.'

. . . Napoleon Buonaparte was then a remarkably strong, well-
built man, about five feet seven inches high, his limbs particularly
well-formed, with a fine ancle and very small foot, of which he
seemed rather vain, as he always wore, while on board the ship,
silk stockings and shoes. His hands were also very small, and had
the plumpness of a woman's rather than the robustness of a man's.

His eyes light grey, teeth good; and when he smiled, the expression of his countenance was highly pleasing; when under the influence of disappointment, however, it assumed a dark gloomy cast. His hair was of a very dark brown, nearly approaching to the black, and, though a little thin on the top and front, had not a grey hair amongst it. His complexion was a very uncommon one, being of a light sallow colour, differing from almost any other I ever met with. From his having become corpulent, he had lost much of his personal activity, and, if we are to give credit to those who attended him, a very considerable portion of his mental energy was also gone. It is certain his habits were very lethargic while he was on board the *Bellerophon*; for though he went to bed between eight and nine o'clock in the evening, and did not rise till about the same hour in the morning, he frequently fell asleep on the sofa in the cabin in the course of the day. His general appearance was that of a man rather older than he then was.[1]

A boy named John Smart living in Brixham had cause to remember all his life the day when H.M.S. Bellerophon, *with Napoleon on board, anchored in Torbay.*

In July the *Gazette* came down with the lists of killed and wounded at Waterloo. The coach from Exeter brought the first copy, and quite a crowd surrounded the landlord of 'The London Inn', who read aloud in his large parlour the names of those regiments that contained any Brixham men.

In common with most English schoolboys of that Waterloo year, we had an extra week's holiday at midsummer, and this was fortunate for me, as it tided me over my birthday on 24 July. It was a bright summer's morning when I sallied out after breakfast, with two half-crowns in my pocket, to meet Charlie Puddicombe and his younger brother Dick. Charlie was the biggest boy in our school; Dick was almost the smallest, and I and they were great chums.

We met by appointment on the quay, and at once began to discuss how we should spend the day and my money. Suddenly we spied two ships coming round Berry Head and into the bay — the first a large man-of-war, and the other a three-masted sloop. The ships were coming in quickly with wind and tide, but we

[1] A month short of forty-six.

heard faintly the sound of the boatswain's whistle, and in a moment the sailors were scrambling up the rigging and out on the yards to take in sail. Then, within half a mile of Brixham Quay, the anchors were let go, and the ships swung round with the flood tide, the large ship being the nearer to the shore. How thankful we were that no school bell would drag us away, but that we might stay to see all the fun! 'Run up to Mrs. Hawkins' (the baker's wife), said I to Dick, 'and tell her some King's ships have come in, for she and Michelmore are sure to go off in her boat, and I know she will let us go too.' 'And we will shove off the boat meanwhile,' said Charlie. Already several boatmen were unmooring their boats; but just then we saw a boat shove off from the ship, and we all gathered round the steps at the pierhead, for which she was making. As the boat came near we saw it was a large gig, pulled by eight sailors, and in the stern sheets sat three officers. 'Way enough,' said one of them; the oars were tossed, and the coxswain brought the boat as neatly alongside as if he had studied the run of the tide at Brixham all his life. Two of the officers jumped ashore: the one a tall man of about thirty-five, with a cloak on his arm, and the other a younger man, apparently of inferior rank. A portmanteau was handed ashore, and then at once the younger officer gave the order 'Push off!' and as the bow-man, who was ready with his boathook, obeyed, he added to the young midshipman who was sitting in the stern, 'I shall be back in ten minutes; remember orders; no talking.' Then, addressing himself to one of the shore boatmen, who had already shouldered the portmanteau, he asked which was the principal inn where a postchaise could be obtained. Being directed to 'The London Inn,' the two officers proceeded there, and went in together.

Now, it was rather disappointing, and certainly unusual, that the boat did not stop by the quay, for generally Jack is fond enough of putting foot on shore, asking and telling news, besides doing a little shopping. However, the midshipman kept his boat moving a little way off, within easy hail of shore, and seemed to avoid the boats that were putting off to the ships. The officers at the inn proved the attraction for us, and we boys formed part of the group there. It certainly could not have been more than ten minutes before the horses were put in the old yellow postchaise that was as familiar to us as King William's Stone.[1] The two officers came out

[1] William of Orange, King William III, landed at Brixham on November 5th, 1688.

directly the chaise was ready, the younger one reading from a newspaper to the other, as the latter got into the chaise. Then, while the postboy mounted, the landlord, who would fain have seen more of them, came out with a bottle and poured out a glass of wine for each. 'Good-bye, Dick,' said the one in the chaise; 'here's to our next meeting!' 'Here's to your safe arrival in London!' said the younger one, 'and good-bye,' he added, as the chaise rolled away up Fore Street. Then, walking back to the pierhead, he held up his hand as a signal to the boat, which speedily came up.

In a letter to General Sir Charles Hastings, Lady Charlotte Fitz-gerald, a daughter of the 1st Earl of Moira, described how she and her husband saw Napoleon transfer ship off Plymouth.

August 11, 1815. I have seen Bonaparte distinctly, I was quite close to him for above three minutes, and witnessed the whole business of his transfer from one ship to another!!! But previous to giving you a detail of what I was an eye witness to, I will answer some of the questions contained in your letter as to *the effect* produced by this wonderful man in this part of England. Believe me the most unwise step our government ever took was showing John Bull that Bonaparte had neither horns nor hoofs! One used to hear the epithets 'Monster,' 'Rascal' or 'Roast him alive' tacked to his name, but that time is gone by, and he is now mentioned as 'Poor fellow, well do I pity him' or 'What an air of grandeur he has tho' he is so dejected.' Such are the remarks amongst the common people and in not one instance has a severe opinion been passed upon him; his appearance seems to have effaced the recollections of the British blood he has spilt and to have removed *the just* as well as *the unjust* prejudice we had to this man.

During his stay at Plymouth the popular tide in his favour ran alarmingly high, and one evening the mob won by his smiles cheered him with enthusiasm; after that all visitors were enjoined to preserve silence and neither to rise up in their boats or to touch their hats when he came forward. How the appearance of Napoleon could thus soften their hearts rather surprises me, as his effect on mine was so different. I went to see him, admiring him through all his crimes, compassionating him as a prisoner and one whom I thought had been harshly treated since he gave himself up to the British clemency, but I came away with my heart considerably steeled against him and with many fears lest the lion should again escape from his cage! The true reason of their bringing him back to Dartmouth was, that *they durst not* attempt changing him from one ship to another amongst his Plymouth partizans, therefore they brought him to our retired regions. . . .

FitzGerald and I went in Captain Nisbett's vessel off Dartmouth. We reached the ships at half past one and an officer of the 53rd whom we met in a boat civilly told us that B was still on board the *Bellerophon* but had been expected by the *Northumberland* since ten o'clock. The confusion of boats was very great and a schooner commanded by a lieutenant was employed to keep off all from approaching, but by a *miracle of chance* the schooner was at that moment occupied in keeping off some other vessels and we slipped in between the two ships at the moment of all others most desirable. Two minutes afterwards they threatened to fire into us unless we moved from our station, which we readily did having seen everything! The *Bellerophon* and *Northumberland* were about a quarter of a mile asunder (we lay exactly between them). B descended the side of the former leisurely and the barge passed as close to us as their oars would admit of. Napoleon sat in the stern, Lord Keith[1] on one side of him, Captain Brenton on the other, then *Madame* Bertrand, her husband, maid, and a young French officer; these with the cockswain and bargemen filled the boat. Napoleon's dress is described in the papers, so I will only say he was scrupulously neat, and his person was evidently attended to. He is growing full though not quite fat, his chest and shoulders have great muscular breadth and strength. He resembles no human being I have ever seen, I can trace a look of him only in the little picture of Richard the 3rd at Donington (in the dining room). He has *pale* brown hair, is very dark but his complexion is *so clear* an olive that it gives the effect of a fairer man. His eyes are dark and round, with very little of the pupil visible — his face narrow at the temples and broad at the lower part (the shape vulgar); all prints, coins and busts I have seen of him exaggerate the projection of his nose and chin, they are blunter than they represent them, indeed there are none in the least like him — he is not handsome but he is not plain — in short in everything he is *apart* from the rest

---

[1] George Keith Elphinstone, Admiral Viscount Keith (1746–1823), was intermediator of the British Government in its dealings with Napoleon on his being sent to St Helena.

of mankind — to say he *wants* expression is silly — the truth is his countenance *reveals nothing* — it seems as if matchless in the art of dissembling or self government he had resolved we should learn none of his feelings from his face. I never saw so *immovable* a countenance; there sits in it solemn composure blended with stern determination. He has not the least of a military air nor yet of a royal one, but *a something* greater than either, more imposing, more extraordinary than any creature I have ever seen. No person in the boat articulated a sentence, all seemed absorbed in the wonderful combination of events that brought them there together.

Napoleon was received on board the *Northumberland* only as a lieut.-general! He touched his hat to the sentry as he passed the gangway, he desired Lord Keith to introduce the officers of the *N.* to him, and if he felt his situation concealed it. You will be curious to know if I think he has abandoned hope. Oh no, I never saw a man look less hopeless — so far from it he gave the impression of his planning future vengeance on his enemies — others may suppose his career finished but I am sure he does not — he appears most to resemble a bust of marble or bronze *as cold* and *as fixed*, he seems quite inaccessible to human tenderness or human distress — still he is wonderful! This hasty sketch is I am sensible full of contradictions, but I sketch him as he appeared to me . . .

Postscript. — Bonaparte is bald at the back of his head, his figure and legs are good. Bertrand I never once looked at. Madame Bertrand did really attempt to throw herself into the sea but there was stage effect in it as assistance was so near at hand. During the removal of Napoleon the most awful silence prevailed, you could have heard a pin drop in the sea.

KEY TO THE SOURCES OF EXTRACTS

The Emperor Returns from Elba

Reiset, iii, 74–6
Fantin des Odoards, 422–3
Coignet, 273–4
Girod de l'Ain, 371–4
Saint-Chamans, 277
Oudinot, 359–62

Walcot MS.
Bonneval, 111–12
Carnot, ii, 404–5
Lavallette, 343–5
Henckens, 216–19
Barrès, 211–12

The Armies Assemble

Mainwaring, 514
Mercer, i, 2–17
The Bath Archives, ii, 480–3 [Jackson]
Lieber, 151–3
Saltoun, iii, 44
Wellington, *Dispatches*, xii, 358, 435

Scheltens, 196
Gronow, i, 64–5
Müffling, 212–14
Creevey Papers, 228
Gibney, 174–5

The Opening Moves

Delbrück, iv, 521 [Gneisenau]
Niemann, 541
Wider Napoleon!, ii, 313–14

Mauduit, ii, 29–30, 32–3
Ross-Lewin, 253
De Lancey, 42–5

The Duchess of Richmond's Ball

Richardson, 373–4 [Verner]
Müffling, 230
De Ros, 122–4, 132–3

Maxwell, ii, 13 [Dalrymple]
Young, 306–8
Malmesbury, ii, 445–6 [Bowles]

The Call to Arms

Eaton, 18–21 [Waldie]
Kincaid, 310–11
Jackson, 14–15
Frazer, 536–8

Albemarle, 136–7 [Keppel]
Mercer, i, 230–3
Bannatyne, 319–20 [Macready]

The Battle of Quatre Bras

Battle of Waterloo, 1, 56–8 [Batty]
Anton, 190–5
Morris, 197–8, 201–3

Macready, 389–90
Grouchy, 102–4 [De Vatry]
Lemonnier-Delafosse, ii, 369–70

The Battle of Ligny

Mauduit, ii, 38–41
Reiche, ii, 183–4
Maxwell, ii, 19–20 [Wellington]
Fantin des Odoards, 430–2
François, ii, 879–81
Lieber, 155–6

Reuter, 45–7
Ollech, 139–40 [Wussow]
Wider Napoleon!, ii, 318–19
Reiche, ii, 201–3
Delbrück, lv, 522
Stanhope, 110

June 17th: The French Pursuit

Wider Napoleon!, ii, 320–1
Hope, 236–8
Malmesbury, ii, 447 [Bowles]
Jackson, 31–2

Mercer, i, 264–74
Mauduit, ii, 230–2
D'Erlon, 96–7

The Night before the Battle

The English Army in France, i, 119–22 [Smith]
Cornhill Magazine, 1899, 727–8 [Carey]
Wellington, *Supplementary Despatches*, x, 501
Napoleon, *Mémoires*, 120–2

Foy, 278–9
Gibney, 183–5
Kelly, 275–6 [Decoster]
Pétiet, 195–6, 213–14
Clay, 219–20
Kincaid, 325–9
Albemarle, 140–1 [Keppel]

Phase One — The Assault on Hougoumont

Waterloo Letters, 261–5 [Woodford]
Clay, 220–2
Waterloo Letters, 268–9 [Standen]

Maxwell, ii, 73 [Wellington]
Waterloo Letters, 19–20 [Seymour]

Phase Two — D'Erlon's Corps attacks the Allied Centre

Scheltens, 201–2
Duthilt: Quoted in *Waterloo illustré*, No. 5 (2/II), 41–2
With Napoleon at Waterloo, 141–5 [Dickson]

Dalton, 258 [Ewart]
Ainslie, 158–9 [Kennedy Clark]
Cavalry Journal, 1926 [Clarke]

Brussels, Ghent and Antwerp during the Battle

Creevey, *Life and Times*, 17–18 [Ord]
Capel, 114–15
Chateaubriand, iv, 19–21

Reiset, iii, 211–14
Eaton, 62–77 [Waldie]

Phase Three — Prodigal Cavalry Charges

Leeke, i, 30–3
Lawrence, 208–10
Gronow, i, 69–72, 190–1

Battle of Waterloo, i, 199–201 [Lewis]
Waterloo Letters, 233–4 [Rudyard]

Phase Four — The French capture La Haye Sainte

Beamish, 453–9 [Baring]
Waterloo Letters, 406–9 [Graeme]
Albemarle, 148–51 [Keppel]

Reiche, ii, 209–13
Mercer, i, 309–16

Phase Five — The Guard Attacks

Bannatyne, 343–4 [Macready]
Macready, 400–1
Leeke, i, 39–41
Levasseur, 303–4
Ney, 179–81
Waterloo Letters, 254–6 [Powell]
Napier, i, 178–80 [Churchill]

Kincaid, 341–3
With Napoleon at Waterloo, 163–4 [Robertson]
Tomkinson, 311–3 [Marshall]
B.M. Add. MSS. 34,703, ff. 31–3 [Taylor]
Leeke, i, 67–8

In the Hour of Victory and Defeat

English Historical Review, vol. xviii
  [Petit]
Levasseur, 305–6
Robinaux, 209–11
Lemonnier-Delafosse, 398–401, 404
Fleury de Chaboulon, ii, 190–6
Napoleon, Lettres inédites, ii, 357–8
Ollech, 256–7 [Julius]

Dallas, 140–4
Three Years with the Duke, 217–8
  [Hume]
Camden Miscellany, vol. xviii
  [Wellington]
Creevey Papers, 236–7
Blücher, 151
Smith, 275–6

How the News reached Belgium, France and Britain

Eaton, 72–5 [Waldie]
Labretonnière, 268–70
Thiébault, v, 351–2, 360–1
Lavallette, 364–5
Young, 142–4

Trench, 316–7
Simpson, iv–vi
Ward, 96–8
Wellington, Supplementary Des-
  patches, x, 553–4 [Prince Regent]

Care of the Wounded

Fleischman & Aerts, 114 [D'Hoogh-
  vorst]
Tellier, 45–6
Gordon, ii, 273–5
Simmons, 365–8, 374–5

Hope, 268–72
Costello, 195–6
D'Arblay, vi, 240–1
Bell, 230, 241–3, 246–8

The Advance on Paris

Boldero MS.
Wellington, Dispatches, xii, 499–500
Blücher, 154–5

Farmer, 169
Gronow, i, 201
Müffling, 251

The Occupation of Paris

Broughton, 298–9 [Hobhouse]
Smythies, 201 [Wray]
Leeke, 151–4
Foy, 287

Fantin des Odoards, 427–8
Labretonnière, 286–8
Shelley, 102
Cadell, 237–8

Napoleon takes Leave of Europe

Maitland, 56 [Napoleon]
Maitland, 69–71

Napoleon and his Fellow Travellers,
  295–7 [Smart]
Hastings, iii, 307–9 [Fitzgerald]

BIBLIOGRAPHY

PUBLISHED SOURCES

N.B. The place of publication is London unless stated otherwise.

Ainslie, General Charles P.: *Historical Record of the First or the Royal Regiment of Dragoons* (1887)

Albemarle, George Thomas, Earl of: *Fifty Years of my Life* (3rd ed., 1877)

Anton, James: *Retrospect of a Military Life during the most Eventful Periods of the Last War* (Edinburgh, 1841)

Bannatyre, Lieut.-Colonel Neil: *History of the Thirtieth Regiment 1689–1881* (Liverpool, 1923)

Barrès: *Souvenirs d'un Officier de la Grande Armée* [J.-B. Barrès], publiés par Maurice Barrès, son petit-fils (Paris, 1922)

Barrett, C. R. B.: *History of the XIII Hussars* (2 vols., 1911)

Bath Archives, The: A Further Selection from the Diaries and Letters of Sir George Jackson, K.C.H., from 1809 to 1816. Edited by Lady Jackson (2 vols., 1873)

Battle of Waterloo, The, also of Ligny, and Quatre-Bras, described by the series of accounts published by Authority with Circumstantial Details, by a Near Observer. Also important particulars, communicated by Staff, and Regimental Officers, serving in different parts of the field, with every connected official document; forming an Historical Record of the Campaign in the Netherlands, 1815; from the Testimony of Eye-Witnesses, and of those who had the honour to share in its operations (10th ed., 1817)

Beamish, North Ludlow: *History of the King's German Legion* (2 vols., 1837)

Becke, Captain A. F.: *Napoleon and Waterloo. The Emperor's Campaign with the Armée du Nord, 1815. A Strategical and Tactical Study* (2 vols., 1914)

Bell: *Letters of Sir Charles Bell, selected from his Correspondence with his Brother, George Joseph Bell* (1870)

Blücher: *Blücher in Briefen aus den Feldzügen, 1813–1815, herausgegeben von E. von Colomb, General-Lieutenant* (Stuttgart, 1876)

Bonneval: *Mémoires anecdotiques du Général Marquis de Bonneval, 1786–1873* (Paris, 1900)

Boulger, D. C.: *The Belgians at Waterloo* (1901)

Broughton, Lord (John Cam Hobhouse): *Recollections of a Long Life. With Additional Extracts from his Private Diaries.* Edited by his daughter, Lady Dorchester (2 vols., 1909)

Bullock: 'Journal of Robert Henry Bullock, 11th Light Dragoons' (*The English Historical Review,* Vol. III, 1888)

Cadell, Lieut.-Colonel Charles: *Narrative of the Campaigns of the Twenty-Eighth Regiment since their Return from Egypt in 1802* (1835)

Calvert: *An Irish Beauty of the Regency,* compiled from 'Mes Souvenirs' — the unpublished journals of the Hon. Mrs Calvert, 1789–1822 — by Mrs Warrenne Blake (1911)

Capel: *The Capel Letters. Being the Correspondence of Lady Caroline Capel and her Daughters with the Dowager Countess of Uxbridge from Brussels and Switzerland, 1814–1817.* Edited by the Marquess of Anglesey (1955)

Carey, Tupper: 'Reminiscences of a Commissariat Officer' (*The Cornhill Magazine,* new series, Vol. VI, 1899)

Carnot: *Mémoires sur Carnot par son fils* (2 vols., Paris, 1865)

Chateaubriand, François René, Vicomte de: *Mémoires d'Outre-Tombe* (new ed., 6 vols., Paris, 1880)

Clarke, Lieut.-Colonel I. B.: 'Waterloo Letters from the Royal Scots Greys' (*The Cavalry Journal,* January, 1926)

Clay, Private Matthew: 'Adventures at Hougoumont' (*Household Brigade Magazine,* 1958)

Coignet: *Les Cahiers du Capitaine Coignet (1799–1815),* publiés par Loredan Larchey d'après le manuscrit original (Paris, 1883)

Copin, Jean: 'Waterloo: le Folklore de la Bataille' (*Le Folklore Brabançon,* Nos. 143, 146, 148, 151, Brussels, 1959–61)

Costello: *Adventures of a Soldier, written by himself. Being the Memoirs of Edward Costello, K.S.F., formerly a non-commissioned officer in the Rifle Brigade, late Captain in the British Legion, and now one of the Wardens of the Tower of London* (2nd ed., 1852)

Cotton, Sergeant-Major Edward: *A Voice from Waterloo. A History of the Battle fought on the 18th June, 1815* (Brussels, 9th ed., 1900)

Creevey Papers, The. A Selection from the Correspondence & Diaries of the late Thomas Creevey, M.P. Born 1768–Died 1838. Edited by Sir Herbert Maxwell (3rd ed., 1 vol., 1905)

Creevey: *Creevey's Life and Times. A further Selection from the Correspondence of Thomas Creevey.* Edited by John Gore (1934)

Dallas: *Incidents in the Life and Ministry of the Rev. Alex R. C. Dallas, A.M., Rector of Wonston;* by his Widow (3rd ed., 1873)

Dalton, Charles: *The Waterloo Roll Call with Biographical Notes and Anecdotes* (2nd ed., 1904)

De Bas, Colonel F., and Le Comte J. de T'Serclaes de Wommerson: *La Campagne de 1815 aux Pays-Bas d'après les rapports officiels néerlandais* (Brussels, 3 vols., 1908)

De Lancey: *A Week at Waterloo in 1815. Lady de Lancey's Narrative. Being an Account of how she nursed her Husband, Colonel Sir William Howe de Lancey, Quartermaster-General of the Army, mortally wounded in the great Battle.* Edited by Major B. R. Ward (1906)

Delbrück, Hans: *Das Leben des Feldmarschalls Grafen Neithardt von Gneisenau.* Fortsetzung von G. H. Pertz (Berlin, 6 vols., 1880)

D'Erlon: *Le Maréchal Drouet, Comte d'Erlon. Vie militaire écrite par lui-même et dédiée à ses amis* (Paris, 1844)

De Ros: *A Sketch of the Life of Georgiana Lady de Ros, with some Reminiscences of her Family and Friends, including the Duke of Wellington.* By her daughter the Honble. Mrs J. R. Swinton (1893)

Duthilt: *Les Mémoires du Capitaine Duthilt,* publiés par Camille Lévi (La Société dunquerquoise pour l'Encouragement des Lettres, des Sciences et des Arts, Lille, 1909)

Eaton, Charlotte A.: *The Days of Battle, or Quatre Bras and Waterloo* (1853)

Ernouf, Baron: *Maret, Duc de Bassano* (2nd ed., Paris 1884)

The English Army in France; being the Personal Narrative of an Officer: comprising the Journal of Adventures connected with the Battle of Waterloo, and with the subsequent Events down to the Period of the Occupation of France by the Allied Forces (new ed., 2 vols., 1831)

Fantin des Odoards: *Journal du Général Fantin des Odoards. Etapes d'un Officier de la Grande Armée, 1800–1830* (Paris, 1895)

Fleischman, Théo: *Le Quartier Général de Wellington à Waterloo* (Charleroi, 1956)

Fleischman, Théo, et Winand Aerts: *Bruxelles pendant la bataille de Waterloo* (Bruxelles, 1956)

Fleury de Chaboulon: *Mémoires pour servir à l'histoire de la vie privée, du retour, et du règne de Napoléon en 1815* (2 vols., London, 1820)

Foy: *Vie militaire du Général Foy, par Maurice Girod de l'Ain* (Paris, 1900)

François: *Journal du Capitaine François (dit le Dromadaire d'Egypte) 1793–1830,* publié d'après le manuscrit original par Charles Grolleau (Paris, 2 vols., 1903–4)

Frazer: *Letters of Colonel Sir Augustus Frazer, K.C.B., commanding the Royal Horse Artillery in the Army under the Duke of Wellington, written during the Peninsular and Waterloo Campaigns.* Edited by Major-General Edward Sabine (1859)

Gibney: *Eighty Years Ago, or the Recollections of an old Army Doctor. His Adventures on the Field of Quatre Bras and Waterloo and during the Occupation of Paris in 1815.* By the late Dr Gibney of Cheltenham. Edited by his son, Major R. D. Gibney (1896)

Girod de l'Ain, Général Baron: *Dix Ans de mes Souvenirs militaires, de 1805 à 1815* (Paris, 1873)

Q

Gleig, G. R.: *The Light Dragoon* [George Farmer, 11th Light Dragoons] (1850). This also appeared as 'Reminiscences of a Light Dragoon' in Colburn's *United Service Magazine*, 1841-2.

Gordon, Pryse Lockhart: *Personal Memoirs, or Reminiscences of Men and Manners at Home and Abroad during the last Half Century* (2 vols., 1830)

Gronow: *The Reminiscences and Recollections of Captain Gronow, being Anecdotes of the Camp, the Court, and the Clubs, and Society at the Close of the Last War with France* (First to Fourth Series, 1862-6. Two-volume edition, 1900)

Grouchy: *Mémoires du Maréchal de Grouchy*, par le Marquis de Grouchy (Paris, 4 vols., 1874)

Hay, Captain William: *Reminiscences, 1808-1815, under Wellington.* Edited by his Daughter, Mrs S. C. I. Wood (1901)

Hastings: *Report on the Manuscripts of the late Reginald Rawdon Hastings, Esq., of the Manor House, Ashby de la Zouch.* Edited by Francis Bickley. (Vol. 3, 1934. Historical Manuscripts Commission)

Henckens, Lieutenant: *Mémoires se rapportant à son service militaire au 6 ème Régiment de Chasseurs à Cheval français de février 1803 à août 1816* (La Haye, 1910)

Historical Account of the Battle of Waterloo, fought on the 18th of June, 1815; intended to elucidate the Topographical Plan executed by W. B. Craan, Examining Engineer of the Government Surveys of South Brabant. Translated from the French, with explanatory notes, by Captain Arthur Gore, Thirtieth Regiment of Foot (1817)

Historical Records of the 32nd (Cornwall Light Infantry), compiled and edited by Colonel G. C. Swiney (1893)

Hobhouse: *See* Broughton, Lord.

Hope: *Letters from Portugal, Spain and France, during the memorable Campaigns of 1811, 1812, & 1813, and from Belgium and France in the year 1815.* By a British Officer [Lieut. James Hope], (1819)

Houssaye, Henry: *1815: La Première Restauration — Le Retour de l'Ile d'Elbe — Les Cent Jours* (79th ed., Paris, 1927; first pub. 1893)

Houssaye, Henry: *1815 — Waterloo.* Translated from the 31st French edition by Arthur Emile Mann and edited by A. Euan-Smith (1900)

Houssaye, Henry: *1815: La Seconde Abdication — La Terreur Blanche* (26th ed., Paris, 1905)

Jackson, Lieut.-Col. Basil: *Notes and Reminiscences of a Staff Officer chiefly relating to the Waterloo Campaign and to St. Helena Matters during the Campaign of Napoleon.* Edited by R. C. Seaton (1903)

Jérôme: *Mémoires et Correspondance du Roi Jérôme et de la Reine Catherine* (7 vols., Paris, 1866)

Kelly, Christopher: *Memoirs and Wonderful Achievements of Wellington the Great. His Crowning Victory at Waterloo, &c.* (1852)

Kincaid, Captain J.: *Adventures in the Rifle Brigade, in the Peninsula, France, and the Netherlands, from 1809 to 1815* (1830)

Klein: *Die Befreiungskrieg 1813, 1814, 1815. Urkunden, Berichte, Briefe.* Mit geschichtlichen Verbindungen von Tim Klein (Ebenhausen bei München, 1913)

Labretonnière, E.: *Macédoine — Souvenirs du Quartier Latin, Paris, à la Chute de l'Empire et pendant les Cent Jours* (Paris, 1863)

Lavallette: *Mémoires et Souvenirs du Comte Lavallette, ancien aide-de-camp de Napoléon, Directeur des Postes sous le Premier Empire et pendant les Cent-Jours* (Paris, 1905)

Lawrence: *The Autobiography of Sergeant William Lawrence, a Hero of the Peninsular and Waterloo Campaigns*, edited by George Nugent Bankes (1886)

Leeke, William: *The History of Lord Seaton's Regiment at the Battle of Waterloo* (2 vols., 1866, 1871)

Lemonnier-Delafosse, Lieut.-Colonel M.: *Campagnes de 1810 à 1815. Souvenirs Militaires* (2 vols., Le Havre, 1850)

Levasseur: *Souvenirs militaires d'Octave Levasseur, officier d'artillerie, aide-de-camp du Maréchal Ney, 1802–1815* (Paris, 1914)

Lieber, Francis: *Reminiscences, Addresses and Essays*, being Vol. I of his Miscellaneous Writings, edited by Daniel C. Gilman (Philadelphia, 1881)

Macready: 'On a Part of Captain Siborne's History of the Waterloo Campaign', by an Officer of the 5th British Brigade [Major Edward Macready, 30th Foot] (Colburn's *United Service Magazine*, 1845, Part I)

Mainwaring: 'Four Years of a Soldier's Life' (*United Service Journal*, 1844, Parts II and III)

Maitland, Rear-Admiral Sir Frederick Lewis: *Narrative of the Surrender of Buonaparte, and of his Residence on board H.M.S.* Bellerophon, *with a detail of the principal events that occurred in that ship between the 24th of May and the 8th of August, 1815* (1826)

Malmesbury: *A Series of Letters of the First Earl of Malmesbury, his Family and Friends from 1745 to 1820.* Edited by his grandson (2 vols., 1870). This contains many letters by Captain George Bowles.

Martin, Jacques: *Souvenirs d'un ex-officier* (Paris, Genève, 1867)

Mauduit: *Les Derniers Jours de la Grande Armée, ou Souvenirs, Documents et Correspondance inédite de Napoléon en 1814 et 1815*, par le Capitaine Hippolyte de Mauduit, fondateur et rédacteur en chef de la Sentinelle de l'Armée (Paris, 2 vols, 1847)

Maxwell, Sir Herbert: *The Life of Wellington. The Restoration of the Martial Power of Great Britain* (2 vols., 1899)

Memoirs of the Tenth Royal Hussars (Prince of Wales' Own), Historical and Social. Collected and arranged by Colonel R. S. Liddell (1891)

Mercer, General Cavalié: *Journal of the Waterloo Campaign kept through the Campaign of 1815* (2 vols., 1870)

Morris, Thomas, late Sergeant 73rd Regiment: *Recollections of Military Service, including some details of the Battles of Quatre Bras and Waterloo* (1847)

Müffling, Baron von: *Passages from my Life; together with Memoirs of the Campaign of 1813 and 1814.* Edited, with notes, by Colonel Philip Yorke (2nd ed., 1853)

Napoleon: *Correspondance de Napoléon 1er*, publiée par ordre de l'Empereur Napoleon III (Vol. 28, Paris, 1869)

Napoleon: *Lettres inédites de Napoléon 1er*, publiées par Léon Lecestre. Tome second (1810–15) (Paris, 2nd ed., 1897)

Napoleon: *Mémoires pour servir à l'histoire de France en 1815* (Paris, 1820)

Napoleon and his Fellow Travellers, being a reprint of certain Narratives of the Voyages of the dethroned Emperor on the Bellerophon *and the* Northumberland *to exile in St. Helena; The romantic Stories told by George Home, Captain Ross, Lord Lyttelton, and William Warden.* Edited by Clement Shorter (1908)

Naylor, John: *Waterloo* (1960)

Ney: *Vie du Maréchal Ney, Duc d'Elchingen, Prince de la Moskowa* (Paris, 1816)

Niemann: 'The Journal of Henri Niemann of the 6th Prussian Black Hussars', edited by Francis Newton Thorpe (*The English Historical Review*, Vol. III, July, 1888)

Ollech, General der Infanterie von: *Geschichte des Feldzüges von 1815 nach archivalischen Quellen* (Berlin, 1876)

Oudinot: *Récits de Guerre et de Foyer. Le Maréchal Oudinot, Duc de Reggio.* D'après les Souvenirs inédites de la Maréchale, par Gaston Stiegler (Paris, 1894)

Pétiet: *Souvenirs militaires de l'histoire contemporaine*, par le Général Baron Auguste Pétiet (Paris, 1844)

Petit: 'General Petit's Account of the Waterloo Campaign', edited by G. C. Moore Smith (*The English Historical Review*, Vol. XVIII, 1903)

Pfister, Dr Albert, Generalmajor z.D.: *Aus dem Lager der Verbündeten, 1814 und 1815* (Stuttgart and Leipzig, 1897)

Reiche: *Memoiren des königlich preussischen Generals der Infanterie Ludwig von Reiche*, herausgegeben von seinem Neffen Louis von Weltzien (Leipzig, 2 vols., 1857)

Reiset: *Souvenirs du Lieutenant Général Vicomte de Reiset, 1814–1836*, publiés par son petit-fils (Paris, 3 vols., 1902)

Reuter: 'A Prussian Gunner's Adventures in 1815', edited and translated by Captain E. S. May (*United Service Magazine*, Oct., 1891)

Richardson, Ethel M.: *Long Forgotten Days (leading to Waterloo)* (1928).

This contains extracts from the Diary of Lieut.-Colonel Sir William Verner.

Robinaux: *Journal de Route de Capitaine Robinaux, 1803–1832*, publié par Gustave Schlumberger (Paris, 1908)

Ropes, John Codman: *The Campaign of Waterloo. A Military History* (New York, 1892)

Ross-Lewin, Harry: *With 'The Thirty-Second' in the Peninsula and Other Campaigns.* Edited by John Wardell (Dublin, 1904)

Saint-Chamans: *Mémoires du Général Comte de Saint-Chamans, ancien aide-de-camp du Maréchal Soult, 1802–1832* (Paris, 1896)

Saltoun, Alexander Fraser, of Philorth, seventeenth Lord: *The Frasers of Philorth* (Edinburgh, 3 vols., 1879)

Scheltens: *Souvenirs d'un grognard belge (1804–48). Les Mémoires du Colonel Scheltens*, publiés avec une introduction historique par le Vicomte Charles Terlinden (3rd ed., Brussels, n.d.). Originally published in 1880 as *Souvenirs d'un vieux soldat belge de la garde impériale.*

Shelley: *The Diary of Frances Lady Shelley, 1787–1817*, edited by her grandson Richard Edgcumbe (1912)

Siborne, Captain William: *History of the War in France and Belgium in 1815: containing Minute Details of the Battles of Quatre Bras, Ligny, Wavre, and Waterloo* (1844)

Simmons: *A British Rifleman. The Journals and Correspondence of Major George Simmons, Rifle Brigade, during the Peninsular War and the Campaign of Waterloo.* Edited by Lt.-Col. Willoughby Verner (1899)

Simpson, James: *Paris after Waterloo. Notes taken at the time and hitherto unpublished, including a revised edition — the tenth — of a visit to Flanders and the Field of Waterloo* (Edinburgh, 1853)

Six, Georges: *Dictionnaire Biographique des Généraux et Amiraux français de la Révolution et de l'Empire (1792–1814)* (Paris, 2 vols., 1934)

Smith: *The Autobiography of Lieutenant-General Sir Harry Smith, Baronet of Aliwal on the Sutlej, G.C.B.* Edited by G. C. Moore Smith (2 vols., 1901)

Smythies, Captain R. H. Raymond: *Historical Records of the 40th (2nd Somersetshire) Regiment from its Formation, in 1717, to 1893 (Devonport, 1894)*

Stanhope, Philip Henry, 5th Earl: *Notes on Conversations with the Duke of Wellington, 1831–1851* (1888)

Tellier, Pierre-Joseph: 'Un Témoin de Waterloo' (Société belge d'études napoléoniennes, *Bulletin* No. 8, Mai, 1953)

Thiébault: *Mémoires du Général Baron Thiébault*, publiés sous les auspices de sa fille Mlle Claire Thiébault d'après le manuscrit original, par Fernand Calmettes (Paris, 5 vols., 1893)

Three Years with the Duke of Wellington in Private Life, by an ex-aide-de-camp [Lord William Pitt Lennox] (1853)

Tomkinson, Lieut.-Colonel William: *The Diary of a Cavalry Officer in the Peninsular and Waterloo Campaigns, 1809–1815*, edited by his son, James Tomkinson (1894)

Trench: *The Remains of the late Mrs Richard Trench, being Selections from her Journals, Letters and other Papers* (1862)

Vivian, Hon. Claud: *Richard Hussey Vivian, First Baron Vivian. A Memoir* (1897)

Waldie: *See* Eaton, Charlotte A.

Ward, Harriet: *Recollections of an Old Soldier: A Biographical Sketch of the late Colonel Tidy, 24th Regt.* (1849)

Waterloo illustré: Publication historique (Nos. 1–11, Brussels)

Waterloo Letters. A Selection from original and hitherto unpublished Letters bearing on the 16th, 17th, and 18th June, 1815, by Officers who served in the Campaign. Edited by Major-General H. T. Siborne (1891)

'Waterloo Letters from the Royal Scots Greys' (*The Cavalry Journal*, January 1926)

Waterloo Memoirs; or Record of all the Events connected with, and arising out of, the Battles fought on the 16th, 17th, and 18th of June, 1815, in the Netherlands. With the Biographies and Military Services of the most distinguished Officers (2 vols., 1817)

Wellington: *The Dispatches of Field Marshal the Duke of Wellington during his various Campaigns.* Compiled by Lieut.-Colonel Gurwood (Vol. 12, 1838)

Wellington: *Supplementary Despatches, Correspondence, and Memoranda of Field Marshal Arthur Duke of Wellington, K.G.* Edited by his son, the Duke of Wellington (Vols. X, XI, 1863, 1864)

Wheeler: *The Letters of Private Wheeler, 1809–1828.* Edited and with a Foreword by Captain B. H. Liddell Hart (1951)

Wider Napoleon! Ein deutsches Reiterleben 1806–1815. Herausgegeben von Friedrich M. Kircheisen (Stuttgart, 2 vols., 1911). Originally published in 1861.

With Napoleon at Waterloo, and other unpublished documents of the Waterloo and Peninsular Campaigns. Edited with an Introduction by Mackenzie Macbride (1911)

Young, Julian Charles: *A Memoir of Charles Mayne Young, Tragedian, with extracts from his son's Journal* (2nd ed., 1871)

PERSONAL INDEX

(Bold figures indicate authorship of an extract)

235

INDEX OF ARMIES